A Practical Guide to Using Computers in Language Teaching

A Practical Guide to Using Computers in Language Teaching

JOHN DE SZENDEFFY
Boston University

UNIVERSITY OF MICHIGAN PRESS
ANN ARBOR

To Audrey

ISBN 0-472-03048-5

Published in the United States of America by
The University of Michigan Press

Manufactured in the United States of America

2008   2007   2006   2005   4   3   2   1

Acknowledgments

Many friends and colleagues generously contributed ideas for this book and gave me valuable feedback on chapters. Dorothy Lynde, of Harvard University, contributed her tour and student recording activities for low-level students and read several chapters, giving me frank and valuable comments on tone and focus early on. Doug Kohn, of Berklee College of Music in Boston, refined my understanding of and approach to using film in language teaching and demonstrated the value of video-editing projects in class. Pamela Couch, of Mission College in Santa Clara, lent me several of her tried-and-true activities for low-level ESL writing. Michael Feldman, of Boston University, through his addiction to teaching on the bleeding edge of technology, served as the inspiration for many of the Internet activities, and his classes validated the usefulness of this rich medium for language teaching. Chris Antonellis, Barbara Bliss, and Doreen Miller have conducted the ongoing experiment that is the CELOP Semester Book at the Center for English Language and Orientation Programs at Boston University. I'm grateful for their ideas on and experience with producing content for the elaborate Semester Book as a model for desktop publishing activities that incorporate journalism skills for high-intermediate ESL students.

I've been fortunate to have access (we're talking a few meters) to Jonathan White at Boston University, who daily proves himself a font of up-to-date technical minutiae, a keen observer of computer industry developments, and a critical thinker when it comes to implementing technology in education. Shawn Provençal, the systems administrator at the Geddes Language Center at Boston University, dispatched critical comments on the chapter on platform from the perspective of a network administrator in a cross-platform lab environment integrated into a complex university network. Eugenie Wejntrob, in the CALL Research Group at Technion, Israel Institute of Technology in Haifa commented on the chapter on platform from a non-technophile perspective. Terry O'Neil, the CALL Lab Director at Koç University in Istanbul, scrutinized the activities and demanded more details, examples, and rationale—always keeping an eye out for what terms or procedures might throw a CALL tenderfoot, or anyone else, for a loop. His critical suggestions contributed toward the objective of what this book aspires to be: an accessible guide. He also, admittedly, helped me tone down language that exposed my occasional frustration with certain self-induced problems teachers and students repeatedly face as computer users. I'd like to acknowledge as well the many LLTI listserv members around the world—language teachers and CALL lab directors—who detailed scenarios that rounded out my research addressing CALL challenges in a great variety of teaching and computing environments.

In Kelly Sippell at the University of Michigan Press I was lucky to have a supportive, flexible, and patient editor, who also made decisions I was incapable of in whittling down the book from its original unwieldy heft. Thanks as well to the magnificent Bates Hall at the Boston Public Library for providing an inspiring, contemplative space to work on weekends. And, finally, to my wife Linda go the deepest thanks of all for those countless nights and weekends she spent as a book widow taking care of our girl, Audrey.

Grateful acknowledgment is given to the following authors, publishers and individuals for permission to reprint previously published materials.

Apple Computer, Inc., for screenshot of Apple QuickTime Player.

Stewart Arneil for screen image from MacIntosh version 5 of *Hot Potatoes* at *http://www.web.uvic.ca/hrd/hotpot*. Reprinted by permission.

Duncan Charters for "Typical Rules for Mailing List Postings (netiquette)" from the 11 rules at SL-LISTS at LaTrobe University, *sl-list.net*. Reprinted by permission.

Google for screen shot of search results for *thwart* and Changing interface language in Windows XP and Mac OS x. Reprinted by permission.

LexisNexis for screen shots. Reprinted with the permission of LexisNexis Academic & Library Solutions. LexisNexis and the Knowledge Burst logo are registered trademarks of Reed Elsevier Properties, Inc., used with the permission of LexisNexis.

Merriam-Webster for screen shot of *audible* by permission. From the Merriam-Webster OnLine Dictionary ©2004 by Merriam-Webster, Incorporated *(www.Merriam-Webster.com)*.

MIT for screen shot of "Park Sleep" by J. Donath. Used with permission by MIT.

Pearson Education, Inc., for screen shot from the definition of *audible* from *Longman Dictionary of Contemporary English, 4th ed.*

University of Victoria for screen shot of Business English: Meetings from *North American Idioms* CD, *(http://www.uvcs.uvic.ca)*. Used with permission.

World Book Encyclopedia for screen shot of "dog behavior."

Yahoo! Inc. for screen shot of *Yahoo! mail screen*. Reproduced with permission of Yahoo! Inc. ©2004 by Yahoo! Inc. YAHOO! and YAHOO! logo are trademarks of Yahoo! Inc.

Every effort has been made to contact the copyright holders for permission to reprint borrowed material. We regret any oversights that may have occurred and will rectify them in future printings of this book.

Contents

PART 4 Appendices

Introduction

Computers—the most powerful dimension of the second or foreign language learning experience since the advent of the teacher—serve as tireless *portals* to limitless target language models and, more important for the classroom, as tools for activities that draw students together to cooperate on activities that interest them and stimulate their creative language production and comprehension, all while challenging them to overcome obstacles in a complex environment in the target language. In the computer-assisted language learning (CALL) classroom, students don't study language as much as use it to cooperate and solve problems not unique to the language classroom. If we recognize the value in the *process* more than *product*, then we can appreciate that when a CALL class activity gets messy, and it does, it's realistic: It reflects real language use and life in general with unforeseen problems and the need for creative solutions using a tool central to modern life.

What are the greatest obstacles to realizing this learning potential of the CALL classroom?

1. Users not appreciating these challenges in the *process* as being valuable to language *use* and therefore learning. These challenges may take many forms for students:

   - following verbal and written instruction
   - needing to gain comprehension in one step in order to get to the next
   - consulting each other for clarification
   - helping struggling neighbors with secondary instruction
   - translating concepts (activity ideas) into action (specific procedures)
   - working through challenges and problems with language and procedures
   - being immersed in the target language on screen, content, and interface

2. Teachers not being adequately oriented to this relatively new, challenging environment in terms of their own comfort with personal computing, as well as effective CALL pedagogy, practical activities, and relevant resources.

Why This Book?

I wrote this book because I couldn't find one to recommend to the hundreds of teachers, graduate students, and administrators I've met over the years trying to solve the mystery of how to integrate computers into their language teaching curriculum in second and foreign language environments. What would I have liked to recommend? *A concise, accessible, practical guide to using computers in language instruction;* one that gives context and meaning to the computer environment; one that includes the Internet but is not limited to it; and one that addresses the immediate needs of teachers faced with having to integrate computers into their curriculum, whether by choice or not. Teachers often don't have the time to scramble for pieces of this puzzle through journal and web articles, *listserv*[1] archives, or inquiries (where general ones never get answered anyway) or through computer activity texts that tend to focus on one resource (usually the Internet) without capitalizing on the richness of the computing environment as a whole. Other texts, conversely, speak in a scholarly theoretical or retrospective vein about CALL and its effectiveness.

While teachers scramble for activities they can take into the classroom tomorrow, they also need a practical perspective that connects these ideas with an understanding of the wider context for language learning offered in this relatively new environment. As teachers gain some appreciation for the richness of the immersion environment offered by CALL, in combination with the practical challenges to students communicating in the target language, their fears of not completing an identifiable or predetermined lesson objective within a controlled environment (the analog lab or conventional classroom) subside. That is, the usefulness of the lab in building communicative competency can be seen in the *process,* the struggle with activities, at least as much as in the *product,* or the completion of an activity.

Who Needs This Book?

Educators using computers to teach any language, foreign or second, or to develop curriculum with computing resources, will find practical advice on the subject. Although most of my experience is with large college-based language centers and departments, most of the discussion and activities maintain relevance across a broad spectrum of users and environments. These include small, independent language schools, even ones with no dedicated lab staff, that have a small number of machines (perhaps not constituting a "lab" at all), no Internet access or local network, and a tiny budget for software.

Prospective language teachers—primarily those in graduate modern foreign language departments and schools of education (such as educational technology and TESOL)—will find application to their study of language pedagogy in a working context in specific discussions on classroom techniques, activities, and pitfalls.

---

[1] In this book, I am using *listserv* in a generic sense to mean electronic discussion list.

A note about the issue of computer *platform*—the operating system (OS) that runs the computer, such as Windows®, Macintosh® (Mac®), and Linux®. In Chapter 10 I try to debunk the myths often driving platform choice and clouding compatibility issues generally. Otherwise, I consider platform issues *irrelevant* for the larger purpose of this book. When I talk about what you can do on "a computer," I'm talking about capabilities commonly available across applications on Macs and PCs (and, to a lesser extent, on Linux, too). The enduring value I hope to impart in this book, which is not a technical manual, cannot be diminished or made obsolete by updated versions of the OS, which, at the application level, is largely inconsequential.

Technical terms that are glossed in Appendix A are in boldface italics in the text.

A Note on Sources

Online resources provided the bulwark of research sources for this book. Content from magazines, journals, newspapers, and user groups available on the web offered fast and free access to a great deal of current information. Through Boston University's subscription to LexisNexis®, I was also able to access text from virtually any newspaper, magazine, journal, or industry report of interest. In addition, the CALL community generously shares its practical technical, pedagogical, and curricular knowledge through listservs[2] and individual and lab websites. If any field demonstrates the usefulness of the academic model of free exchange of ideas and information enabled globally, instantaneously, and free thanks to the Internet, it is CALL. (See Appendix H, Selected CALL Resources for selected online resources.)

Notes on Typographic Conventions and Terms

Menu Commands

Insert > Picture > From File...

The main *menu* of an application stretches across the top of the screen from left to right, usually including the categories **File, Edit, View,** etc. In this book, menus and commands found in the menu drop-down boxes are in **bold**. The right arrow (>), or greater than symbol, indicates a submenu. For example, execute the command above by clicking on the **Insert** menu, then choosing **Picture** within that drop-down menu,

---

[2]A listserv operates like an e-mail group. A message sent to the listserv goes out to all subscribers. Some listservs are moderated, meaning that an editor reviews each message for appropriateness before posting it to the community. (See Chapter 5, Activity 5, Mailing Lists.) Two excellent CALL listservs are Language Learning Technology International (LLTI), operated by Otmar Foelsche at *http://iall.net*, and CALLIS, the CALL interest section of TESOL, *www.tesol.org.*

and finally choosing **From File...** from the resulting submenu. The expansion of sub-menu items to the right or left is known as *cascading menus*. The minor ellipses (...) indicate a *dialog box* (where you make further choices) to follow that command. A colon (:) between items indicates not another menu to follow but a specific tab or field choice within the resulting dialog box.

Keyboards

Enter/return refers to the key with one of those labels on a computer's alpha key-board, formerly known as the "carriage return" key on typewriters. Most Mac keyboards label this key **return**, while most PC keyboards label it **enter.**

Shortcut Key Commands

Control-C (or Ctrl-C)

Control (Ctrl) and **C** are each keys on the keyboard. *Keyboard shortcuts* call for pressing the given combination (hold down **Control** then hit **C**, but don't be con-cerned with depressing both precisely simultaneously). By convention, a hyphen usually separates separate keys in representing the shortcut but is itself not typed.

Software Versions

An italicized lowercase x, *x,* represents something of a wildcard character, or short-hand, in denoting software versions. For example, Mac OS® 10.*x* represents all ver-sions of the Mac OS in that particular version generation, including 10.0 to 10.3 (and beyond). Likewise, Windows Server™ 200*x* represents versions of that soft-ware from 2000 to 2004 (and beyond).

Web Address Format

The global address of a page or other file on the web is often referred to as its *URL* (uniform resource locator). When typing a URL in a *web browser* location line or in an open page dialog box (**File** > **Open** > **Location**) to load a particular page, you do not need to type the entire address. For example, the complete URL of the Center for English Language and Orientation Programs at Boston University

http://	*www.*	*bu.*	*edu*	*/celop/*	*index.html*
protocol	web server	domain name	domain	website folder	page file name

can be expressed as

bu.edu/celop

The **protocol**, *http*, is assumed by the web browser; the *www* name of the web server is usually assumed as default, so *bu.edu* resolves to (or forwards to) *www.bu.edu*; and when you specify a location that ends in the folder name instead of a specific file within the folder, most web servers automatically display the file named *index.html* or *default.html* to prevent a visitor from viewing a directory list. (We know that *celop* is a folder and not a file because it does not include a ***file extension*** [what follows the period] identifying its type, such as .html or .htm, .pdf, .ra, etc.). With so many URLs to write and follow in life, we need to take all the shortcuts we can. Note further that most web browsers assume the domain *.com* where none is indicated, because the vast majority of pages on the web are found in that domain, thus simply typing *apple* should resolve to *apple.com* and thus the full URL, *http://www.apple.com/*. In this text, this site might be referred to as *apple.com*.

Web Addresses for Reference

URLs for in-text references are given at the end of each section or chapter.

Character Case

Most keyboard shortcuts are case sensitive, meaning that **Ctrl-c** will not work as **Ctrl-C (Control-Shift-C)**. In a web address (URL), only a part of it is case sensitive. Everything after the domain, representing folders and files on the web server, is case sensitive. The part of the following URL after .edu *is* case sensitive. Be sure the CAPS LOCK key is not on when typing a URL.

WWW.BU.EDU/celop/resources/faqs/indcx.html

not case sensitive | case sensitive

Internet Resources

Unlike print media, which remain on the shelf or archived, Internet resources come and go, some staying longer than others. Where I've supplied websites (URLs) or e-mail addresses, I've attempted to stick to ones that have a track record of at least a few years and have affiliations with institutions or established professionals in their field.

PART 1

What Is Computer-Assisted Language Learning?

1 The Wonderful World of Computer-Assisted Language Learning (CALL)

* ❖ Are computers effective at helping students learn language?

* ❖ Why not use the simpler tape-based lab? It worked for a long time.

* ❖ Does the teacher's role diminish when computers teach students?

Computers are playing an increasingly important role in second and foreign language instruction as they are in virtually all fields of instruction. No longer a specialty among a clique of language teachers, computer use for instruction, in some capacity, is widespread. The *digital* format of audio, video, images, and text (*multimedia*) enables a student to randomly access practically limitless pedantic and authentic models of target language materials and, through the Internet, to do so from any connected computer in the world. A student can individually adjust the pace of his or her work to accommodate different proficiencies, aptitudes, and learning styles while receiving the same relative challenge as another student working at a different pace.

3

While the means of access become more efficient and modes of electronic communication among teachers and students increase interaction—in the target language—many students become more engaged in the learning process with computers, where they are in control, whether in a class working on a group project or individually in a self-access lab.

What Computers Bring to Language Learning

- Delivery of a wide variety of multimedia content with pedantic and authentic language models, accessed with individual control
- Another source of target language knowledge and examples relieving the teacher as the sole font of target language knowledge in the classroom
- Other channels of communication between class members and distant learners
- Supplemental practice exercises and tutorial feedback
- Sophisticated tools for creation of individual and group projects
- Outlet to publish student writing and projects to a larger audience via e-mail and web pages

An Evolution of the Analog Lab

In the "old" language lab—that is, the tape-based or *analog* lab—teachers might have played audiocassettes at a master console and broadcasted or copied the audio out to student workstations. At other times, students used their own audiocassettes or ones borrowed from the language library to listen to on their own at a lab carrel. The beauty of this equipment was the dual-mode head in the tape decks that played audio from one

Figure 1.1 ■ The magnetic tape on a standard audiocassette had two sides, or "tracks." Each half played in one direction. In the tape-based lab, one track played while the other recorded simultaneously in the same direction, similar to multiple-track recording tapes used for music recording.

track of the tape while simultaneously recording student input on the other track. When students played the tape back, they could readily compare their production to the model.

An audiocassette tape has two tracks, each occupying half the width and all of the length of tape, which not only squeezes more audio onto the tape but allows for continuous play when you flip the cassette at the end of one side and continue on the other without having to rewind. We can think of the tape as a two-way highway where the audio signals go in opposite directions. Language lab tape decks exploited this second track to record the student response while the first track played the model, thus both signals went in the same direction instead of opposing directions. This technology facilitated *listen-repeat-compare* activities informed by the audiolingual approach, a repetition of contrived examples that demonstrated particular forms without necessarily facilitating opportunities to communicate in the target language.

It's more than merely the technology that differentiates an analog lab from a CALL lab. The possibilities for interacting with more capable computers affects not necessarily *what* is taught but *how* it's taught—the classroom dynamic. Analog lab equipment largely delivered predetermined audio or video material to students as a model to repeat or decipher in comprehension exercises. The activity was between the student and his or her machine, with the lab teacher exerting more control over what material the student accessed, when it was accessed, and how it was accessed. Using computers as tools to produce collaborative projects shifts the focus to the relationship between students working together and away from a student working alone with a machine.

Where the analog lab broadcasted information in one direction, the computer serves more as a pliable tool displaying a vast array of information and stimuli on demand while also providing constant opportunity for input and more creative expression. Teachers can tap into this power to orchestrate challenging activities

---

TECHNOTE ■ **Analog vs. Digital Technology**

Analog audio or video resides on magnetic tapes, like audiocassettes or VHS. *Digital* audio or video resides in computer files on magnetic (hard drives) or optical (*CD* or *DVD*) drives. Analog information is continuous while digital is discrete—that is, made up of many smaller parts. An analog clock has hands that move in a continuous motion around the clock face, while a digital clock displays only certain points in time, usually hours and minutes, but no smaller unit and nothing *in between*. (In an analogy to grammar, we might think of analog conceptually as a noncount noun and digital as a count noun.) An analog audiotape represents sound as a continuous wave recorded by a microphone. Digitizing this sound *samples* the wave at regular intervals, or takes snapshots of it. The 44.1kHz rate of CD audio samples a sound 44,100 times per second, enough to make our ears perceive it as continuous, and describes it in a *binary* file made up of 1s and 0s. Analog tapes, furthermore, degenerate each time they are played, and copying introduces recording flaws. Thus a copy of a copy of an original recording is third generation, each generation being cumulatively inferior to the original. Conversely, all copies of digital files are identical to the original.

that involve and empower students, stimulate thought and production, and create more instances of authentic interaction between students using the target language than might be the case in the analog lab or conventional classroom.

Computers, as tools, facilitate an **integrative approach** to language learning by the nature of access they provide to materials and interaction they promote between students. Mark Warschauer described "three historical stages of CALL":[1]

- **Behaviorist** (1960s–1970s): repetitive drills, using the computer as a self-paced mechanical tutor
- **Communicative** (late 1970s–early 1980s): immersion in the target language, focus on forms for original production, implicit grammar instruction
- **Integrative** (late 1980s–present):
  - use of authentic environments
  - integration of all skills in a holistic approach
  - use of multimedia and hypermedia in a nonlinear manner
  - greater student control
  - task-based, content-based, project-based activities
  - communication with native speakers and other learners by synchronous and asynchronous means
  - integration of technology into process (e.g., as content)

Integrative CALL provides the theoretical underpinning of the approaches taken in this text.

The Teacher's Role

With this new set of possibilities, computers can invigorate curricular development and encourage interested faculty members to rethink their approaches to teaching. MIT President Charles Vest offered such prospects, surely voicing the experience of many CALL teachers:

> Faculty engaged in these new approaches [using educational technology] do believe that they have become better teachers—but not so much because of the technological extensions of their capability but because the process of designing the programs forces them to think in fresh ways about ancient techniques.[2]

---

[1] Warschauer, M. (1996). Computer-assisted language learning: An introduction. In S. Fotos (Ed.), *Multimedia language teaching* (pp. 3–20). Tokyo: Logos International.

[2] Vest, C. M. (2001). *Disturbing the educational universe: Universities in the digital age—Dinosaurs or prometheans?* Retrieved July 20, 2004, from the MIT website: http://web.mit.edu/president/communications/rpt00-01.html

Far from being replaced by computers, teachers actually take on more responsibilities in a CALL environment than in a teacher-centered, lecture-based class. They add to their content knowledge and pedagogical skills a familiarity with a certain range of computer functionality and adroitness at managing a student-centered, student-empowered classroom.

The responsibilities of a CALL teacher include to:

- arrange project- or task-oriented activities stressing student interaction
- manage the time that individual students or groups spend on activities and accommodate those who finish early
- instruct students in proper, effective use of applications
- train students to think critically about problem solving
- guide students through resources for language learning
- encourage an environment where students help each other before seeking help from the teacher (particularly for computer-related problems)
- help students appreciate the language learning opportunities in the computing interface itself

Thus the CALL environment requires different teaching skills, those involving facilitation and project management more than content expertise. This stimulating, challenging, student-centered interactive environment calls for new pedagogy. Chapter 3, Ten Suggestions for Teachers with Limited CALL Experience, highlights the key approaches.

Other Rationale for CALL

There are at least five other factors motivating a language program to use computers in its instruction, either deploying dedicated language labs or arranging access to public labs (i.e., owned or managed by another department or the institution).

1. *Replacing the analog lab.* In the case where a tape-based lab needs replacing because maintenance exceeds the current value or has become obsolete in that it does not meet current needs, the opportunity presents itself to compare an analog replacement with a new computer lab. While the factors influencing such a decision are complex, the decommissioning of an outdated lab precipitates a decision to replace it with *something*, one possibility being a CALL lab.[3]

---

[3] Of the many factors to consider in deciding between dedicated language lab hardware and a computer lab, two among them are cost and technical support. The proprietary hardware associated with dedicated language lab systems, so-called "turn-key" systems, are generally more expensive to purchase and install, and their maintenance requires a technician whose specialized skills could not be as widely applied as those of a technical coordinator of a computer lab, who could address the general computing needs and support of faculty and staff as well.

2. *Taking advantage of content development.* Since the appearance of multimedia computers in the mid-'80s, but especially since the widespread adoption of the Internet by educators for content and communication in the mid-'90s, there has been an inexorable flood of authentic content, activities, and pedantic material appropriate for language learning. Adopting CALL allows teachers and students to capitalize on this windfall.

3. *Teaching relevant skills.* Computers can be used as tools to teach language through content or skills, such as general computer-use concepts, word processing, and effective Internet browsing (see Appendix D, Web Browser Basics, for examples). Students will take these skills into their continuing academic work, careers, and personal lives.

4. *Keeping up with students' expectations.* Students are coming to class with increasing computer expertise and sophistication. They expect to continue to be challenged and expand their computing abilities while they learn other content.

5. *Competing with other programs.* Most schools and programs compete for students with other institutions. Along with selling the expertise and experience of their faculty, language programs often tout their facilities. For some students, computing facilities, access to computers, and integration of computers into the curriculum may be deciding factors in where they enroll. In addition to being a marketing advantage, access to computers and CALL expertise may attract talented teachers interested in a place to explore cutting-edge CALL pedagogy.

2

Getting Started

> ❖ I teach language, not technical skills. Isn't it the tech guy's job to deal with students' computer questions?
>
> ❖ I use a computer, but I'm not a technophile. How can I possibly teach with computers?
>
> ❖ We have no lab staff in my department. How can I get training?

Many teachers may be apprehensive about using computers in class because they feel responsible for dealing not just with their own technical challenges, as they do when they use a computer themselves, but for the technical challenges of *all* students in the class—a prospect as daunting to some as a chess master playing dozens of simultaneous games with opponents in an exhibition. Consequently, they may feel that only a technical master could handle such responsibilities on top of the challenges of the content and of managing a student-centered class.

9

Toward the other end of the spectrum lie teachers who tend to regard the technical skills required to use these tools as the purview of technical support staff, with their own efforts being reserved for dealing with the content. In between these extremes lie teachers whose excitement about the power and potential of CALL far outstrips their apprehensions about their readiness to use computers in class. For teachers of the first group, those daunted by the challenges, CALL creates authentic problem-solving and language learning opportunities *whether or not* the activity proceeds without technical or procedural hang-ups, as a comedy routine might be at its most hilarious when it unintentionally diverts from the script and ad-libs.

Computers as *Tutor* vs. *Tool*

To understand the value of computers in education, especially language learning, we must first distinguish between the two functions, or modes of use, of these machines: *tutor* and *tool*. Teachers use computers in class as **tools** for producing collaborative or creative projects that encourage authentic student-student and student-teacher interaction. The teacher plays an active and integral role in the students' activities, usually circulating around the room while students work, guiding and helping as needed. As a tool, a computer enables a specified activity, much like a chisel enables a woodworker to carve; it doesn't carve by itself. (We might see some justification for leeway in the use of tutor programs in class in environments where teachers have more contact hours—such as, typically, teaching English abroad, EFL—and simply do not have time to construct original, custom activities for every meeting.)

Students, generally working in a self-access lab or at home, use the computer as a *tutor* in the *absence of a teacher*. In this mode, the computer instructs, provides content and exercises, guides the student, and gives feedback. Just as students don't have a tutor in class, neither should the computer see much duty in the tutor mode in a teacher-led class. Though this happens frequently, in the interest of providing quality human instruction, it really shouldn't. A teacher can, nonetheless, add value to a student's experience with tutor applications by *introducing* selected programs, their strengths and operations, to students who can use them on their own time or as assigned homework as a supplement to other activities. (See Tip 9, *Be a Resource Guide*, in Chapter 3 for more discussion on the use of tutor programs.)

Concepts vs. Procedures

Computers are complicated systems demanding that the user navigate the operating system, different applications, peripheral devices, and a network. It's not sufficient to expect to operate in this environment effectively simply by following a set of rote *procedures*, either written or memorized, for a given outcome. The user must understand the context and *concepts* of each environment and why some things work the way they do. An understanding of the concepts can be applied to many computing environments rather than a specific one addressed by a set of procedures that work only when followed precisely with no unforeseen problems or diversions from the steps. When we understand how programs work, we internalize the functional logic just as we want our students to internalize grammar to produce original language, not simply repeat learned phrases.

Appreciate What You Already Know

Language teachers facing the prospect of teaching with computers most likely have used common personal computing applications and are well positioned to extend the use of the computer as a tool to class after an introduction to the pedagogical approaches of this environment (see Chapter 3) and carefully chosen activities to start with.

Range of possible teacher computing experience before *venturing into CALL*

- Word processor or spreadsheet program: to create class materials, tests, and syllabi, and to write correspondence
- *Web browser:* to research class activities, gather content and language examples; conduct personal research, business, and entertainment
- Browser *plug-ins:* to play web audio or video, view certain graphics or animations, read formatted documents
- Internet-based communication tools (e.g., e-mail, *chats*, mailing lists): to communicate with colleagues, students, and friends
- Database program: to complete student evaluations, record grades, keep attendance, and track assignments
- Photo viewer or album program: to view, arrange, and store digital camera or scanned photos for personal or teaching purposes
- **Slide show** program: to provide visuals for classroom lectures or conference presentations
- Content or reference programs: to access **CD-** or **DVD-**based dictionaries, encyclopedias, educational programs, children's programs, and so forth
- Financial or spreadsheet programs: to compute personal taxes and keep personal or business budgets

So with some sampling of the computing experience listed here, it's clear that most teachers are not starting from zero as they contemplate CALL. Most may well know enough to get started. It's said that a private pilot's license does not confer upon the flyer who has passed the qualifying exams and Federal Aviation Administration (FAA) flight test all the knowledge required of a pilot but the minimum required to *start learning* how to fly on his or her own (i.e., without killing himself or herself), which is a never-ending process. Likewise, a teacher with a smattering of computing skills may be ready to start learning about CALL by logging hours in the CALL classroom. Those with little computing experience or confidence can buddy up with a colleague with more.

Tools of the Trade

While teachers need not be technophiles, geeks, or gurus to use CALL effectively, they need to understand that computers have already become a tool of the trade as common as copy machines. In many cases, computers aren't an option or add-on: A certain level of proficiency in their use is expected as a factor in measuring a teacher's competency, both from a student's and a supervisor's perspective. Thus there lies a demarcation between what a teacher is expected to know—more *practical* than technical knowledge, actually—and what a lab or technical administrator should take responsibility for, a distinction that varies by environment and conditions but one that should be recognized nonetheless.

Sample practical responsibilities of a CALL teacher

- Be proficient at using applications that students will use in class for activities (e.g., word processor, web browser, audio and video players).
- Understand basic **Desktop** (PC) or Finder (Mac) operations, including locating files or launching applications residing on the computer hard drive or inserted CD or DVD.
- Know how to switch between open applications and documents using the Start bar (PC) or Dock (Mac) (See Figure 2.1).
- Be familiar with changing *view* settings in applications used, such as the *zoom* percentage in a word processor (making the text appear larger without affecting the print size) or the view *mode* in a slideshow application (e.g., single slide edit, slide sorter, outline, full screen presentation—see Figure 2.2).
- Know where students should save their work (e.g., to floppy or Zip® disk, USB *flash* (or "keychain") **drive**, local folder on the hard drive, folder on a network server, or folder associated with a user login).

Figure 2.1 ■ Launch applications or switch between open ones with the Dock in Mac OS X (top) or the Start bar in Windows (bottom). You can customize the appearance and functioning of both.

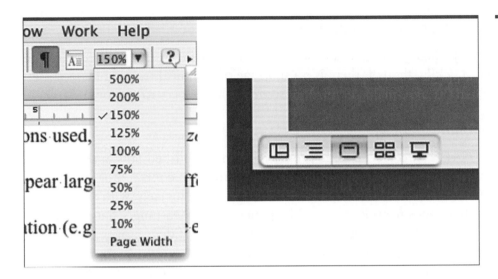

Figure 2.2 ■ The zoom adjustment in Microsoft Word's toolbar (left) adjusts how large type appears on-screen without affecting printing. The view mode buttons on the bottom left corner of a PowerPoint window (right) change how you view a slide show for editing but do not affect the finished presentation.

- Know how to use players for audio or video files students access (e.g., QuickTime Player, RealPlayer, Windows Media® Player).
- Know how to adjust the volume for listening material and change needed sound input settings for recording with a microphone.
- Understand student login procedures and common errors, if applicable, or other procedures set up by technical personnel to control access to material or applications.

Sample responsibilities of technical or lab personnel[1]

- Set up and maintain all student and teacher workstations and network servers.
- Install, configure, and maintain all software.
- Address any hardware failures or software glitches.
- Set up and maintain login or other material access procedures.
- Set up printing and saving options and procedures.
- Manage digitizing of audio, video, image, and text material for class use.
- Ensure proper setup and functioning of all peripheral equipment (e.g., headsets, external drives, scanners, cameras, projectors, speakers).

---

[1] Of course, computer environments differ widely in language learning. Small programs or language departments in schools or colleges might not have the luxury of a dedicated full- or even part-time technical staff person. In many cases, these duties are assumed by a teacher who may or may not receive release time from a portion of his or her teaching to administer the lab. If this person does not have adequate technical training or experience, as is often the case, then the computing facilities may not be effectively utilized, despite this person's dedication. Without an investment in qualified technical staffing consistent with the investment in hardware, software, and infrastructure (an investment many administrators are, alas, skittish about), students and teachers will likely see far less pedagogical value from a lab than could otherwise be the case. The sample responsibilities described here, then, refer to an *ideal* division of labor between technical and teaching personnel.

Get Training When You Need It

This book serves as a pedagogical guide and source for activity ideas, not as a technical or application manual. Luckily, though, there is no shortage of technical training material on any aspect of computing as well as many other resources for teachers to explore.

Resources for computer training

- *Lab staff or CALL teachers.* In large programs with established labs, a teacher interested in CALL perhaps has no better friend than a lab coordinator or fellow teacher with some lab teaching experience. Consult them for help with specific activities (such as ones from Part 2) and be patient about learning what you need to know for each, accumulating expertise, and with it confidence, over time.

- *Academic computing support center.* Colleges, universities, and many large schools have centers and staff that support faculty use of computers for their teaching and research. Often affiliated with offices of information technology (IT), the academic computing support centers may offer workshops, self-guided tutorials, primers, or one-on-one assistance on various aspects of computer use, usually for free.

- *Centers for adult or continuing education.* In many large cities these nonprofit, usually city-subsidized centers offer a wide range of classes with knowledgeable teachers for a nominal fee.

- *Books.* Most general purpose bookstores and computer superstores have burgeoning sections on computer use and application manuals of all kinds. While some volumes offer intimidating bindings, other series specialize in more concise, user-friendly works for nontechnical users.

- *Online help.* Most software no longer comes with paperbound manuals but include help files instead on the CD (usually in **PDF** or web page format). Look for "tutorial," "learning," or "help" folders on the CD or in the **Help** menu of the application itself. The usefulness of these resources varies by application and is sometimes more cumbersome to navigate and read than a concise book.

- *Internet resources.* The Internet references section at the end of every activity or chapter in Part 2 will point you to free resources, including general computer use, specific application use, techniques, and teaching ideas.

- *Conferences.* CALL has been growing in use, acceptance, and sophistication for years, a fact attested to by the large number of conferences organized around it or including it. These conferences include paper presentations, workshops, poster sessions, and software fairs that give details of successful approaches and activities. See Appendix H, Selected CALL Resources, for a sample of organizations hosting conferences.

3 Ten Suggestions for Teachers with Limited CALL Experience

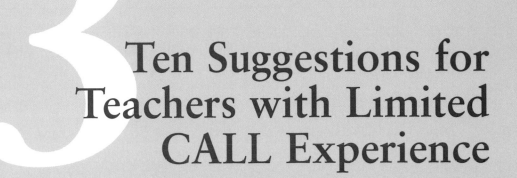

> ❖ **What computer programs are there for ESL?**
>
> ❖ **Don't students waste a lot of time figuring out how to use programs?**
>
> ❖ **What do I do with students who finish activities at different times?**

The suggestions offered in this chapter were fashioned in the spirit of Strunk and White's *Elements of Style*, the classic style manual that defines conciseness. I suggest pedagogical guidelines for implementing classroom activities, with applications for each suggestion found in Part 2. These guidelines don't discount competing views of experienced or inventive teachers but simply frame an integrative approach to CALL. Following these or any other "rules" matters less than their role in encouraging critical thinking about CALL pedagogy as a reinterpretation of conventional language classroom techniques.

☑ TIP 1

Focus on activities, not software titles.

Effective lab classes generally revolve around a well thought-out activity that involves content accessed via computers with stimulating student interaction in the target language.

📖 Class Example

Many language classes have a skill focus. Think first about what *kind of activity* you want your students engaged in that provides exercise for that skill development, and then find a lab activity that supports that objective. Don't do it the other way around. If you're teaching a listening/speaking elective, for example, determine at least four things first:

- the kind of material students will use (authentic or pedantic—usually determined by level)
- how they should engage it (answering cloze or comprehension questions, writing a response essay, or making a verbal response)
- if they will work alone or collaborate in pairs or small groups
- how long they have to complete it

Language teachers routinely set up these types of activities. The new factor in the CALL equation is primarily the *means of delivery*. Answer each of these questions in the lesson planning stage (with ideas from Chapter 6, Audio/Video Activities) and discuss their implementation with lab personnel or experienced CALL teachers a day or more before class.

📝 Pitfalls for New CALL Teachers

With a growing choice of language instruction programs (tutor applications, mostly) offering more and more dazzling capabilities, some teachers new to CALL might pass along their own enthusiasm about such programs to their students or concede to student expectations of multimedia. Telling students to use such a program and work for a set period of time is not a lab class—it's a study hall, which may have a place in students' language learning, but not in a class where human instruction is expected. (See Computers as *Tutor* vs. *Tool* in Chapter 2.) If this were how labs worked, then they wouldn't require language teachers as much as technically proficient lab monitors. The problem isn't in *using* tutor applications, but *when* they're used. If students use these programs in class, then they're doing so *in lieu of* interacting with and getting instruction from the teacher they're paying for, amounting to poor instruction value. Students can use these programs in a self-study lab or buy them on the Internet and use them at home, but they can't get a live teacher and other students to interact with at home.

Grammar practice, pronunciation, vocabulary, and test-preparation applications, content programs, and other pedantic material (such as packages billed as "language systems" or "integrated-skills programs") demonstrate title-based, not activity-based, approaches. Most of these programs don't allow for adaptation, and an overreliance on them may even contribute to a teacher's lack of confidence to construct or carry out activities where the computer is used in class as a tool—a fossilization, if you will, of CALL development—allowing the assortment of programs available in the lab to define what students do in lab class, rather than first determining a language objective for students and then exploring ways to use computers to achieve this objective in an interesting, stimulating way.

Furthermore, rigid adherence to completion of the objective-type exercises (multiple choice, cloze, etc.) in these programs as a measure of lab activity discounts their usefulness in providing practice and reinforcing forms and gives a sense of progress in the most simplistic quantifiable terms. Such activities (sometimes derided as "drill and kill"—repetitive drills informed by a behaviorist model of language instruction) by themselves may well fail to inspire learning, instead reducing language study to a monotonous task completed for its own sake. If activities aren't interesting and challenging to teachers, they aren't likely to be to students either. See Tip 9 for the proper role of tutor applications.

☑ TIP 2

Wade in slowly.

Teachers new to CALL are often put off by the perception that they must be technical gurus, that they must know how to do everything in order to do anything. They don't.

📖 *Class Example*

Most teachers are familiar with word processing, e-mail, or web browsing. Start with one of these. Text-based activities—reading, grammar, vocabulary, and writing—generally offer lower technical demands than those involving multimedia projects or online interactive activities. Many language lab classes make use of a word processor. Fortunately, even people with minimal exposure to computers have likely used one, and they are all fundamentally the same. Microsoft® Word, AppleWorks®, Nisus® Writer, Corel® WordPerfect®, and so on, share the same basic functionality. Some commands may appear in different menus, but they all function the same once they're found, much like driver controls in cars—windshield wipers, cruise control, trunk release—appear in varying locations but work the same in any car.

Writing classes in the lab, furthermore, readily expand into other skills. Incorporate speaking and listening, for example, by having students interview each other and write short biographical pieces. These documents can later include pictures and other information to illustrate the class experience, eventually becoming part of a class book that students take home—even involving a desktop publishing component as well. Such activities—teamwork, interviewing—also facilitate the social nature of language study. Start simple; build in complexity in manageable steps as necessary. (See Chapter 4 for specific ideas on writing projects, or Chapter 7, Project Activities: Class Books on page 139.)

Pitfall for New CALL Teachers

Wade in slowly with simple activities that can be expanded—explore these thoroughly before moving on to something else. Look to colleagues for ideas of what works in the lab, especially activities involving procedures not overly technical or involved. Don't rely on lab personnel to simply create a smorgasbord of application choices available for your class; many will be beyond your skills at first or inappropriate for other reasons (such as tutor applications).

☑ TIP 3

Teach.

Lab class should provide human instruction time and contact with each student.

Class Example

Lab teachers should be quite busy. They should

- circulate
- talk to each student
- look at what students are doing on-screen
- have a student first help another student asking a question
- make sure students are using the target language
- keep abreast of what's happening and who might need help
- let students know that they're not on their own

Teachers should ask questions because questions are the basis of a communicative activity exercising students' speaking, listening, and vocabulary skills. The nature of most lab work is ideally suited for teachers to interact one-on-one with each student or group, providing more individual attention than in the lecture-discussion class.

Pitfall for New CALL Teachers

Lab class isn't a time for computers to babysit students or for the teacher to sit at a computer working on other class preparation, writing e-mail, or doing some other business unrelated to actively managing the current class activity.

☑ TIP 4

Appreciate the richness of the computing environment.

The means to the lesson *is* a lesson. If the computers students use in class have a *localized* version of the *OS*[1] and applications—where the ***menus, toolbars, dialog boxes,*** and so forth, are in the target language—then the interface itself provides stimulus for practical language development and the computer becomes an immersion environment where a student works entirely in the target language. The student must understand the language used in this environment in order to function, and that understanding is reinforced by repeating actions. The complexity of this environment frequently leads students to seek help, either from the teacher or, preferably, from a classmate—thus the importance of pairing students or at least seating them according to unlike L1s. Pairs, if seated adjacent, might work better than groups because students can communicate without leaving their computers. Ideally, in addition to not sharing an L1, pairs should have complementary computing skills—the know-it-all with the neophyte.

📖 *Class Examples*

1. Use versions of the OS and applications that are localized to the target language. So if you teach French in Turkey, use the French version of the OS and applications, such as the word processor and web browser. The target language should surround the students, their eyes and ears. In an ESL course on web development, for example, students are likely exposed to more new vocabulary in the course of discussions and activities than they might be in a course with "vocabulary" in its title. Although some of the terms have primarily technical applications, most are common English words and expressions used in contexts with many other analogous uses. Talk about the derivation of terms and their less technical uses. For example, when a web browser renders a background by *tiling* the background image, compare it to tiling a floor, repeating a small unit in a predictable pattern to cover a large area. Similarly, before we can cut or copy a word or sentence, we select it, or *highlight* it with the cursor—that is, make it stand out as the highlight of a vacation stands out in our memory.

2. Use the target language to teach the relevant computing skills required by your lab activities and beyond as language through content. For example, use the target language to discuss how to use the computer, access resources, and carry out basic functions (such as printing, saving, accessing network servers, formatting papers and business letters, working with multiple documents or applications, navigating the desktop environment, recovering from problems, etc.). These computing skills

---

[1] Operating system, such as Mac OS X, Windows XP, and so forth.

will serve students after your class in their continuing education, work, or professional development—a strong motivating factor beyond language learning. In the old *analog* lab, your students left with the practical ability to use a Walkman®. They leave the CALL lab computer literate.

✍ *Pitfall for New CALL Teachers*

In foreign language teaching environments where all students speak the same L1, pairing or grouping risks having students speak their L1. A teacher circulating constantly through the class can keep a check on language use. Otherwise, like-L1 environments may see fewer activities where students collaborate with each other and more where they interact with the target language material individually.

☑ TIP 5

Prepare and be patient.

Know everything you ask your students to do. Be familiar with applications you have students use so that you can answer questions knowledgeably. Work through every activity in advance, and anticipate what problems students might encounter. This familiarity is as much the teacher's responsibility as knowing other materials used, such as textbooks.

📖 *Class Examples*

Have a backup plan, especially for online activities. You must expect that your online resources (websites) will be periodically unavailable or that your entire Internet or network connection may go down. Have an activity planned in reserve that uses *local* resources (i.e., on the computer's hard drive or a CD or DVD) or no computers at all. Otherwise, your class is vulnerable to a host of technical calamities lying in wait.

Teach students—the younger of whom may have an unjustified faith in computers (in contrast, perhaps, to the teacher)—to head off loss of work by saving early and often. Teach them to be compulsive savers with the keyboard shortcut of **Ctrl-S** (PC) or **Apple-S** (Mac). With a good saving routine, a computer or network crash will not result in a chilling loss of original work.

✍ *Pitfalls for New CALL Teachers*

Computers are often unnecessarily complicated and intolerably unstable. That's a fact. Complaining only exacerbates it. When technical problems arise, focus on a "work-around" and salvage the class. Wonder *why* it happened later, not on students' time. Don't criticize the computers or facilities in class or blame technical personnel in the lab (even if warranted). It's bad for the program's image. Students sense a teacher's frustration with technology and may lose faith in the teacher's technical competence, his or her decision to hold the class in the lab in the first place, and the program's resources generally. Labs represent an investment in the quality and effectiveness of your program. So while you probably can't eliminate problems, you can take steps to anticipate them and prepare contingency plans.

☑ TIP 6

Don't let technology drive your class.

Don't use technology for technology's sake, because it's there, or let it become an end in itself instead of a means. Recognize the difference between taking advantage of a stimulating language learning environment and letting it dictate what you do. To reiterate a theme from Tip 1, think of an interactive language activity first, then look to technology to enable it, if possible.

📖 *Class Examples*

One of the first abilities many teachers expect of a CALL lab is a holdover from the analog lab: the student intercom function. They want students, even those sitting next to each other, to be able to communicate verbally through headphones attached to the computers. Forget the technical issues involved for a moment (but know they exist). How would this ability enable a richer language experience than having these students talk face-to-face? "We did it in the old lab," doesn't answer the question.[2]

Some language teachers of web page authoring classes argue that we should teach students in these classes *HTML* (the code of web pages) because this knowledge *may* help them somewhere down the line. Perhaps. But is it an appropriate choice for a *language* class? Students may pick up a little vocabulary here and there but that answers the wrong question for a teacher to ask. *Any* language method will teach *some* language, but the key is to find the methods that *most effectively* teach language.

Although not providing an adequate substitute for an absent teacher, technology can, nevertheless, salvage a class otherwise cancelled. If you set up a web-based communication forum for your class, such as with *courseware* (e.g., WebCT or CourseInfo), a custom website, or an education *portal* (such as **Nicenet**), then you can have students work on a predefined activity in the lab in your absence. Ideally, the absent teacher would be able to communicate with students during class, to take roll and provide assistance, by a

---

[2] Nonetheless, some teachers have justified the use of computer-facilitated audio chatting among students in the same lab class, particularly in foreign language environments with young learners. Duncan Charters, at Principia College in Illinois, supports this use of the technology for many reasons, such as that it provides a fun change of pace to other activities, eliminates non-verbal communication (giving practice for phone conversations that many learners find difficult), reduces student intimidation by allowing them to speak without being watched, tends to keep them focused on the task rather than horsing around with a friend next to them, and allows for greater and more efficient variety in pairing students.

synchronous chat, bulletin board, or simple e-mail group (see Chapter 5, Internet Activities). For example, I observed students working in an ESL lab class in Boston when their teacher was attending a conference in Amsterdam. The students were instructed to go to the teacher's website at the start of each lab class to read the assignment for the day.

On the day of his absence, they were instructed, on the assignment page, to log in to a private text chat room set up for the class, where the teacher greeted them from a **cybercafe** (where it was 9:00 PM). He led them through a discussion of art on display at the Rijksmuseum. While they viewed the images in a separate browser *window,* he directed questions at individual students. The entire text of the chat was logged by the program and later printed by the teacher for discussion. In addition to observing this experiment in distance learning, I assisted students with technical questions, assistance that could otherwise be provided by a lab assistant or a technically proficient student in class—the latter an example of cooperative learning.

> **Nicenet**
>
> Nicenet's Internet Classroom Assistant (ICA) is a free web resource for education. Teachers can create class groups and manage class communications similar to those offered by subscription-based courseware services (WebCT, CourseInfo, etc.). Nicenet offers a bulletin board for students in a class, where they can post messages on a topic, personal messaging, document sharing, scheduling, and link sharing *(www.nicenet.org).*

> **Cybercafe**
>
> A coffee shop where patrons can also rent time on a computer, usually for web browsing or e-mail. Cybercafes, or Internet cafes, didn't catch on in the United Sates to the extent that they have abroad, especially in countries with high telephone rates. They cater especially to tourists and business travelers.

I later used the same distance teaching technique for my class in Boston through a chat interface while at a conference in Turkey. The students had been creating their own web pages. We critiqued each student's work in one browser window while referring to another, which displayed a student's pages. Attendance at both of these distance teaching classes was consistent with the semester average, and participation among otherwise shy students was impressive. Thus we used technology to achieve a teaching objective, not simply because that capability existed.

Pitfall for New CALL Teachers

While technology enhances many activities, in terms of access, interaction, and teaching language through content, it's not a panacea for all language learning challenges and may fail to provide the most effective environment in certain cases or when the teacher does not carefully choose and plan activities.

☑ TIP 7

Invest time in training and orientation.

Teach students how to use tools of the lab classroom, their computers. Taking the time to walk students through the use of a new application or activity as a class will save time because it's easier to say something *once* to the class before an activity than to individually instruct *each* student during an activity. Time invested initially on orientation will pay off with less confusion later that must be addressed one student at a time. Use a show-and-tell method with a projector, if possible. Don't assume that students know computers or each program because they're young. They don't. As discussed in Tip 4, this instruction is a listening comprehension and vocabulary activity in itself.

📖 *Class Example*

A lab administrator could head off problems relating to insufficient lab orientation by scheduling *all* classes for orientations by lab staff at the beginning of the semester. Large programs might benefit from creating an orientation video or presentation slide show for students, one made available on the computers on a self-access basis. Such a video or presentation could be produced in the lab with digital video footage, still shots, screen shots, titles, and voice-over narration. Students could watch the program individually replaying segments as needed, and complete a worksheet of salient points. A lab assistant could discuss the answers with the group and respond to any other questions as well.

🗒 *Pitfall for New CALL Teachers*

Students with extensive computing experience may bring a false sense of confidence into the lab, skip orientation sessions, or pay little attention to instructions and directions in the lab. These students may fail to appreciate that their knowledge of computers bears little relevance to the specific procedures and learning resources of a particular lab. Such attitudes should not be given a pass by the teacher. Labs also have a right to expect students to know and respect the rules of using the facilities so that they can be maintained for all students.

☑ TIP 8

Pace activities.

There are two issues relating to pace:

1. *Students finish at different times.* Allowing students to complete activities at their own pace is part of the beauty of CALL. The challenge comes not with students taking too long to complete tasks but with those finishing before the others. What to do with them? Have *buffer* activities ready for these students—anything

providing some language learning stimulation of short or variable duration and requiring little or no direction. (See Chapter 5, Internet Activities: Pedantic Language Practice on page 77 for buffer activity ideas.)

2. *Transitioning from one activity to another takes time.* Choose your activities carefully for how much lab class time they will occupy, noting that many lab activities span several classes. Students are slow to change gears when they're at the wheel (that is, the mouse), so segue from one activity to another without abruptly interrupting their momentum. New activities must overcome the inertia of the preceding one while addressing the technical overhead of the new one. Allot more time to activities in the lab than you would in a conventional class, and be careful of rushing into another activity without sufficient class time to finish it. This approach differs from the less interactive conventional audio lab where we needed to mix things up to keep students awake.

📖 Class Example

The more complicated the activity, the greater the spread of finishing times among students will be. While buffer activities are the easiest to implement and provide flexibility, there are other options to try, depending on the students, their level, and the environment:

- Ask those finishing earlier to help a neighbor, though this may only work with students exhibiting leadership or helpfulness; otherwise, it's not much of an incentive for more proficient students.

- Ask early finishers to help with material preparation or to follow up on some tricky question not fully answered in a class discussion—an assignment especially attractive to students if the answer is to be found on the Internet.

- Have multiple projects in progress at any one time to provide work for these students to alternate between.

- Have students keep track of their lab work with an activity log, one that gives them direction for the next or buffer activities.

📑 Pitfall for New CALL Teachers

While finishing times for activities may differ among students, the *relative challenge* may still be the same for students of varying proficiencies; that is, one student may take longer than others to complete a listening comprehension cloze activity because the level of the exercise could have presented more of a challenge for him or her. The student didn't necessarily do less work. A student who finishes earlier and then moves on to complete another of the same type of activity, likewise, can't simply be seen as doing twice the work because it was, perhaps, easier for him or her.

☑ TIP 9

Be a resource guide.

A lab teacher's skill is largely exhibited in his or her ability to choose appropriate and effective materials and activities and to teach access skills and epistemology, particularly of the enormous Internet resources. As a lab teacher, you are the librarian of the lab in that it is partly your responsibility to introduce students to appropriate lab resources, whether used in class or not, in fact, especially for relevant materials you won't have time to use in class. Your role in the use of a content program, such as a grammar or pronunciation program, for example, is to *diagnose* individual student needs and *assign* the appropriate area to focus on for each. They can then work through activities on their own in a self-access lab. (See the discussion on the use of content activities in Chapter 9.)

Many software programs suffer from some degree of poor instructional design or lack intuitive navigation and function. You must bridge the gap between the value a program has to offer and a student's ability to tap into it by understanding the procedures for using it and being aware of the resources and features available.

📖 Class Example

A teacher of a test-preparation class (such as for the TOEFL®) might be inclined to have students use one of many available computer-based test (CBT) preparation programs in lab class. While this use of lab time for tutor programs defies Tip 1, there is value in *introducing* students to the resource and encouraging them to work with it *on their own time*. Preview these programs to learn exactly how they work including, for test-prep software, if a test can be paused and resumed later, if results include explanations of correct and incorrect responses, and if these annotated results can be printed. Demonstrate for students, ideally with the use of a projector, how to use and navigate the program, its strengths and weaknesses, including glitches that might waste student time.

📑 Pitfall for New CALL Teachers

While familiarizing students with content or pedantic programs as resources available for their use outside of class, don't forget to move on to introducing other programs or doing other activities. That is, keep Tip 1 in mind and don't let students roll from learning how to use one of these tutor programs into spending the whole class using it, though it may be difficult to curb their momentum.

☑ TIP 10

Orchestrate communicative activities.

Some second language teachers see language teaching as at least as much of a performance art as an academic discipline. This notion—sure to stir opposition—holds that a CALL teacher's job is to orchestrate communicative activities that are student centered and student empowering. In a CALL lab, students have an expectation of hands-on work and active participation more than passive listening; they are more predisposed to *doing* something. Give them instructions for an activity, and let them have at it. Develop open-ended activities where students create as much as possible and are not arbitrarily restricted to a narrow, predefined model. And pairing proves critical here, because if they are at least speaking the target language (in unlike L1 pairs, if possible), then they are getting valuable speaking and listening practice in the process regardless of their progress on the activity itself.

📖 *Class Example*

Using the Socratic method in class, you can demonstrate how useful students can be to each other and how they should look to each other first to answer their computer or activity questions. Why answer a student's question when you can get another student to do it for you? It takes more finesse to facilitate understanding through productive query and interaction than it does to simply be a font of knowledge. But teachers know that already.

📋 *Pitfall for New CALL Teachers*

Getting students' attention in a lab class can be difficult. You're competing with the computer in front of each one of them. Make announcements and give instruction at the beginning, and keep it short. If your lab has the ability to lock students' screens temporarily, use it (but judiciously—students may be gritting their teeth till they can get back to the computer).

Keep these ten suggestions in mind while you consider implementing any of the class activities from Part 2.

Assessing Lab Effectiveness

How do you know that your labs are working? Is there a special test to indicate progress? How do you know your regular classroom teaching is effective? Assessment is the same: improved ability and inclination to communicate in the target language, higher test scores, good attendance, etc. Keep in mind that in most situations the lab component (not including individual access) makes up a small percentage of a student's language instruction time overall. Also, look at your attendance in lab classes versus other classes, read what students write about the lab in their evaluations, and try to pick up what they're saying to each other about the lab.

PART 2

CALL Classroom Activities

Introduction

While theoretical discussions of CALL and hypothetical scenarios may help define the role of computers in language learning, they don't provide teachers with classroom activities, at least not in any immediately applicable form. The six chapters in Part 2 offer practical activities, resources, and techniques to take into a lab class. These activities represent a *selection* from many options. Once you're comfortable with one, try another to expand your repertoire. Fortunately, teachers make extensive use of the Internet to publish their ideas, techniques, and sometimes complete curricula.

Breakdown of Activities in Part 2

Chapter 4—Writing Activities

Chapter 5—Internet Activities

Chapter 6—Audio/Video Activities

Chapter 7—Project Activities

Chapter 8—Text-Based Activities

Chapter 9—Content Activities

These chapters do not organize activities around discrete language skills, a notion that would betray the theme of this book, of CALL providing a more realistic, engaging, and communicative environment for language learning—*multi*skill in other words. The very nature of this multiskill environment—challenging, interactive, full of stimuli—provides a certain underlying justification for doing a particular activity in the lab versus in a traditional classroom, though qualified by the teacher's effective use of this environment. This view of CALL prefaces a response to the question, "How does this activity help my students learn language?" That is, the challenging nature of the environment and interactive nature of the activities combine for a stimulating and communicative language experience. What's learned can be judged by the *process,* the struggle with activities, at least as much as by the *product,* or the completion of an activity.

For the most part, the focus in the following chapters remains on activities and ideas that can be widely adapted, not on specific software or procedures (though the features of a few popular programs are explored). Most can be modified or expanded to suit the target language and level of student. Each chapter includes example activities of several variations, with suggestions for teacher skills, student level, and software needed:

- **Teacher skills:** suggested computing experience of the teacher
- **Student level:** suggested range of student's target language proficiency
- **Content objective:** computing skills introduced or reinforced
- **Software (and/or equipment):** minimum applications (and equipment) required for activity

The activities in Part 2 are presented with the following components:

- **Introduction:** a brief description of the activity
- **Pedagogical Rationale:** the learning potential this activity may offer
- **Teacher Preparation:** recommended steps for the teacher to take prior to the activity
- **Steps for Students:** concise procedures for students to follow in the activity

Some activities do not include all of these components, such as where a prior activity has already provided pedagogical rationale for a variation or where it is self-evident, or where student steps can be derived from the teacher preparation steps or where they would most meaningfully be adapted by teachers for a particular setting. Additional technical information and tips are presented in sidebars.

Two important variables in how teachers implement these activities concern (1) the *teacher-student burden balance* and (2) the *coordination of lab activities with class activities*.[1]

1. Shifting activity setup and tasks from the teacher to students increases their responsibilities and the challenge of the activity while decreasing teacher preparation or at least giving the teacher more time in class for one-on-one work with students.

2. The degree to which lab activities support or correspond to regular classroom activities depends on where labs fit in the structure of classes—whether they are electives or core classes and whether they are taught by the same person that teaches non-lab classes or a different teacher. Elective lab classes and those taught by someone other than the core or classroom teacher may have less of a connection to classroom work. Coordinating lab activities with classroom work may give

---

[1] Terry O'Neil, director of the English Learning Center lab at Koç University, Istanbul, Turkey, suggests an awareness of these variables to increase the effectiveness and practicality of lab activities.

more continuity to activities and make more efficient use of lab time, where preparation that doesn't require computers (e.g., planning projects, choosing topics) won't be distracted by them.

Computer Requirements

All of the activities can be done using PCs or Macs in a variety of lab setups and with a variety of software. The computers you use for class should have the language kit (character set) installed for the language you're teaching. Ideally, they will also have a *localized* version of the OS, too (one that uses the target language for the interface). Many activities would also benefit from the availability of a projector for the teacher or student to project his or her computer screen for the entire class to see at once. A projector shows students what you're telling them, a visual demonstration supporting a verbal explanation, which is especially useful for detailed, step-by-step instructions and for student presentations.

Above all, this book is not designed to serve as an application manual and thus makes certain assumptions about the availability of other resources to address those particular needs.

4

Writing Activities

- ❖ Students don't need to be taught how to use a word processor, do they?
- ❖ The only program we have is a word processor. What can we do in class?
- ❖ What are document templates used for?

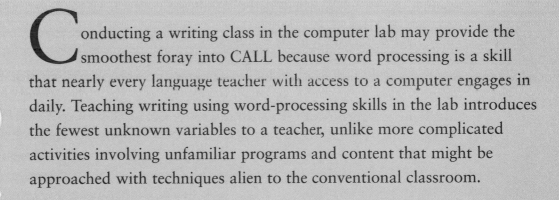

Conducting a writing class in the computer lab may provide the smoothest foray into CALL because word processing is a skill that nearly every language teacher with access to a computer engages in daily. Teaching writing using word-processing skills in the lab introduces the fewest unknown variables to a teacher, unlike more complicated activities involving unfamiliar programs and content that might be approached with techniques alien to the conventional classroom.

The eight writing activities in this chapter involve writing for a wide range of communicative purposes. Writing activities that rely on an Internet connection are covered in Chapter 5, Internet Activities. Also note that these ideas bring computer capabilities to bear on established writing activities rather than represent techniques for teaching writing generally.

	ACTIVITY 1 ■ Word-Processing Basics[1]
	Teacher skills: basic word-processor use
	Student level: high-beginning to advanced
	Content objective: basic text manipulation
	Software: word processor[2]

This activity combines instruction on word-processor use with explicit language instruction and can easily be adapted to any language, level, or grammar focus on any word processor. Students will correct a paragraph while learning to manipulate text.

Teacher Preparation

- Write a short paragraph or use one from a recent reading in class, such as the **example paragraph** (uncorrected) that follows.
- Do not capitalize any word or letter.
- Jumble (i.e., move out of order) one or more sentences.
- Remove several words at random or according to a recent grammatical or lexical focus.
- Add some extraneous words or phrases to sentences.

---

[1] Pamela Couch, at Mission College, Santa Clara, California, generously provided comments and supplied the first two activities of this chapter, which she regularly uses with her ESL writing students at the beginning of the semester.

[2] Commercial word processors, such as Microsoft Word, AppleWorks, Nisus Writer, or Corel WordPerfect, are preferable for these activities, though free programs included with Windows (WordPad) or Mac OS (SimpleText, TextEdit) or *freeware* (free programs) available online will work, albeit without some advanced features, such as spell-checkers, a thesaurus, document templates, collaborative tools, headers/footers, footnotes, print styles, and so forth. Note that Word in Microsoft Works (PCs only) lacks some of the features of Word in Microsoft Office.

- Save the document as a *template* (see **TECHNOTE: Template** on page 35) and distribute to each student according to the document-sharing procedures for the class (such as via a shared network volume, e-mail *attachment,* class website, or *courseware* site). Or simply e-mail the text in a message to each student and have students copy and paste this text into a new word-processing document.

Example paragraph (uncorrected)

the wampanoags, a native american tribe, inhabited the before european settlers arrived in the 17th century. the settlers fished hunted the bountiful waters around the island, and nantucket developed as a fishing and boat-building port the. in the 18th century, it became one of the most important whaling ports in the world. men set out on ships for up to water four years to hunt whales. whale fat, or blubber, was used to produce lamp oil, candle wax, perfume, of and other products. the island's inhabitants no longer make a living by fishing or whaling. since the early 20-century, tourism, not, has been the primary industry. people come to at its beautiful beaches and admire the elegant ship captains' mansions the town center. nantucket is an island off the coast of massachusetts, south cape cod.

Example paragraph (corrected)

Nantucket is an island off the coast of Massachusetts, south of Cape Cod. The Wampanoags, a Native American tribe, inhabited the island before European settlers arrived in the 17th century. The settlers fished the bountiful waters around the island, and Nantucket developed as a fishing and boat-building port. In the 18th century, it became one of the most important whaling ports in the world. Men set out on ships for up to four years to hunt whales. Whale fat, or blubber, was used to produce lamp oil, candle wax, perfume, and other products. The island's inhabitants no longer make a living by fishing or whaling. Since the early 20th century, tourism, not whaling, has been the primary industry. People come to swim at its beautiful beaches and admire the elegant ship captains' mansions in the town center.

Steps for Students

- Open the document and identify the problems with the paragraph (sentence order, capitalization, missing and extra words).
- Follow the teacher's demonstration on how to make the necessary changes to the text, which will include
  - selecting or "highlighting" text
  - moving selections
  - cutting

- copying
- pasting
- inserting
- replacing

■ If you make a mistake, use the **Edit > Undo** command immediately to take back the action.

■ Compare your edited paragraph with a partner's to verify.

■ Save a copy in the appropriate saving location, giving the file a descriptive name.

Glitches

Teachers in the lab sometimes assume that students know what they need to know to use any word-processing program effectively. While possibly true for some, this assumption will likely lead to wasted time and interrupted activities by repeatedly instructing many students individually instead of instructing the group once on the use of a program.

Saving

Save early and often. Writing is a cumulative process and saving an incremental one. Use the **Save** not **Save As...** command (see Figure 4.1), because the first time you save a document, the **Save** command invokes the **Save As...** *dialog box* (see Figure 4.2) anyway (the ellipses indicate a dialog box follows) since you must establish a *name* for the file and the saving *location* (hard drive, removable disk, server volume, etc.). Subsequent saves require only the **Save** command (**Apple-S** on Macs or **Ctrl-S** on PCs) again because the file name and location are already established.

Know your saving location; the file has to be stored *somewhere*. Some applications point to their application folder for saving by default (i.e., until you change it in the **Save As...** dialog box). Be organized and create folders in the initial **Save As...** dialog box if necessary (click on the **Create New Folder** icon or button). Many applications remember the last ten or so documents opened in that application. Find these "Recent Documents" under the **File** menu of the application.

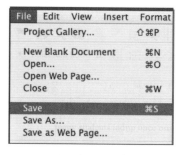

Figure 4.1 ■ Use the **Save** command from the **File** *menu* the first and subsequent times you save a document unless you want to change the file name, type, or location.

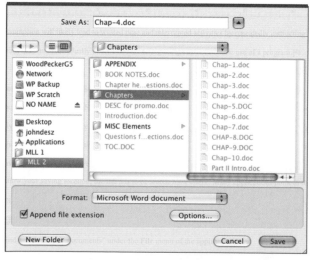

Figure 4.2 ■ The **Save As...** *dialog box* is used the first time a document is saved to name the file and choose a saving location and file format.

TECHNOTE ▪ **Template**

A template is a file format option in the **File** > **Save As...** dialog box of many applications. Saving any document as a template (also called *stationary*) permits it to be opened by more than one user on a network at the same time, such as if the class uses a shared network folder on a server for class documents. A template document opens as an untitled copy, so the original file is not changed. Templates (or locked files, depending on the application) may need to be copied to a new document to be editable using the **File** > **Save As...** command.

To convert an existing document to a template

Open the document, go to **File** > **Save As...** "Document Template" or "Stationary" from the file type options, if available. Otherwise:

• (Mac) Click once on the file in the Finder and choose **File** > **Get Info** (or **Apple-I**) then click in the "Stationary" box (see Figure 4.3).

• (PC) Right-click the file in a directory view, choose **Properties** from the pop-up menu, check "Read only" (see Figure 4.4).

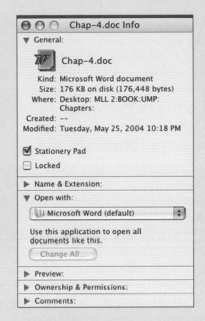

Figure 4.3 ▪ (Mac) Change any file to stationary with the file information box (**File** > **Get Info**). Check the Stationary box.

Figure 4.4 ▪ (PC) Making a file read-only effectively makes it stationary. Right-click on the file, choose **Properties**, and check the Read-only box.

TECHNOTE ■ File Format	
There are many types, or formats, of word-processing documents. The default, or *native*, format is the one identified with that application, such as Microsoft Word (.doc) or WordPerfect (.wpd). Other common formats include earlier application versions, and the nonproprietary rich text format (.rtf) and text-only (.txt).	*RTF* retains document formatting, such as character size and style, line spacing, and alignment. The "text-only" format strips the document of all formatting, leaving only the plain text characters. Both can be read by any word processor on any computer.

✎ ACTIVITY 2 ■ Academic (Manuscript) Formatting	
	Teacher skills: word processing, academic formatting conventions
	Student level: low-intermediate to advanced
	Content objective: formatting academic papers
	Software: word processor

Students, especially those beginning postsecondary education, need to know how to format a paper, partly to meet the expectations of teachers and others reading them and partly to shift their focus from how the text *looks* (big, funky, colorful fonts) to what it *says*. The first writing assignment for such students, no matter the length or difficulty, can serve as a vehicle to teach acceptable formatting for papers. Use the same paragraph from Activity 1 in this chapter or use a short writing assignment to demonstrate how to make basic formatting changes to text.

Typical paper formatting conventions for U.S. schools

- Include on top of first or title page: name, class, paper title, date.
- Use default or common 12-point *serif* font (Georgia, Times New Roman, Palatino) in black.
- Use appropriate case (sentence, proper noun, and acronym capitalization; no text in ALL CAPS).

- *Justify* (align) text to left only (leave jagged on right).

- Double-space lines with paragraph formatting command (select all text first).

- Let the end of lines wrap automatically (no *hard returns* with **Enter/Return** key except for the end of paragraphs).

- Do not add an extra paragraph return between paragraphs.

- Indent the first line of paragraphs 1/2" with the **Tab** key or paragraph formatting.

- Number pages when there is more than one (for long documents, use a header or footer for name, title, and page).

- Use default margins for a new document (usually 1" all around).

Formatting Marks

These are nonprinting marks to indicate spaces, tabs, paragraph returns, etc. (see Figure 4.5). Most word processors have a toolbar button to display or suppress these marks. Have students display these marks to reveal whether they are using the word processor correctly, for example, by letting the program wrap text automatically at the end of the line instead of hitting the **Enter/Return** key, double-spacing lines, and centering text, such as a title, with the text alignment tool instead of the space bar. Seeing formatting marks allows a teacher to quickly assess document layout or printing problems. Students often don't like seeing these nonprinting characters, mostly because they can't image that they *don't* print.

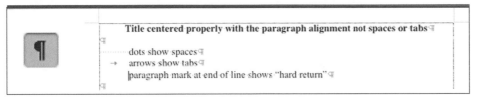

Figure 4.5 ■ The **Show/Hide** formatting button from the Word toolbar (left) and a Word document with formatting marks revealed (right).

📓 ACTIVITY 3 ■ Using Built-in Language Tools	
	Teacher skills: word processing, using a spell-checker and a thesaurus
	Student level: low-intermediate to advanced
	Content objective: using proofing tools
	Software: word processor

If you're using a word processor that includes language tools, such as a spell-checker, the-saurus, and grammar-checker, *and* you allow your students to use them in their writing, show students how to use these tools properly.

A **spell-checker** only looks for words that do not exist in its built-in dictionary or the *user* (custom) dictionary, to which you add words with a **Learn** or **Add** button in the spell-checker dialog box, as shown in Figure 4.6. It does not detect inappropriate use or erroneous grammar or syntax (*to* for *too* or *your* for *you're*). Most spelling tools suggest alternative words based on those with similar spellings or sounds of the questionable word.

The **thesaurus** tool ostensibly offers the prospect of introducing students to new words (see Figure 4.7), but must be used carefully and with a dictionary and usage examples.

Figure 4.6 ■ The spell-checker in Word adds words to your personal dictionary or corrects them based on given suggestions. The **Options** button allows the users to ignore it.

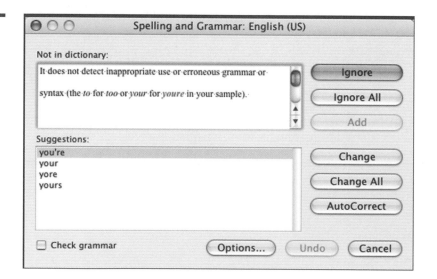

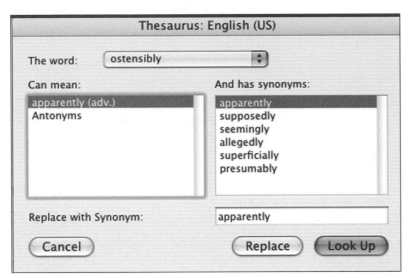

Figure 4.7 ■ The thesaurus in Word suggests synonyms for a selected word. Search for synonyms of selected synonyms as well by double-clicking on one.

Grammar-checkers may point out errors such as incomplete sentences, comma splices, faulty subject-verb agreement, or case mistakes. They highlight problematic phrasing and then offer prescriptive notes.

Teacher Preparation

- Create a document with text from a class reading or other source.
- Save it as a template and distribute to all students (as in Activity 1).
- Include misspelled words, misuse of correctly spelled words, and proper nouns not likely to be in the word processor's built-in dictionary.
- Include word choices you would like them to change with the assistance of the thesaurus (e.g., *support* for *assistance* in this sentence).
- To demonstrate the grammar-checker, include grammatical errors (such as sentence fragments, faulty agreement, and case mistakes).
- Have students open the document (as a copy) and demonstrate the use of the tools on the paragraph.

Steps for Students

- Open the document template.
- Listen as the teacher demonstrates the use of each tool.
- Start the spell-checker (with the toolbar button or menu command).

- Determine if a suspect word is actually misspelled or if it's a proper noun not in the dictionary.

- Select suggested spellings as appropriate.

- Reread the document for incorrect use of correctly spelled words.

- Find words that do not seem to be the correct choice for the context.

- Click on such a word, and then invoke the thesaurus for suggested replacements.

- Look up thesaurus suggestions in the dictionary before choosing them.

- If using the grammar-checker, look at the problems identified and read the suggested notes.

- See if the grammar-checker still identifies problems with the corrected sentence.

- Verify your corrected text with a partner's corrected text.

Glitches

The danger of misleading students using these **proofing tools** lies not with the rules presented in the grammar-checker or in options provided by a spell-checker or thesaurus but the *application* of a rule where the tool cannot possibly analyze the larger context, tone, or intent. All of these tools have utility for writers but only when used carefully. Teachers should not assume that students know *how* to use a tool just because they know where to find it.

Spell-checker: Some students take a *suggested* word in a spell-checker as *recommended* and accept a nonsensical replacement—and one that doesn't show up in future spell-checks as questionable.

Thesaurus: Students might refer to synonyms in the thesaurus simply to avoid repetition without consulting a dictionary or usage manual or consider how the changes might confuse the reader.

Grammar-checker: A grammar-checker may lead inexperienced writers to believe that it can do what most writers and teachers know can still only be done by humans. Grammar-checkers may find errors where they do not exist, such as identifying a clause as a sentence fragment if the subject is separated from its verb by commas, as with an appositive or a noun clause. They also tend to loathe the passive voice in English, opposing every instance, even where it is not a style choice but an appropriate device for emphasizing *what* was done, not *who* did it or to avoid attributing it.

📖 Activity 4 ■ Using Other Writing Resources	
	Teacher skills: word processing, using dictionary and encyclopedia programs
	Student level: low-intermediate to advanced
	Content objective: using dictionary and encyclopedia programs or sites
	Software: word processor, dictionary and encyclopedia program or online versions

This writing activity employs an encyclopedia and reinforces paraphrasing techniques.

Many **CD-** and free web-based dictionaries offer audible pronunciation of words and *hyperlinked* definitions (where words within a definition are linked to their own definitions). More elaborate dictionary programs, such as the *Longman Dictionary of American English CD-ROM for ESL/EFL*, offer interaction between dictionary entries, pictures, and exercises, and integration into Microsoft Word as a toolbar command. A reverse dictionary function allows students to search for a word based on its definition. For example, typing in a search field *dry* and *weather* would result in *drought*. Main dictionary entries include audio pronunciation (see Figure 4.8). Other disk-based encyclopedias contain audio and video clips with separate captioning or a transcript of the audio, reinforcing listening (see Figure 4.9).

Figure 4.8 ■ The *Merriam-Webster Online Dictionary* provides a definition for each entry for a word, but, more important, an audio of a native speaker pronouncing it (click on speaker icon). By permission. From the Merriam-Webster OnLine Dictionary ©2004 by Merriam-Webster, Incorporated (www.Merriam-Webster.com).

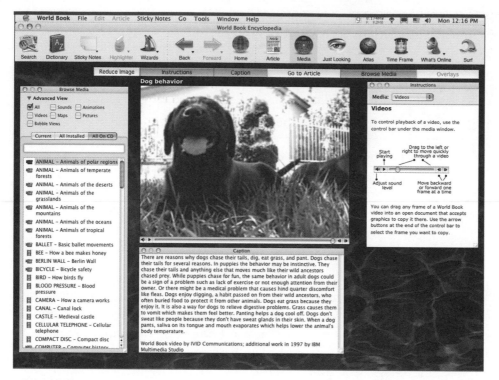

Figure 4.9 ■ An article with video from an encyclopedia CD. Transcript of video appears in window below image, instruction for using the video controller appears to the right, and the search/browse tool appears to the left. (World Book 2004 CD, Mac OS X version)

Pedagogical Rationale

A second language learners' dictionary—as opposed to a bilingual or native dictionary—will offer more utility to a language student than simple definitions, such as grouping words (e.g., weather-related terms), a reverse dictionary function, pronunciation, usage notes, and example sentences. Encyclopedias in the target language, either online or on CD or *DVD*, provide good, general resources to language students in writing classes and encourage exploration of related or adjacent items or random discovery. Acquainting students with the use of an electronic encyclopedia may entail differentiating the use of a dictionary versus that of an encyclopedia, that is, how some entries may be represented in both but the expectation of the information sought in each differs.

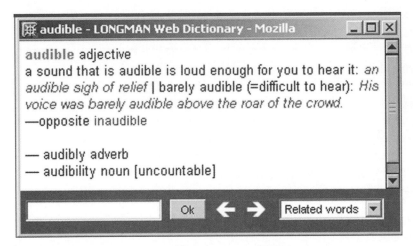

Figure 4.10 ■ The free *Longman Web Dictionary* gives definitions especially for second language learners without part-of-speech abbreviations and with an antonym, example usage, related words, and information such as whether a noun is count or noncount. *(www.longmanwebdict.com) From the definition of* audible *from* Longman Dictionary of Contemporary English, 4th ed., *Pearson Education.*

Teacher Preparation

- Demonstrate to students how to look up a term in the encyclopedia program or site used, including accessing **multimedia** material if available.

- Assign to each student an entry to look up, something that is otherwise unfamiliar to the student.

- If the encyclopedia includes exercises for entries, in the form of comprehension questions or quizzes following the article, assign them to students as well.

Steps for Students

- Read the encyclopedia entry until you understand it. Look up unfamiliar words in a dictionary.

- Take notes but don't copy complete sentences.

- Close the encyclopedia program or page.

- Write your own description using the word processor.

- Exchange entry descriptions with your partner and verify each other's description with the encyclopedia entry.

Glitch

Paraphrasing is difficult. It may be helpful for students to learn to fully understand something first, to the point where they can then repeat it or explain it to someone else, without referring to the original text. Thus it's critical that they close the encyclopedia program or web page before they start writing their description of their entry.

✎ ACTIVITY 5 ▪ Story Starter	
	Teacher skills: word processing, spell-checking, using a thesaurus
	Student level: high-beginning to advanced
	Content objective: collaborative writing
	Software: word processor, e-mail program

Students write a story whose first line has been given to them. To connect the lab activity to the classroom curriculum, use one from the beginning of a short story that the students will later read in class.

Pedagogical Rationale

Story starters get the ball rolling on a creative writing project while giving students practice with writing either as a *synchronous* (working at the same time) or *asynchronous* (working separately in turn) activity—see **TECHNOTE: Synchronous and Asynchronous Communication** in Chapter 5 on page 75). With one student's contribution following another, you have the opportunity of introducing students to collaborative writing tools built into programs such as Word and WordPerfect (see Activity 8 later in this chapter), where students can comment on the contributions of others. (In word processors that don't support these features, students can simply add comments in the text manually using an agreed-upon color code—for example, red for text to delete, green for text to add, and blue for comments.)

Pairs vs. Groups

A *pair* of students can work together at the same time at the same computer. Both contribute, but only one is at the keyboard at a time. Such an in-class writing activity could be completed in one or two classes. Higher-level students and *groups* of three or more might be better suited to collaborating on the writing but not sharing a computer. Each student works on the story individually in turn, on a computer either in class or as homework. The student passes it along to group members by e-mail or through the designated saving location for the class. Each group member makes his or her own contribution until the project is finished. The group members can meet together for a final reading and make changes and corrections as well as standardize the formatting. This collaborative approach assumes that students will have other tasks or activities to occupy them in the lab while they're not working on their contribution or that they will work on it exclusively as homework. In either case, the project will take longer to complete as a group collaborative effort than the pair approach.

Teacher Preparation

- Organize students into pairs working together or teams of three or four collaborating but writing their own text (see **Pairs vs. Groups** on page 44).

- Choose a story from which to take the first line.

- Copy this story starter to a document and save it as a template where students can access it.

- Decide on project parameters and discuss them with the class:

  - use of external sources (references, other stories)

  - length of story

  - involvement of each member

  - use of collaborative writing tools to edit and comment on each other's contributions (for group work)

  - deadlines for passing the story off to the next student (for group work)

  - when the completed project is due

- Assign one writer in each team the responsibility of formatting the completed story—making the font, margins, and spacing consistent throughout and conforming to formatting guidelines (see Activity 2).

✎ ACTIVITY 6 ■ Interview	
	Teacher skills: word processing, using a spell-checker and a thesaurus
	Student level: high-beginning to advanced
	Content objective: interviewing, note-taking, writing interviews
	Software: word processor

At the beginning of the semester, an interview activity can serve as an icebreaker while reinforcing word-processing skills and formatting conventions. Students interview each other in pairs or in a chain where *a* interviews *b* who interviews *c* who interviews *a*. The subject can be simply biographical or a position on a topic and can become part of a class book later in the semester (see Chapter 7, Project Activities: Class Books on page 139).

Teacher Preparation

- Assign pairs or groups to interview each other.
- Give students hints on questions and demonstrate how to ask follow-up questions.
- Show them examples of how to take quick notes without taking dictation.

Steps for Students

- Interview your partner or group member.
- Take notes but not dictation.
- Type up the interview, observing the formatting guidelines learned in Activity 2.
- Give a draft of your interview to your interviewee so he or she can check it for accuracy and comment.
- Correct your draft.
- Save the interview file for a possible class book later.

EXPANDING ACTIVITY 6 ■ Adding Photos

Expand interviews to include a photo or other graphic in the text document. Most word processors can import common graphic file types (*JPEG*, *GIF*, *TIFF*, PICT, or bitmap). They can be resized in the word processor after being inserted into the document. Add other *relevant* graphics using students' digital or scanned photos or images from the web found with image *search engines* (such as **Google > Images**). (See Activity 6, Class Books, in Chapter 7 for details on working with images in text documents.)

ACTIVITY 7 ■ Business Writing	
	Teacher skills: word processing, using a spell-checker and a thesaurus
	Student level: high-intermediate to advanced
	Content objective: using business templates
	Software: word processor

Programs like Microsoft Word, AppleWorks, Corel WordPerfect, and other word processors have templates for many different kinds of documents, such as business correspondence, interoffice memos, resumes, newsletters, brochures, manuals (see Figure 4.11).[3] *Templates* set up document layout and type styles, so students can concentrate on adding their content to placeholder text without getting distracted by formatting, yet when they're finished, their content is in the appropriate form. Access these templates (or stationary) when you create a new document (in Word, **File > New from template**).

If the word processor you use does not include templates, you can find many examples on the web, such as at an OWL (online writing labs—see Chapter 5, Writing Activities). Writing textbooks, especially business writing books, also include samples of various business forms.

Teacher Preparation

- Coordinate this activity with class work on writing business correspondence, memos, resumes, etc.

- Determine a template to use (see Figure 4.11) and make sure students can access them as well.

- This activity could also be a printed form of Activity 3, Letter of Complaint, in Chapter 5 on page 64. Have students write a letter in business form complaining or commenting positively about a company's product or service. Follow the steps in that activity and print the letter instead of sending it by e-mail.

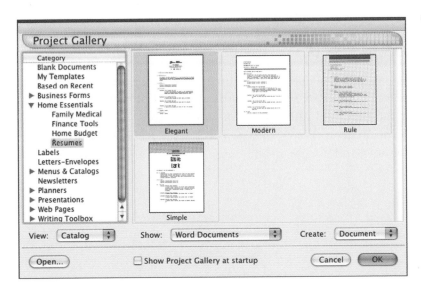

Figure 4.11 ■ To base a new document on a built-in template in Word or any other Microsoft Office template, such as for Excel, PowerPoint, or Front-Page, open the Project Gallery from Word's **File** menu. Here are the templates for Word only, resume formats in particular, from the **Home Essentials** template folder (Mac OS X).

---

[3]Some versions of Microsoft Word require custom installation of many of these templates from the application CD or from the Microsoft website.

📓 ACTIVITY 8 ▪ Editing Student Writing	
	Teacher skills: word processing, using comment and track changes feature
	Student level: low-intermediate to advanced
	Content objective: using proofing tools
	Software: word processor with comment and track changes features

More and more, students in regular writing classes (where the class physically meets) as well as in online classes submit their writing assignments electronically to their teacher as e-mail attachments or through a *courseware* site. Some word processors offer teachers an alternative to writing directly on students' printed papers and physically handing them back.[4] Teachers can comment on a student's paper using features built into the word processor and then send a copy back to the student by e-mail or by saving to the designated saving location for the class. The student gets a copy of his or her paper with comments and changes clearly identified. In addition to students in writing courses, people collaborating on writing projects and even those working in the same office, commonly use these features.

Comment Feature in Microsoft Word

The **Comment** feature inserts comments into a document exactly as you would with a pen, except that they're editable and face no space limitations as handwritten margin notes do. If you are using the comment and track changes features regularly, it will save time to add these tools to the Word toolbar: **View > Toolbars > Reviewing.** Buttons to quickly accept or reject changes and add or delete comments will appear (see Figure 4.12).

---

[4]Both Microsoft Word and Corel WordPerfect have the features to add comments and track editing changes discussed here, though the procedures in Word, for PC or Mac, are detailed here (see the sidebar on **Version Variations,** page 52). Both of these programs have in their **Help** menus assistance for switchers from the other program. For example, WordPerfect presents a two-column table with Word functions on the left and the corresponding WordPerfect functions on the right, with links to specific help files.

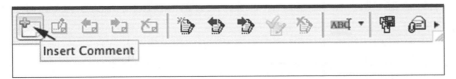

Figure 4.12 ■ The Reviewing *toolbar* in Word gives easy access to buttons for working with Comments or Track Changes (**View** > **Toolbars** > **Reviewing**).

Teacher Preparation

- Use any student writing assignment on which to comment electronically instead of conventionally (i.e., writing on the hard copy in pen).

- Have students submit their papers to you electronically, either by saving to the class-saving location or by sending via e-mail.

- If you *and* your students both use Microsoft Word or Corel WordPerfect, then follow these instructions for using the Comment and Track Changes features.

- If you and your students both do not use either of the these applications, then follow the instructions under Manual Comments for Other Word Processors on page 51.

Steps for Teachers—Using Word's Comment Feature

- Open the student's document in Word.

- Add the comment and track changes buttons to your toolbar: **View** > **Toolbars** > **Reviewing**. (Hover the mouse over any of the buttons to see its function in the balloon description—see Figure 4.12.)

- Be sure the view mode is Print Layout (**View** > **Print Layout**).

- Place the cursor exactly where you would like the first comment to appear in the text.

- Click the **New (or Insert) Comment** button on the toolbar.

- Write your comment in the special box or colored bubble that appears.

- Comments can be edited or deleted later.
  - To edit, click on the Comment text.
  - To delete, click on Comment, then click the **Delete Comment** button or right-click (PC) or **Ctrl**-click (Mac) on the Comment and choose **Delete** from the *pop-up menu.*

- When finished commenting on the document, save the file under a different name or location, indicating that it's the teacher's commented version (**File** > **Save As...**).

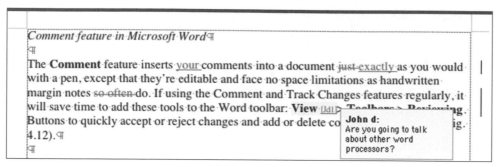

Comment feature in Microsoft Word¶
¶
The **Comment** feature inserts your comments into a document just exactly as you would
with a pen, except that they're editable and face no space limitations as handwritten
margin notes so often do. If using the Comment and Track Changes features regularly, it
will save time to add these tools to the Word toolbar: **View** [Jd] ᐅ Toolbars > Reviewing.
Buttons to quickly accept or reject changes and add or delete co   ig.
4.12).¶

> **John d:**
> Are you going to talk
> about other word
> processors?

Figure 4.13 ■ Text marked up with Word's Comment and Track Changes
features. Deleted text will appear in red on screen with a line through the middle;
added text will appear in red and underlined; comments are inserted where the
text is highlighted in yellow, with the comment appearing when you *mouse over*
the highlighted text.

Steps for Students—Correcting a Paper with Word Comments

- Open the essay document corrected by your teacher.

- Be sure the view mode is Print Layout (**View** > **Print Layout**).

- Read the teacher's comments and edit your document accordingly.

- You do not need to delete the comments. They will not print unless you want them printed (see **Viewing and Printing Word Comments** on page 51).

- To delete comments, right-click (PC) or **Ctrl**-click (Mac) on a comment, and then choose **Delete** from the pop-up menu.

---

[5] "Classic" is the Macintosh operating system before OS X, specifically OS 9 as it runs within a window of OS X. Applications designed to run on older versions of the Mac (pre- OS X) can run within OS X as long as that computer also has the Mac OS 9 system ("Classic") installed as well. (See Chapter 10 for a discussion of computer *platform*.)

Audio Comments

As an alternative to text comments, you can also record them into a document, especially long, complicated comments that need to be explained and might overwhelm the text if written out. In most versions of Word with this feature, insert a recorded comment just as you would a text comment, but click on the audiocassette icon in the comment box to begin (and stop) recording each comment. An audio comment icon will appear in text like an icon appears for a text comment. Audio comments will considerably increase the file size of the document and may affect your ability to transfer it, such as by e-mail attachment. Other writing tools, such as the Daedalus® Integrated Writing Environment (discussed later in this chapter), offer audio comments as well. (Your computer will need to be set up to record with a microphone. Look in the **Control Panel** > **Sound** (PC, Mac Classic)[5] or **System Preferences** > **Sound** (Mac OS X).

Manual Comments for Other Word Processors

- Open the student's document in your word processor.

- Place the cursor in the text where you want to place a comment, just as with Word comments.

- Type the comment and then select the comment text and change the text color either with a toolbar color selector or from the **Format** menu (usually **Font** or **Character** > **Color**).

- Use a consistent color scheme, e.g., blue = comment only, red = text to delete, green = text to add.

- Save the file as a copy (**File > Save As…**).

- Comments entered in this manual way *will* print, so the student will need to delete them before printing.

Viewing and Printing Word Comments

Comments appear only in the Print Layout view (from the **View** menu). They do not appear in the Normal view. Depending on the version of Word and View mode selected, comments appear in the right margin with an arrow to the exact location in text referred to or in a bubble that appears when the pointer passes over a comment symbol in the text (or yellow highlighted text). Otherwise, *right-click* (PC) or **Ctrl**-click (Mac) on the comment indicator in the text to read it. Comments print with the text only if you select that option in printing (see Figure 4.14).

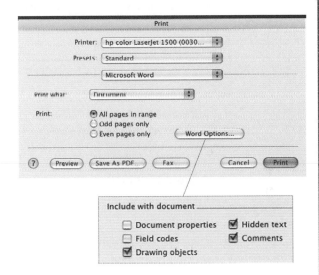

Figure 4.14 ▪ To print comments and tracked changes, choose the Word options in the print dialog box and then check the boxes to print comments and hidden text.

Track Changes Feature in Microsoft Word

Another editing feature of Word and WordPerfect is **Track Changes,** a visual record of changes made to the text, a tool used by teachers, editors, and writers collaborating on projects. With Track Changes enabled, Word marks up a text document just as you might with a pen (but more legibly), with words to delete crossed out, added words underlined or appearing in a bubble, and all changes color coded (see Figure 4.13). If more than one person edits the same document, different colors can be used for different editors. Passing the mouse over changed text will identify the editor in a pop-up box. An editor's changes do not take effect until the writer accepts them.

Teachers reviewing student writing drafts—ones to be edited again by students—may find the Comment feature more appropriate than this feature (see **Glitches: Pedagogical Concerns** on page 53).

Steps for Teachers—Using Word's Track Changes Feature

- Open the student's document in Word.

- Add the Comment and Track Changes buttons to your toolbar: **View > Toolbars > Reviewing.**

- Click the **Track Changes** button to toggle it on (click again to toggle off later).

- Track changes marks appear in Normal or Print Layout view (in **View** menu). Choose the look you prefer.

- Begin editing the document: add, delete, change, or move any text as needed.

- Track changes will automatically indicate your changes:
  - Deleted text will appear colored with a ~~line through it~~.
  - Added text will appear in the same color as above but <u>underlined</u>.
  - Moved text will have colored arrows indicating where it moved from.
  - The look these changes takes can be customized: **Tools > Options > Track Changes.**

- When finished editing the document, save the file under a different name or location, indicating that it's the edited version (**File > Save As...**).

> **Version Variations**
>
> The exact look and functioning of the **Track Changes** and **Comments** features in Word may vary by the version (e.g., XP, 2004), by the suite that it's a part of (Office or Works), or by the platform (Mac or PC), though the general concepts and functionality remain the same. Consult the **Help** menu in the version of Word you're using if you have trouble using these features.

Steps for Students—Correcting a Paper with Track Changes

- Open the edited document.

- Be sure the view mode is Normal (**View** > **Print Layout**) for a more simplified view.

- Read the teacher's changes and decide which changes to accept and which to reject:

  - To reject/accept a change, click on it and then click the **Reject** or **Accept Change** button or right-click (PC) or **Ctrl**-click (Mac) and choose from the pop-up menu.

  - To reject or accept *all* changes in the document, choose that option from the reviewing toolbar buttons.

- As with Comments, you have the option of printing these changes as visible or not. In the Print dialog box:

  - To print comments: in the **Print What** field, choose Document showing markup.

  - To not print comments: in the **Print What** field, choose Document (see Figure 4.14).

Glitches: Pedagogical Concerns

Knowing *how* to use a tool does not in itself impart wisdom on when or where to use it.

Track Changes. While comments on a native speaker's writing typically include its organization of ideas, development of topic sentences, word choice, clarity, variety, and complexity of sentences, non-native speaker (NNS) writing may call for wholesale restructuring to accommodate the appropriate rhetorical style. Simply changing words and adding comments might not suffice. Teachers of NNS writing often choose to speak one-on-one to students about their papers, helping them draw out ideas and ways of expression.

Comments. On paper, there's limited space to write comments in the margins or between the lines. No such limit exists with electronically embedded comments and changes, a capacity that may exacerbate the danger of overwhelming students with long comments or numerous changes, discouraging more than guiding them. Use electronic comment and change features to construct *concise* advice, since they remain editable and can be deleted.

Editing instead of guiding. When a teacher changes text in a student's paper with the Track Changes feature, the student must go through the edited document, click on each change, and accept or reject it. How many writing students have the confidence or desire to *reject* their writing teacher's suggested change? For those that don't, the teacher becomes less of a guide or facilitator of process writing than a copy editor doing what the writer should learn to do for her- or himself. Track Changes may, therefore, find more appropriate use with native speakers (NSs) or near-NSs or among a team of writers collaborating on a piece, where participants are coequals in the process, such as students working on a group project. One technique to foil the student strategy of merely accepting all changes involves inserting a number of false or "distracter" changes, much as they are used in incorrect answers in multiple-choice questions.

Manual Track Changes for Other Word Processors

- To indicate text to delete, select it and change the color to red (don't actually delete).

- To indicate text added, type it in, select it, and change the color to green.

- To indicate moved text, select it and change the color to blue.

- After the student or writer sees the edits, he or she makes the necessary changes.

- Before printing, select all of the text (**Edit > Select All**) then change the color back to black.

TECHNOTE ■ **File Transfer**

In most environments, students should be able to work on their writing in class and out of class, such as during open lab times (i.e., not scheduled lab class), in library labs, or on their computers at home. There are many options for transferring files from one computer to another.

- *E-mail attachment.* If students have Internet access at home <u>and</u> in the lab, they can attach their word-processing document to an e-mail message to themselves using any web-based e-mail account (e.g., Yahoo!® Mail) and then retrieve the attachment from their account while connected at home.

- *Portable drives.* Small, inexpensive, high-capacity storage drives can fit in a purse or pocket. The *USB* "key-chain" or *flash drive* plugs into a USB port on PCs and Macs with no software needed.

- *Folder on a lab or school server.* Students at some institutions may be able to access from the lab as well as from home a network storage account maintained by the school.* If a student uses a different word processing program at home from what's used in the lab, he or she can save the document in both places as rich text format (RTF), which any word processor can read. (See **Saving** sidebar on page 34.)

* Virtual private network *(VPN)* software might be required to access lab servers from outside the campus network (e.g., using a commerical ISP). VPN *client* software employs encryption and *authenticate* users (makes sure they are members of the school community).

Integrated Writing Programs

While many native or foreign language writing classes make use of a word processor and its built-in tools, some labs use more complex writing programs. "Collaborative writing" programs help students generate and organize ideas, share ideas and drafts with others to gain feedback, and build appropriately formatted bibliographies. They integrate into a word-processing program *heuristic* tools to assist students in developing their ideas, guiding them in tutorial fashion through the process with discovery and problem-solving techniques. One popular program for PCs and Macs, Daedalus® Integrated Writing Environment (DIWE), bundles language reference material and collaboration and communication tools with a word processor. Other programs that writing teachers might use, such as FirstClass®, offer only communication tools, most notably some variety of a *threaded* discussion (where messages are grouped by topic), bulletin board, or private chat. While offering language resources and collaborative tools not found in common word processors, collaborative writing programs have their drawbacks (see Table 4.1).

TABLE 4.1 ■ Collaborative Writing Programs

Advantages	*Disadvantages*
Integrate many writing tools into one environment	More expensive than word processors
Initial investment in time learning how to use them effectively becomes more acceptable the longer the programs will be used, particularly beyond one semester	Require more demanding technical setup, maintenance, training, and support of users
May reduce student anxiety with writing assignments	May involve a student login procedure in addition to other lab logins
Disciplines outside of writing and language learning, such as the humanities and the sciences, use collaborative programs as well	Use in a class may blur the line between using the computer as tutor vs. tool
	Students are not likely to encounter them in the workplace
	Students and teachers can only use in the labs, not at home, unless the site adopts a web-access version

The "integrated" in DIWE refers to the various components, called "modules," that make up the whole package. Each module can be used independently or in combination with others, depending on the features and functionality of interest to teachers and students. Many teachers use DIWE only for the conferencing tools, such as InterChange, described in the following list, or adopt the modules one at a time. Whatever modules are used, students log-in to their own account.

The six modules of DIWE 2007 include:

> **Suites**
>
> Packages of related programs from the same company that work together to some degree are known as a *suite* of programs, much like Word, PowerPoint®, Excel, FrontPage®, and Access make up the Microsoft Office suite or how the word-processing, drawing, painting, database, and spreadsheet programs make up the AppleWorks suite.

- **Invent.** Helps students brainstorm, explore, and develop topics and plan their writing through a series of questions. This module offers the heuristic tools to assist students in producing text, guiding them through the writing process with discovery and problem-solving techniques. A teacher can customize this module by adding his or her own prompts for students' prewriting activities.

- **Write.** The word processor. Documents created in Write can be exported to other file formats, such as RTF (see the **Saving** sidebar on page 34).

- **Respond.** A tool for peer editing that guides students through the process of critically reading another student's draft writing and suggesting revisions. These functions roughly correspond to the Comment and Track Changes feature in Microsoft Word.

- **Mail.** A bulletin board for student messages about class activities, readings, and group projects. This feature corresponds to e-mail groups and may also be used for private e-mail.

- **InterChange.** Threaded online discussions for readings, brainstorming topics, and collaborating on projects. Instructors set up virtual conference rooms for groups of students or the entire class. The discussions are *synchronous,* meaning they occur in real time, like a phone conversation. The discussions are logged, and the transcript is available at any time.

- **Bibliocite.** Creates formatted works cited and references pages through simple forms students complete.

In addition to the modules, DIWE provides utilities for teachers, students, and administrators.

- With **Instructor Utilities,** teachers can post class assignments, manage InterChange discussions, and modify prompts for the Invent module.
- **Student Utilities** provides a dictionary and a thesaurus and a means for document management and exchange.
- With **Administrator Utilities,** faculty or lab personnel create classes, configure class preferences, and archive all writing, discussions, and so forth at the end of the course.

Colleges or programs that adopt DIWE generally provide detailed instructions to students on its use and training (or training material) and support to instructors.

Other Writing Tools

"Interactive writing environments," such as Grammatica (formerly Sans-Faute), Système D, Le Correcteur, Antidote (all for writing in French), and Interactive English present users a less complex palette of features than a collaborative writing environment such as

Plagiarism

While plagiarism in second or foreign language writing may be as big a problem as it is in native language writing courses, it may be easier to detect, since several sentences of completely idiomatic language will likely stand in greater contrast to the L2 student's other writing. Technical solutions include the use of free or fee-based online plagiarism search services that try to match a **search string** from a student's writing (about seven or more consecutive words) with other texts available online, including academic papers, published articles, and web pages. Most services offer free trials, and some universities subscribe to one, making it available to faculty at no cost. These services claim to combat the large number of papers purchased by students from term-paper mills by comparing passages from a student's work with online sources. While these verification services can't possibly *certify* that a passage isn't plagiarized, they risk false positives. The fact that students are using the Internet for research more and more presents teachers with a cheaper and easier alternative for plagiarism detection: If students found the information online, you can too.

Plagiarism detection on the cheap

- Use a few popular web search engines, such as Google™ and Yahoo, to enter strings of text you suspect may not be the student's own writing.
- Be sure to put quotes around the string or indicate in the search engine's advanced searching options that you want results only for *all of the words, in order.*
- Follow resulting links, if any, to compare to the student's writing.
- If your school or institution subscribes to the LexisNexis full-text news database, conduct a similar search there.

DIWE. Interactive writing programs combine a simple word processor with some assortment of language reference tools, such as a built-in dictionary (for spell-checking and looking up definitions), a sentence-analyzing grammar-checker, and grammar and usage notes. Interactive English, for example, bills itself as a process-oriented writing environment providing writing lessons, readings, and grammar exercises. Writing assignments range from personal experience narratives to persuasive essays.

Microsoft Word can also be outfitted with "add-in" packages of proofing tools for dozens of languages. They include fonts, spelling- and grammar-checkers, and translation dictionaries. Current Word users may find it hard to justify the added expense and trouble of interactive writing programs; however, they do offer context-sensitive grammar and spelling *instruction* where Word would offer only a suggested alternative to accept or reject without in-depth explanation.

Internet References

Word, Microsoft Corporation, *www.microsoft.com*

AppleWorks, Apple Computer, *www.apple.com*

Nisus Writer, Nisus Software, *www.nisus.com*

WordPerfect, Corel Corporation, *www.corel.com*

Daedalus Integrated Writing Environment (DIWE), *www.daedalus.com*

FirstClass, *www.firstclass.com*

Interactive English (Plato Learning), *www.academicsystems.com*

Grammatica, *www.grammatica.biz*

Système D, *www.heinle.com*

Le Correcteur, *www.futurecommerce.com/documents*

Antidote, *www.druide.com*

Longman Dictionary of American English, *www.longman.com*

The Paper Store, sells research papers to students, *termpapers-on-file.com*

Plagiarism.org, plagiarism detection service, *www.plagiarism.org*

EVE (essay verification empire), plagiarism detection system, *www.canexus.com*

Download.com, distributor of free, inexpensive, or demo software, *www.download.com*

5

Internet Activities

❖ We don't have a lot of expensive software. What can we do for free on the Internet that's focused and effective?

❖ I need projects that my students can finish in one day as well as long-term projects. Can I use the Internet for both?

❖ Are chats helpful to language learners? How can I set one up?

The Internet presents language students with target language stimuli, primarily reading and listening, like no other medium. In addition to the widest variety and greatest quantity of content ever available to language students, the medium also provides an abundant variety of language-through-content learning opportunities and interactive activities, most in authentic contexts.

Some teachers may note that a few of the activities in this chapter could be accomplished without the Internet or even a computer. We use computers in language learning to exploit a powerful resource with stimulating, interactive tools so that we can learn language more *engagingly,* not necessarily more easily or cheaply. One of the assumptions of integrating CALL into a curriculum is that the skills acquired in participating in one activity enhance a student's ability to engage in others. The skills build on each other and reap dividends, in part by making students more efficient users of computers as learning tools for language or any other skill or content area.

Computing Requirements

Most of the activities in this chapter can be performed with modest arrangements.

- **Internet connection:** preferably high speed or "broadband" (e.g., T1, cable, DSL), but a fast *modem* (56k +) will suffice.

- **Computer** *hardware:* Most PCs and Macs not more than three or five years old should be fine for all activities. Accessing audio, video, and other multimedia and interactive content online requires recent web browser versions and *plug-ins* (helper applications for the browser), which perform better on faster computers.

- **Software:** Web browsers (e.g., Microsoft Internet Explorer, Apple's Safari™, Mozilla [Netscape®], Opera, AOL® browser) are free as are the most common plug-ins (RealPlayer, QuickTime, Windows Media Player, Flash, Shockwave, Acrobat®).

Writing Activities

📖 ACTIVITY 1 ■ Electronic Postcards	
	Teacher skills: basic web browser, word processor, e-mail use
	Student level: high-beginning to intermediate
	Content objective: writing postcards
	Software: web browser (Internet connection), word processor

A short, personal writing activity makes use of free postcard or holiday card websites. For example, the MIT Media Lab hosts a postcard engine free of advertisements or other annoying solicitations (the drawback to using free commercial sites) and is typical of how others work.

Teacher Preparation

- Find an electronic postcard site appropriate to the language and interests of your students (see **Internet References** at the end of this activity).

  - Free electronic postcard sites exist in many languages. Refer students to postcard engines in the target language.

  - Use a search engine in the target language, for example the Google France site *(www.google.fr)*, which is designed not just to search sites *based* in France but *francophone* pages as well (from Canada, Belgium, Switzerland, Algeria, etc.).

  - Use *key words* in the target language.

Steps for Students (Using MIT Postcards as an Example)

- Go to *persona.www.media.mit.edu/ Postcards*.

- Go to Postcard Rack to send a card.

- Select a design from a category (e.g., holidays, photography, art).

- Type the recipient's e-mail address and your teacher's (so he or she gets a copy).

- Compose a short message and send.

Card message topics

- If studying in a foreign city, write a friend or relative about your travels.

- Write to a friend abroad about his or her foreign travel or study.

- Send a greeting appropriate for a close holiday (New Year's Day, Halloween, etc.).

- Make up an occasion to write about (wedding, birth of a child, death or illness, congratulations on a new job, etc.).

- Invite someone to a party with directions to your house or apartment.

- Write a thank you note for a dinner or party attended or people you visited.

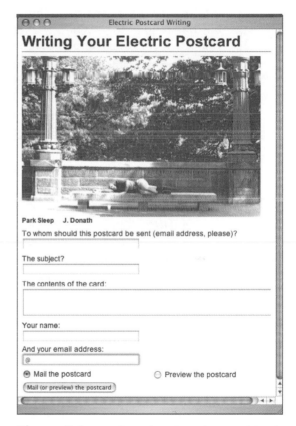

Figure 5.1 ■ After choosing the graphic, the MIT Electronic Postcard is simple to complete, even for beginner-level writing students.

Internet References

MIT Postcards, *persona.www.media.mit.edu/Postcards*

123 Greetings, *www.123greetings.com*

Hallmark, *www.hallmark.com*

French postcards, *www.cybercartes.com*

Multimedia e-cards (many languages), *www.superpostcards.com*

Bookmarking a Site

When you want your students to go to a specific web page, they need the *URL*. The URL (uniform resource locator) is the exact address or location of a page on the Internet, usually begining with "http://...." There are several options, some beginning with copying the URL from the location/address line:

- Send the URL to each student via e-mail. If they use web-based mail or a browser-aware e-mail program (Outlook, Mozilla Mail, OS X Mail, Eudora), they open their mail in class and click on the link in your message to open that page in a browser.
- Put a link to this site on a web page you maintain for the class.
- Use courseware, such as WebCT, CourseInfo, or Nicenet, to add the link.
- If you and the students all use the same web browser (Internet Explorer, Safari, Mozilla) and have a shared network folder, save the actual bookmark file into this folder, where students will click on it to go to the site:
  - Bookmark the site in the browser.
  - Open the shared network folder.
  - (PC) In the bookmarks window (**Bookmarks** or **Favorites** > **Edit** or **Open**), drag bookmark to the shared folder.
  - (Mac) Drag the URL icon directly from the browser address/location line to the shared folder.

📓 ACTIVITY 2 ■ Online Writing Labs (OWLs)	
	Teacher skills: basic web browser, word processor, e-mail use
	Student level: high-intermediate to advanced
	Content objective: using online writing resources
	Software: web browser, word processor

English writing labs at many universities in the United States and elsewhere organize writing resources for students. They offer walk-in services for registered students as well as free resources for all online visitors. One well-known OWL is the Online Writing Lab at Purdue University. It offers many documents in *PDF*[1] and *HTML*[2] format to assist writing students and teachers, such as the *Writing Lab Newsletter*; guides on grammar, spelling, punctuation, research, and documenting sources (MLA and APA styles); ESL issues; and professional writing (such as resumes and cover letters).

These resources are especially useful if your students do not have a writing textbook or reference, or if you're looking for more examples or a different approach to supplement a difficult lesson. In addition, for students that return text and reference books to the school bookstore at the end of the semester (to their teacher's chagrin), OWLs provide continued access to writing resources.

Teacher Preparation

- Find an OWL that offers target language resources.

- Demonstrate the site for students, including navigating its resources and viewing or downloading reference or sample documents. (If your web browser is set up properly, you can view PDF documents "inline" with the Acrobat Reader plug-in installed.)

- For the next student writing assignment, require students to include one reference to a published book, article, or a text used for class.

- Tell them the style convention to use (e.g., APA or MLA).

- Instruct them to use the OWL to find the appropriate format for including the reference in their paper.

- Their partner can check the format of the reference in their paper.

Internet References

Online Writing Lab, Purdue University, *owl.english.purdue.edu*

English Language Centre, Hong Kong Polytechnic University, *elc.polyu.edu.hk/cill*

University of Victoria Writer's Guide, *web.uvic.ca/wguide/Pages/MasterToc.html*

---

[1] PDF: portable document format (.pdf) files open with the free Adobe Acrobat Reader application among others.

[2] HTML: hypertext markup language, the format of document that displays in a web browser—a web page, in other words.

✏ ACTIVITY 3 ▪ Letter of Complaint	
	Teacher skills: basic web browser, word processor, e-mail use
	Student level: high-intermediate to advanced
	Content objective: writing business correspondence
	Software: web browser (Internet connection), word processor

This activity combines writing an argument, word processing, and using the business correspondence form (covered in Chapter 4, Activity 7) with a little Internet research in a realistic scenario, one that any consumer may find necessary.

Teacher Preparation

- As a class, discuss the possibilities for product or service *dissatisfaction*:
  - a recent hotel stay, tour, car rental, or restaurant meal
  - a food product, electronic gadget, clothing, etc.
- Guide students through the letter-writing process.
- Assist them in finding company information on the Internet (look for Contact Us or About Us information on the company website).
- Waiting for a response from a company, if any, may prove impractical. Instead, have students respond to their partner's letter of complaint as if they represented the company.

Steps for Students

- Think of a product or service with which you were not entirely satisfied.
- List the reasons why you were dissatisfied.
- Outline what was expected versus what was actually delivered by the product or service.
- Write a letter detailing the problem versus the expectation.
- Put the letter in the proper business correspondence form (refer to an OWL for examples).
- Save the letter as **rich text format** (RTF).
- Look up the company on the Internet and find the contact information.
- E-mail the appropriate person at the company about your complaint and either paste in the entire text of the letter or attach it as an RTF file.
- Exchange letters with your partner and write a company response to your partner's letter.

🔖 **ACTIVITY 4** ▪ Keypals (E-mail Pen Pals)	
	Teacher skills: basic web browser, word processor, e-mail use
	Student level: high-beginning to advanced
	Content objective: corresponding with a keypal
	Software: web browser, e-mail program

E-mail pen pals (or **keypals,** since a keyboard is used instead of a pen) works like the old snail-mail pen pals: Find someone to exchange letters with, something to write about, and establish a schedule of correspondence. Of course, it's a bit more complicated, like everything else in our hyperlinked, infinitely configurable electronic world. But what better way to capitalize on the worldwide networking potential of the Internet for language learning than with a fast, free, relatively simple system for establishing channels of communication with learners of every age and culture that builds language skills while spreading intercultural understanding? With computer access widespread, and e-mail often a first step in computer use, the practicality of the keypal arrangement equals its appeal. Like many activities in a CALL lab—if not teaching in general—the payoff from keypals as a class activity comes over time as you better understand the resources available and perfect techniques.

Pedagogical Rationale

Motivation. The personal and informal form and authentic nature of e-mail writing is more accessible to students, especially low-level writers, than formal essay writing. Some keypals, furthermore, will continue to correspond beyond their assignments.

Relevant skills. Keypals present an opportunity to teach or reinforce language and skills relevant to academic and workplace success:

- typing (or **keyboarding,** which includes use of the mouse)
- writing clearly
- understanding forms of various kinds of correspondence, address, closure, etc.
- reinforcing vocabulary involved in e-mail
- gaining insight into the perspective of someone possibly of a different language, country, and culture

Multimedia e-mail. E-mail offers an exchange of more than words with the easy attachment of pictures and even small audio files to messages, adding a richer dimension to the exchange. Such attachments technically complicate the exchange somewhat and should be considered only by experienced keypals and CALL teachers.

Foreign vs. second language learners. Foreign language learners typically have a harder time finding local opportunities to use the target language and may therefore benefit more from remote opportunities.

Options in Keypal Arrangements

Class or individual. Teachers can find keypals for students, or students can find them on their own. The former might be preferable to first-time keypal participants and low-level learners, who might have trouble navigating keypal sites and establishing an arrangement in the target language. A teacher can also take certain practical factors into consideration in finding another class to correspond with that students on their own may overlook, as discussed in the following paragraphs. On the other hand, a more advanced student who finds a keypal him- or herself will be challenged by the search activity in the target language and might feel more invested in the arrangement.

Native vs. non-native speakers. Students might be inclined to prefer native speakers as keypals and while this might be more desirable among high-level students, the level of writing from low-level students may leave the native speakers wanting more stimulating conversation. On the other hand, corresponding with non-native speakers may not present your students with good language models and may reinforce faulty structure or use. Two possible solutions:

- Set your students up with *younger native speakers* for less complex language and less sophisticated topics, though interests between students with a *large* age gap may be less likely to intersect.
- Find *tandem* keypals. Tandem learning keypals are native speakers of each other's target language. This option may prove more practical in a foreign language teaching environment, where everyone's L1 is the same (or near native). In an ESL environment, however, finding students who are also learning your students' diverse L1s may prove more time consuming.

Duration. Keypals in other countries and on different school term calendars complicate the project. Possible solutions:

- Conduct the exchanges when the two school *terms overlap*, and schedule the activity more intensively during this brief time.
- Arrange *two different groups* for your class, one roughly for the first half and another for the second.

The resulting shorter keypal projects may be less likely to develop substantive correspondent relationships or be able to follow through on elaborate collaborative projects as with longer-term arrangements.

Failed matches. Whenever one keypal has vastly different expectations than the other, responds with a different frequency, doesn't like his or her keypal, or experiences other personal problems, the match has failed and your student needs another keypal. Another problem arises in a class-to-class matchup when one class is bigger than the other. One possible solution to both problems: Assign the higher-level or more motivated and responsible students more than one keypal each, so that these students have a writing load that corresponds with their ability. The extra keypals provide spares for other students whose keypals fail.

Frequency of writing. Arrange how often students will write to each other and how quickly they are expected to respond. One might assume that the greater the frequency of writing, the greater the chances of non-response; however, many students maintain heavy e-mail loads, responding to dozens of messages or more daily. Responding less frequently, say weekly, may pose greater risks as interest may peter out or students may have trouble continuing a dialogue broken up by large gaps. Whatever frequency you establish, be careful about tying a keypal's response to a particular class activity, as some non-response or delayed response is to be expected, and be aware of time zone differences. Other sources of delayed responses include class meeting days not corresponding, differing holidays, and interruptions in network access.

Non-response. The risk of non-response looms as a black cloud over keypal projects, and some students take it personally.

- Assess your students' motivation and commitment to this activity beforehand.
- Discuss the possibility of non-response with them in advance.
- Convey the importance of not presenting such a problem for another class.
- Arrange with the partner teacher to have students do all or most of the required writing during class time and monitor students to ensure each has written his or her keypal as scheduled.
- Teachers should agree on a compatible weight for the project; it won't work if it's a core class project for one class and an add-on for the other.
- Make contingency plans, such as arranging for more than one keypal per student.
- For class-to-class projects, keep in close e-mail contact with the partner teacher, keeping her or him apprised of non-response problems and progress on assignments.

Scope of project. Keypal projects can range from casual writing supplements to a core component of a writing class, or some compromise. A simple determination of scope considers the quantifiables:

- frequency of correspondence
- length of each correspondence
- duration of project

Evaluation of student writing. The problems with evaluating keypal writing include those stemming from the ephemeral nature of e-mail, the fact that the teacher might not be in the exchange loop, or the voyeuristic quality to being included in the exchange. Require your students to CC you (see the **E-mail Options** sidebar on page 69) a certain number of times when writing to their keypals, perhaps only significant correspondence soliciting or responding to information central to the project, rather than more frequent friendly chatter.

What to write about? Topics will depend on variables, such as students' language proficiencies, age, academic disciplines, and the length and scope of the writing activity. The sensitivities of both cultures need to be considered in presenting topics such as religion, dating, abortion, civil liberties, politics, etc.

Possible writing topics

- (Icebreaker) Each keypal writes a short description of his or her town and then removes certain words to create a cloze activity for his or her keypal, who guesses at answers or tries to research them online. Later, they exchange correct answers.
- (Icebreaker) Describe the teacher in detail, including his or her background, experience, teaching style, strengths, and weaknesses (tactfully).
- Societal or family customs. Describe a specific custom, such as one related to eating, praying, meeting people, or a holiday. Discuss variations on this custom within your culture or changes in it over time.
- Discuss travel done or planned.
- Discuss academic or professional plans.
- Discuss movies, songs, TV, or radio programs available to both keypals online.
- Exchange research papers for peer review (requires similarity of academic discipline and high-level language learners evenly matched).

<u>Sources for Teachers Looking for Keypal Classes</u>

- other students in the same class
- another class in the same department or center
- native speakers attending the same school

- the class of a teaching friend or colleague at another school
- students living in a country of the target language (especially ones studying your students' L1 for tandem exchanges)
- the class of a teacher found through a *listserv*[3] announcement (such as LLTI or FL Teach)
- students arranged through a pen pal project (see Internet References on page 71)

E-mail Options

Any e-mail user knows that the recipient's address goes in the **TO:** line and that the **REPLY** button automatically addresses a message back to the person whose message you're reading (see Figure 5.2). But there are other options:

CC: (carbon copy) sends a copy of your message to this address also.

BCC: (blind carbon copy) functions like CC except that the recipients don't see any of the other recipients. To list multiple recipients on the CC or BCC line, separate them with a comma.

Reply All: your reply goes to the sender of the message as well as anyone included on the CC: line.

Forward: send a message you received on to someone else (it arrives with you as the sender). The text of the forwarded message may appear in quotes, and the message might not automatically include attachments to the original message.

Figure 5.2 ▪ The mail header, above the message composition window or field, contains the various recipient types: TO, CC, BCC. Use BCC for messages to large numbers of people or to keep the recipients confidential. *Reproduced with permission of Yahoo! Inc. ©2004 by Yahoo! Inc. YAHOO! and the YAHOO! logo are trademarks of Yahoo! Inc.*

---

[3] A *listserv*, also written listserver and list server, is an electronic mailing list (see Activity 5 for a description), most of which are powered by LISTSERV® server software, a product of L-Soft *(www.lsoft.com)*.

Teacher Preparation

Prepare students to use e-mail effectively

- Sign up students for e-mail accounts if they don't already have them.

- Have students write their first message to you to verify their accounts are active and to add you to their e-mail address book.

- Reply to students modeling the form that their messages should take, including salutation, closing, tone, and use of text quoted from the original message.

- Discuss the difference between various recipient lines (TO, CC, BCC), and using the **Reply, Reply All,** and **Forward** commands (see the **E-mail Options** sidebar on page 69).

- Demonstrate spell-checking of messages, viewing and sending attachments, creating mail folders to manage messages, etc.

- Review e-mail etiquette (see Appendix C, A Thinking Person's E-mail).

Establish project parameters

- Clearly outline and discuss the project with students: topic, duration, frequency of writing, deadlines, grading.

- Discuss the tone writing should take with examples, including the use of e-mail shorthand. For example, in English, BTW stands for *by the way* and IMHO for *in my humble opinion.* Characters can also be used in place of words (e.g., :) to express *happy,* :(for *sad, 2* for *to* and *too,* and *4* for *for).* Should your students write to their virtual partners using slang and informal conventions of the electronic age or practice the formal language you're teaching them?

Match up keypals

- Match up your students with the keypals you've found and give them the names and e-mail addresses or discuss a strategy and resources for finding keypals on their own. Individuals looking for keypals on their own may want to engage in subjects of a personal interest (music, movies, books, travel, current events, dating).

  A thin line divides some individual keypal sites with dating sites or keypals with more on their mind than writing or cultural exchange. Caution students about divulging personal information (phone number, home address) to someone they don't know well.

- Have your students draft an introductory message to their keypals but send it to you first for feedback.

- Keep close track of students and keypal writing assignments to head off non-response or other problems.

Internet References

Several ESL/EFL teachers, among others, have written extensively about keypal projects and resources for language learners, much of which can be found on the Internet. Search for "keypal" or "e-mail projects" or see the following.

Ruth Vilmi, The Language Centre, Helsinki University of Technology, *www.ruthvilmi.net*

Kenji Kitao and S. Kathleen Kitao, Doshisha University, *www.lancs.ac.uk/staff/kitao*

Thomas N. Robb, Kyoto Sangyo University, *www.kyoto-su.ac.jp/~trobb*

The Foreign Language Teaching Forum (FL Teach). Listserv discussion of foreign language teaching professionals on pedagogy, activities, curricula, and teacher training, *www.cortland.edu/flteach*

Language Learning Technology International (LLTI). Listserv created and moderated by Otmar Foelsche of Dartmouth College and a service of the International Association of Language Learning Technology (IALLT), *iall.net*

SELECTED RESOURCES FOR TEACHERS ARRANGING CLASS-TO-CLASS KEYPALS

The Intercultural E-mail Classroom Connections (IECC). This listserv provides a service for language teachers seeking partner classes only (no resources for finding individual keypals). Several separate lists deal with announcements for different audiences (K–12, higher education, age 50 plus), discussions of keypal project strategies, and a stage for surveying opinions from an international perspective, *www.iecc.org*.

The Hut Internet Writing Exchange. Ruth Vilmi's writing project for intermediate to advanced students of ESL or EFL. Classes and individual students can register for formal exchanges, discussion forums, and chats, *www.ruthvilmi.net*.

cTandum Europa. This resource matches individuals or classes for *tandem* language learning for any language, where the target language of each learner is the native language of the other, *www.slf.ruhr-uni-bochum.de/etandem*

ePals Classroom Exchange. A multifeatured, multilingual site with pages in English, French, Spanish, German, Portuguese, Japanese, Chinese, and Arabic. Search for classes of students to exchange with based on criteria such as language, country, city, class level, age, school, number in class, and software access. Many other resources for teachers and students, *www.epals.com*

Linguistic Funland TESL Pen Pal Center. Teachers or individual students can complete a form with keypal requirements, including native and target language, language proficiency, and age. You can also add comments related to your search and an expiration date, *linguistic-funland.com/addapal.html*

KeyPals Club. Connecting 50,000 students from 76 countries. Class-to-class or student-to-student, *teaching.com/keypals*

KIDCAFE-School. A thematic list for organized school-to-school keypal exchange. Students may take part in any of the ongoing discussions or begin one themselves. Member schools supervise the list so registration is required. Includes a netiquette guide for keypals, *www.kidlink.org/KIDCAFE-SCHOOL*

Rigby Heinemann Keypal Lists. Connect with students from around the world by class or individually according to age groupings (5–10, 11–13, 14–20), *www.hi.com.au/keypals*

SELECTED RESOURCES FOR STUDENTS ARRANGING KEYPALS ON THEIR OWN

iT's MySpace. Individuals can choose keypals or traditional pen pals from groups organized by age (under 18, over 18) or post messages to forums, *www.its-myworld.com*

InterPals. Search for keypals in a database by gender, age, and country, or spend time first in a chat room to find a suitable keypal. Though most postings are in English, keypals usually list the languages they would like to correspond in, *interpals.net*

Dave's ESL Café E-mail Connection for Students, *www.pacificnet.net/~sperling/student.html*

E-mail Penpals Club. Search the database of keypals by gender, *www.geocities.com/SouthBeach/Pointe/2993*

ACTIVITY 5 ■ Mailing Lists	
	Teacher skills: web browser, e-mail use, mailing list subscription
	Student level: intermediate to advanced
	Content objective: finding, reading, and posting to a mailing list
	Software: web browser

Mailing lists operate like listservs and are also known as *user groups*. Members use their regular e-mail programs to send messages to the list, like any other e-mail message. The list then distributes that message, or *posting,* to all list members, be it 10 or 10,000. Some postings pass through a *moderator,* who reads the message for appropriateness or focus or otherwise categorizes the posting. Many lists do not engage a moderator, resulting in a small number of inappropriate postings.

Pedagogical Rationale

For students with some experience with e-mail, mailing lists present a forum for writing and ideas, authentic exchanges likely to involve a language student into the target culture. Mailing lists essentially bring together people with a particular interest into an online community in as technically simple a format as possible. The motivation for using them in class varies, from simply encouraging students to write *anything* to generating feedback on ideas for a writing project beyond the list.

So when you join a mailing list, you join a community and consequently need to understand the community dynamic. Since postings are distributed to a group instead of an individual, lists tend to lack the personal, one-on-one intimacy of keypal correspondence, though replies to list postings are frequently made "off-list," meaning that the reply goes only to the individual making the posting and not the list group, creating the possibility of a more personal or specific correspondence between just two members. In addition, the dynamic differs from a keypal arrangement in that some messages posted to the list frequently receive no reply or comment, while responses to others may overwhelm the original posting, occasionally spiraling into emotional exchanges ("flaming"). Students can read postings without feeling compelled to respond, unless they have something meaningful to contribute.

One subscribes to or unsubscribes from a list usually with a simple e-mail to the listserv *robot*, a computer program that processes subscriptions. Each list posts instructions for subscribing, unsubscribing, and accessing archived messages or *threads* (a group of postings and replies on a specific subtopic), as well as netiquette guidelines for postings.

Typical Rules for Mailing List Postings (Netiquette)[4]

- Send messages to the most appropriate list.
- Don't cross-post (post the same message to more than one related list whose members are likely to overlap).
- Write a message description in the subject line.
- Keep posts short—a few paragraphs tops.
- Keep quotes short and identify source.
- Identify yourself and your school in the signature line.
- Reread and spell-check.
- Be polite—never use obscene language.
- Don't venture into religious proselytizing, sexual solicitation, or the like.
- Don't attack list members personally (even in reply to a perceived attack).
- Don't reply to a post if all you have to say is "me too" or "I agree."
- Don't include attachments.
- Include in replies only selected, relevant quotes from the original post.
- Include URLs or e-mail addresses when referring to sites or people.

[4]Expanded with permission from the 11 rules at SL-LISTS at La Trobe University, *sl-lists.net.*

Teacher Preparation

- Determine whether you want to find an appropriate list or lists for your students to subscribe to or let them sort one out with options you present.

- Use websites in the Internet References at the end of this activity to locate appropriate lists.

- Ensure that all students have working e-mail accounts and understand how to compose messages (see the **E-mail Options** sidebar on page 69).

- Have students subscribe to the chosen list(s) and read the list rules and instructions.

- Go over list netiquette with students (see the **Netiquette** sidebar on page 73).

- Establish an expected frequency of postings for students (i.e., how often they should post to the list).

- If all students join the same list, then subscribe to the list yourself to monitor your students' postings.

- If students join separate lists, then have each of them CC you on their postings.

Internet References

SELECTED LISTSERVS

International Student Discussion Lists (SL-LISTS) for ESL/EFL students, *sl-lists.net*

Language-Related Mailing Lists, Yamada Language Center, University of Oregon. Compiles lists for several dozen languages, including those less frequently taught, *babel.uoregon.edu/yamada/lists.html*

Association for Educational Communications and Technology (AECT), listservs and other technology resources for teachers, *aect.org/lists.asp*

Topica (formerly Liszt). A mailing list directory (or *meta* list—a list of lists), includes mailing lists, discussion groups, newsgroups, chat rooms, and fee-based services. Find one or start your own, *lists.topica.com*

Tile. A search tool for mailing lists, newsgroups, ftp sites, and other Internet resources, *www.tile.net*

📖 ACTIVITY 6 ■ Chat	
	Teacher skills: basic web browser, word processor, e-mail use
	Student level: high-beginning to high-intermediate
	Content objective: synchronous chatting
	Software: web browser, instant messaging (IM) application

An electronic *chat*, using text, audio, or video, is a spontaneous conversation between two or more people at the same time. Most rely on a simple chat window on a web page or a stand-alone application, such as an instant messaging *(IM)* program. (See Figure 5.3.) *Keypals* and discussion lists rely on *asynchronous* communication (not occurring at the same time), where responses to messages or postings might occur soon after the

Figure 5.3 ■ A text chat window. Compose your message in the bottom field and see your message and those of others in your chat room or private chat above, each identified by an icon. (iChat in Mac OS X, compatible with AOL Instant Messenger and video chatting.)

TECHNOTE ■ **Synchronous and Asynchronous Communication**

We can conceptualize modes of communication in terms of those that are *synchronous* versus *asynchronous*. In synchronous communication, all parties communicate at the same time, such as in person, on the telephone, using instant messaging (IM) software, MOOing (see Activity 7 in this chapter), or chatting. In asynchronous communication, parties send and receive information expecting a significant delay, such as with letter writing ("snail-mail"), e-mail, or through telephone answering machines or voice mail messages; that is, the sender is not dependent on the human recipient being present or aware of the message at the time that it's sent. (The use of these terms here differs from their use in a very technical explanation of how electronic devices transmit and negotiate bits of information, but I refer here to how *humans* use machines to communicate.)

sender sends the message or days later. Conversely, *synchronous*, or real-time communication, is dependent on immediate responses, much like a telephone conversation (see **TECHNOTE: Synchronous and Asynchronous Communication** on page 75). Synchronous communication with your computer can take the form of chat, instant messaging, or a virtual conference. All rely on participants engaged at the same time in sending, receiving, or reading messages appearing in a discussion window available to all participants.

The Nature of Chat Communication

The language of chats differs from e-mail or discussion lists in some of the same ways that verbal conversation differs from written correspondence: The latter allows for more thought and editing of expression. Chat is faster, spontaneous, and may resemble a stream-of-consciousness flow compared to organized, developed written expression. While students may have more fun at chat, because they feel less of the anxiety associated with formal writing, they are also under more time pressure to use the target language to express ideas or reactions, thus the blending of characteristics of verbal conversation with writing. Some language teachers worry that electronic chatting introduces the sloppiness of spoken language into writing and reinforces faulty structure and use. Others argue that text chats provide language practice for verbal communication in that these share some characteristics.

Audio and Video (A/V) Chat

With fast Internet connections and efficient ways of transmitting audio and video, text chat activities could be extended to A/V chats, where students have a verbal conversation instead of a written one and possibly see whom they're speaking to in a small video image on-screen. While public opportunities for A/V chats are far less common than for text chats, you can set up private A/V chats between your students and another group of students (much like keypal arrangements). This synchronous form of communication, moreover, requires both parties to be engaged in the activity at the exact same time, thus you may encounter the difficulties discussed earlier with time zone differences, student attendance, etc. You need A/V chat software as well as good headsets with built-in microphones and small video cameras that work with the lab computers. These added complications might only be justified in a foreign language learning environment, where the target language is not widely spoken outside of class.

Types of Chat Environments

There are *public* and *private* chat "rooms" to enter. A public chat exists online, and members join in as they choose. A private chat is set up by its users, such as a class, for a specific purpose.

Countless public chat rooms exist in dozens of languages and on every conceivable topic. Most require some form of log-in or registration to identify users, often only by pseudonym, where students can enter existing conversations among a number of users present, though a chat room may be empty at times. With public chats, you take what you get: You're entering an existing discussion and do not have control over the makeup of the group, though you can leave a group that doesn't work for you and find another. What you get in a public chat is diversity: people from near and far, native and non-native speakers, interesting and inane discussions, and ready-made groups.

Private chat rooms can be set up by a teacher for free at countless online sites. You designate users, such as a class or group comprising students from various classes or keypals, and control the topic, members, and purpose.

Pedagogical Rationale

Chatting as a writing activity can be an engaging, free exchange that doesn't produce the anxiety of a class discussion or formal writing assignment or the monotony of contrived writing exercises. It can be used as warm-up for more formal writing or to quickly get feedback on ideas or fish around for writing topics.

Buffer Activity

In the lab, a *buffer activity* is any constructive language task or activity done between major class projects or activities, occupying students who finish an assignment early or are otherwise not ready to transition to the next. These activities should be uncomplicated, not require much or any instruction to begin, and be readily completed in a very short period of time or terminated without completion. Example activities include word games (crossword puzzles, hangman, wheel of fortune), self-contained short listening comprehension units, and practice test questions (such as the TOEFL® or other language proficiency tests). Of course, buffer activities do not need to be based on Internet resources at all. Typing practice programs, games, or skill-area practice programs (spelling, pronunciation, vocabulary) can also be used by individuals for *short* periods of time.

Public Chat Activities

Find a public chat group or have students locate their own and then join the discussion.

> *Free-writing practice.* Require a minimum number of messages posted.
>
> *Warm-up.* Use as a warm-up exercise before a longer or more formal writing activity.
>
> *Buffer activity.* Use as a buffer activity for those students who finish an activity early (see the **Buffer Activity** sidebar on page 77).
>
> *Topic exploration.* Since most public chats are topical, mine a relevant one for writing topic ideas. Introduce a question and see what kind of discussion develops.

Private Chat Activities

In setting up a private chat, consider the appropriate size. Advanced learners, who might be expected to write longer and more frequently, might benefit from a smaller group; thus, a class of 15 students might subdivide into groups of three to five.

Focus on structure. For low-level classes, set up a private chat to model and reinforce specific grammatical structures or vocabulary and then analyze the transcript of the chat session with the class or individuals to identify correct patterns and errors. Introduce the structure in the form of a question or statement to get the ball rolling and reenter as necessary to refocus the discussion or provide another model. For example, a discussion using the present perfect verb tense could be initiated by the teacher with the question, "What have you seen in Boston since you moved here?" Responses should use the same tense.

Brainstorming. Use a chat as a medium for students to explore a topic or exchange and flesh out ideas in preparation for a writing assignment, presentation, or other project. Students refer to the transcript of the session later, if necessary.

Encourage participation. Electronic communication can lower some of the barriers to participation for shy students and build confidence to contribute that, ideally, spills over to class discussions. Introduce a topic in a chat and let students write their reactions. Remind them to read other postings, since they represent a conversation among many, not simply a platform to air one's views.

Teacher Preparation

- Decide whether you want students to engage in a public or private chat.
- If you choose public chats, will you find and assign them or will students find them themselves?
- Go over rules for postings (see **Netiquette** sidebar on page 73) with students.

- Discuss what is acceptable language (including slang and abbreviations—see Teacher Preparation for the keypal project on page 70).

- Determine when students will engage in chats (as writing warm-up, buffer activity, etc.) and for how long.

- Join the chat yourself to keep track of student participation.

Tools for Setting Up a Private Chat

- IM applications, such as AOL Instant Messenger™, Yahoo! Messenger, MSN® Messenger, and Apple® iChat

- collaborative writing packages, such as DIWE

- communication packages, such as FirstClass

- courseware products, such as WebCT and CourseInfo

The commercial collaborative writing and communications packages have the advantage of offering *logged* chats, that is, chats whose text can easily be saved and retrieved later as a transcript. IM chats, while generally not logged, do remain available for copying and pasting as long as the session window remains open (i.e., scroll up the window just like a long word-processing document to see the text of the chat from the beginning and copy all or part to paste into a word-processing document to save or print).

Internet References

Dave's ESL Cafe discussion forums and chat rooms for ESL/EFL students and teachers. Dozens of topics. User registration required, *www.eslcafe.com/discussion*

Major search engines, especially Yahoo, maintain a great number of public chat rooms in various languages and topics, *www.yahoo.com > Chat > Interactive Chat*

Some search engines also offer free set up of private chats or bulletin boards, *groups.yahoo.com*

TAPPED IN, an online educational community set up like a visual MOO (see Activity 7 in this chapter), provides virtual classrooms and meetings (chats), *tappedin.org*

Free instant messenger applications (check for compatibility between different applications):

AIM (AOL Instant Messenger), *www.aim.com*

iChat instant messenger, *www.apple.com*

Yahoo Messenger, *messenger.yahoo.com*

MSN Messenger, *messenger.msn.com*

📖 ACTIVITY 7 ■ MOO	
	Teacher skills: basic web browser, telnet use
	Student level: high-beginning to advanced
	Content objective: interactive text-based communication and problem solving
	Software: web browser, MOO client, or telnet

A MOO[5] is a text-based, game-like Internet environment for interaction. Users, or players, interact with each other in real time (*synchronous* communication) by typing questions and reading instructions, clues, and responses using a simple, free MOO *client* application (or telnet). Users respond to text prompts and other users to accomplish tasks and manipulate objects in a virtual space (see Figure 5.4). Many MOOs take on the metaphor of a large, complex space, such as a university or castle, where one has to use clues to move about in order to find something or talk to someone.

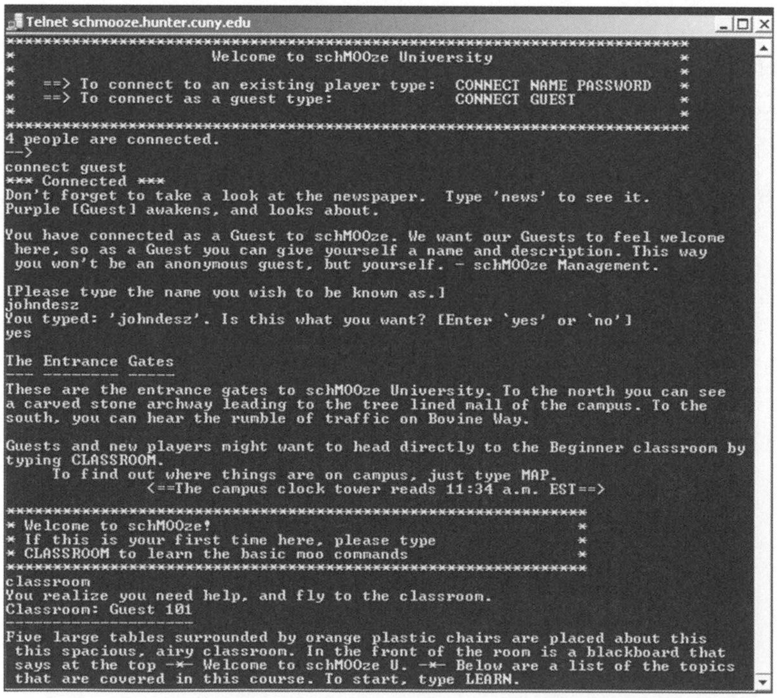

Figure 5.4 ■
Beginning a MOO session at SchMOOze University. After logging in, follow directions for learning basic commands (type CLASS-ROOM) or type commands to move around the space or communicate with others *(telnet://schmooze. hunter.cuny.edu:8888).*

```
Telnet schmooze.hunter.cuny.edu                                    _ □ X
*************************************************************************
*                      Welcome to schMOOze University                  *
*   ==> To connect to an existing player type:  CONNECT NAME PASSWORD  *
*   ==> To connect as a guest type:             CONNECT GUEST          *
*                                                                       *
*************************************************************************
4 people are connected.
-->
connect guest
*** Connected ***
Don't forget to take a look at the newspaper. Type 'news' to see it.
Purple [Guest] awakens, and looks about.

You have connected as a Guest to schMOOze. We want our Guests to feel welcome
 here, so as a Guest you can give yourself a name and description. This way
 you won't be an anonymous guest, but yourself. - schMOOze Management.

[Please type the name you wish to be known as.]
johndesz
You typed: 'johndesz'. Is this what you want? [Enter 'yes' or 'no']
yes

The Entrance Gates
___  _____  _____
These are the entrance gates to schMOOze University. To the north you can see
a carved stone archway leading to the tree lined mall of the campus. To the
south, you can hear the rumble of traffic on Bovine Way.

Guests and new players might want to head directly to the Beginner classroom by
typing CLASSROOM.
       To find out where things are on campus, just type MAP.
              <==The campus clock tower reads 11:34 a.m. EST==>

**********************************************************
* Welcome to schMOOze!                                   *
* If this is your first time here, please type           *
* CLASSROOM to learn the basic moo commands              *
**********************************************************
classroom
You realize you need help, and fly to the classroom.
Classroom: Guest 101
_____
Five large tables surrounded by orange plastic chairs are placed about this
 this spacious, airy classroom. In the front of the room is a blackboard that
 says at the top -*- Welcome to schMOOze U. -*- Below are a list of the topics
 that are covered in this course. To start, type LEARN.
```

---
[5] MOO (MUD, Object-Oriented) is a specific implementation of MUD (Multi-User Dimension) accessed with a *terminal emulator*, such as a telnet application (such as in Figure 5.4) or a MUD client application.

Pedagogical Rationale

MOOs offer a truly interactive environment that educators can exploit for a variety of problem-solving objectives. Users have to operate within a primarily text-based environment, respond to numerous text prompts, and visualize the scenario based on their interpretation of the text.

Steps for Students—Typical MOO Scenario

- Open telnet or a MOO client application.
- Connect to a MOO site:
  - Enter the address in the New Connection (**File > New Connection**) dialog box (e.g., *schmooze.hunter.cuny.edu*).
- Identify yourself with a screen name and provide other information as needed.
- Follow instructions and screen commands given (or options to get them), including instructions for sending messages to other users.
- Make inquiries and read messages from other players to help you achieve the stated objective (e.g., finding something, locating someone).

MOO No More?

Transmitting only text, MOOs once had the advantage of working over slow *modem* connections to the Internet, when that was the norm, an advantage dissipated today by widespread fast access. Now, web browser-based, real-time chats draw many former MOO users for their ability to motivate students to write in the target language, especially if they can engage native speakers. The concept of the multiplayer online game, moreover, has evolved from the text world of MOOs to one more in tune with our colorful, multimedia, point-and-click *GUI* (graphical user interface) environment. The Internet now offers Massively Multiplayer Online Role-Playing Games (MMPORGs), a multimedia virtual reality world, exemplified most popularly perhaps by the commercial application The Sims™. The Sims generates simulated players for a human user to manipulate as a proxy in a virtual world. The Sims Online connects Sims users over the Internet to interact in the same space, or virtual reality.

Internet References

SchMOOze University (for ESL/EFL learners), *schmooze.hunter.cuny.edu*

Diversity University (for ESL/EFL learners), *www.du.org/dumoo/imooinfo.htm*

Yamada Language Center, University of Oregon (foreign language MOO listing), *babel.uoregon.edu/yamada/interact.html*

MundoHispano (for learners of Spanish), *www.umsl.edu/~moosproj/mundo.html*

MOOfrançais (for learners of French), *www.umsl.edu/~moosproj/moofrancais.html*

Deutsche Gemeinschaft virtueller Welten (for learners of German), *www.mud.de*

Educational VR (MUD), School of Psychology and Education, University of Geneva, *tecfa.unige.ch/edu-comp/WWW-VL/eduVR-page.html#Educational*

The Sims, Electronic Arts, *thesims.ea.com*

Telnet. There are many free and shareware telnet applications. See the National Center for Supercomputing Applications (NCSA), *ncsa.uiuc.edu* and c/net download center, *download.com*

Content Activities

🖾 ACTIVITY 8 ■ Media News	
	Teacher skills: web browser, accessing media sites
	Student level: high-intermediate to advanced
	Content objective: accessing media sites for listening and reading
	Software: web browser, browser plug-ins

The Internet offers nearly the same variety and number of news outlets as print media, with major radio, network and cable TV, magazine, and newspaper outlets having a significant Internet presence as well in the form of text, audio, or video content and other resources and services, which are often free. In addition to immense stores of material, many sites, such as PBS, also provide transcripts of audio or video programs and resources for teachers, educational links, and even lesson plans and quizzes. While some content is available only by subscription or fee, suitable free alternatives can usually be found. Some online versions of print publications charge for archived articles (content prior to the current issue). For print publications and transcripts in several languages, LexisNexis, a massive database of news and information text, provides access to institutions that subscribe.

Pedagogical Rationale

Online news sources represent a wealth of authentic target language material appealing to every conceivable interest: current events, news analysis, politics, technology, finance, sports, entertainment, etc. Media news activities use stimulating reports to teach students how to access and evaluate such resources for future academic research or personal or professional needs. Work with online news sources also introduces students to the idea of differing news sources having particular economic or political biases or expectations of their audience in terms of education and interest.

Combining Transcripts with Audio

Some news sources that provide audio or video also provide accompanying transcripts, though many for a fee. CNN, for example, charges for access to its video content but not for its extensive transcripts, while NPR charges for transcripts but not for access to its extensive audio archives.

For ESL/EFL students, many radio and TV news and information broadcasts available online can become part of listening comprehension activities with transcripts available through LexisNexis. For example, NPR's *All Things Considered* presents three- to five-minute audio news segments, available online with a text synopsis, which can be used in conjunction with free online transcripts found through LexisNexis (see Figure 5.7 on page 86).

Foreign Language Versions

Some international news outlets, such as CNN, BBC, and Voice of America, are available online in many languages, offering text, audio, and video content in those languages (see Figure 5.5). Foreign media outlets online (e.g., Radio France, Radio Prague) provide perhaps a more logical first stop for foreign language news content. Choose sources you use based on the variety of content, ease of navigation, format of audio and video, and cost of access.

Figure 5.5 ■ Choose a language on the main navigation bar of the CNN website.

Teacher Preparation—Using Online News Sources

- Do you want students to read news text or listen to audio or video reports?

- Find relevant and reputable news sites in the target language that do not charge for content.

- Test the selected site to make sure that students can access content and that their computers are set up to play the audio or video files (if used) with the necessary media *plug-ins* installed (e.g., QuickTime, Windows Media).

- Demonstrate for students how to navigate sites for current and archived content.

- Younger students might be less likely to be regular consumers of current events information, especially political, economic, or public policy news. These students may need more of an orientation to news sources.

Summarizing Reports Activity

Teacher Preparation

- Find an appropriate site for students to pick out their own stories.
- This site should offer articles or reports of an appropriate length and difficulty for your students (see Figure 5.6).
- Demonstrate for students how to browse the site and choose a report that interests them.
- Do you want students to take notes while reading or listening to the report? If so, they need to avoid simply copying text verbatim or transcribing the audio.
- Do you want students to write their summary of the text or audio report in a word processor or record it to an audio file? (For the latter, see Chapter 6, Audio/Video Activities.)

Figure 5.6 ■ The NPR program *All Things Considered*. Each program offers about a dozen or more short reports (3–5 min.) with a short text synopsis and a link to the audio for each.

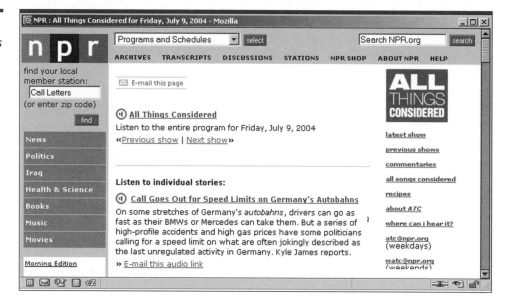

Steps for Students

- Go to the media news site the teacher has assigned.
- Browse the articles or reports and find one that interests you.
- Make note of its title and page address (URL).
- Read or listen to the report one or more times.
- Close the web browser and audio player.
- If writing a summary of the report, open a new document and begin writing.

- If recording an audio summary, open the audio recording program and begin recording.
- Do not refer back to the web report.
- Let a partner read or listen to your summary and write what he or she thinks would be an appropriate title for the report.
- Did your partner understand your summary well enough to give it an accurate title?

Discerning Editorial Slant Activity

Teacher Preparation

- Find two different news sources about the same event or issue, ones that differ from each other in perspective.
- Analyze coverage of the same story from these different sources.
- *Bookmark* these sites and tell students to read or listen to both reports.
- Discuss vocabulary with students, such as *liberal* or *conservative*, as needed.

Steps for Students

- Go to the two online news reports.
- Read or listen to each. Take notes.
- How do the stories differ?
  - Do they exhibit obvious sympathies with one party or another in a conflict?
  - Do they refer to the same people or events with different names?
  - Which story seems written from a conservative perspective, and which seems written from a liberal perspective?

Transcript Cloze Activity

Teacher Preparation

- Find an online audio or video news report for which the transcript is also available (see Figure 5.7).
- Bookmark the page with the report for students.
- Locate the transcript for this report and save it as a text file.
- Open the transcript file in a word processor and replace selected words with blanks for students to fill in.
- Distribute the cloze exercise to students by printing it, e-mailing it as an attachment, or saving it as a template in a shared network folder.

Figure 5.7 ■ The full-text transcript from LexisNexis of the *All Things Considered* report about the German autobahn. (See Chapter 8 for information on getting transcripts of web media broadcasts.)

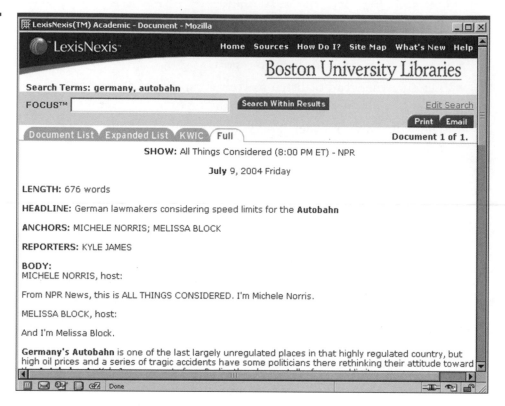

Steps for Students

- Open the web browser and go to the assigned web page.
- Read or listen to the entire news report assigned.
- Get the paper or text file of the fill-in activity.
- Read or listen again while filling in the missing words.
- Verify your answers with your partner.

Internet References

WorldNews.com. A global news service reporting business, politics, sports, technology, and current events. The news is available in more than 20 languages, with access to international radio channels. Site includes a search by topic and language, *worldnews.com*

Voice of America (VOA). A broadcasting service funded by the U.S. government. VOA claims to broadcast to 94 million people worldwide news, educational, and cultural programs in English and over 50 other languages. The site is also offered in each of these languages. Find audio reports with transcripts online. The "Special English" section provides audio reports in simplified English spoken slowly for non-native speakers or learners, *www.voanews.com*

BBC (British Broadcasting Corporation). A variety of radio programs and specials, including news and reports in dozens of languages, *www.bbc.com*

NPR (National Public Radio). A variety of news, cultural, and entertainment programs, with extensive archives, in English, *www.npr.org*

CNN (Cable News Network). Extensive news coverage with text, audio, photographs, background descriptions, analysis, etc. Though transcripts are free, most streaming video is available to subscribers to CNN online only (as of this writing), *cnn.com*. CNN International is available in a half-dozen languages, *edition.cnn.com*

FOXNews.com. A distinctly conservative perspective, *www.foxnews.com*

News Directory. A guide to all online English-language media. Includes newspapers, magazines, television stations, colleges, visitor bureaus, governmental agencies, and more, *newsdirectory.com*

Tehran Times International (English), *www.tehrantimes.com*

China View, Xinhua News Agency (China), English version (also in Arabic, French, Russian, and Spanish), *www.chinaview.com*

Al Jezeera.Net (Qatar), English version, *english.aljazeera.net*

The Jerusalem Post (English, also French version), *www.jpost.com*

❖ Activity 9 ■ Effective Browser Use and Web Searching	
	Teacher skills: strong web browser skills, effective searching
	Student level: intermediate to advanced
	Content objective: formulating intelligent web searches, evaluating sources
	Software: web browser

Effective web searches benefit from conscious decisions made *before* the search about *where* to look for information. Using a search engine, such as Google or Yahoo, is only one option and not always the best one, yet it is the one many students associate exclusively with locating information on the Internet. Instead, we can approach the search for information on the Internet as we would elsewhere—by trying to determine a logical and reputable source first and then going to that source. Otherwise, searches can get bogged down in lengthy, fruitless tangents or lead to sites that appear to provide answers but are not known as authoritative sources. Just because you found it on the Internet doesn't mean it's true or accurate. Anyone can put anything on a web page with no editorial oversight.

To find out current currency exchange rates, for example, we might refer to the business section of a newspaper. Using the Internet, we could go to a financial news site. To find out where Pablo Picasso was born, we might refer to an encyclopedia for this static fact. Using the Internet, we could go to an online encyclopedia. A web searching quiz, or scavenger hunt, can reinforce strategies for locating trusted sources. The value in these activities derives not from the product but the process, that is, not the correct answer that students find but *how* they find it.

Pedagogical Rationale

Despite the fact that younger students now have grown up on the Internet, they aren't necessarily its most savvy users. In particular, they may not consider the *epistemology* of the Internet or the *validity of sources* without explicit instruction. Guided web searching activities combine instruction in the use of a critical tool, the web browser, with search techniques and evaluation of sources. The content or particular tasks involved can be customized to tap into interesting, relevant topics in students' lives as well as their practical needs outside the classroom.

Of course, we don't need the Internet or even computers for reading activities; we have texts and periodicals. But the Internet offers practically limitless choices of topics, materials, and links to related material, and the medium exercises skills at nonlinear navigation in search of specific information.

Teacher Preparation for All Activities

- Write questions that can be answered by Internet research.
- Demonstrate basic browser operations to students. (Use Appendix D, Web Browser Basics, as a guide.)
- Pair students up by unlike L1s, if possible, and by complementary computing and Internet expertise (i.e., the experienced with the inexperienced).
- Give clear directions, a narrow topic focus, and a time for completion of each task.
- Use resources, such as search engines or news and information sites, that have versions in the target language. Yahoo and Google, for example, have dozens of language versions. Otherwise, use native resources known to target language speakers.
- Distribute only one copy of handouts to each pair or team to compel them to work together.

Steps for Students for All Activities

- Read through the assignment questions with a partner.
- Go to the assigned website or category of sites.
- Search the site(s) for answers, write them on the handout, and verify each one with your partner.
- Verify your answers with another team.

Tip: Site-Specific Activities

These activities specify the website to be searched and limit students to that site. See **Bookmarking a Site** sidebar on page 62 for distributing URLs to students. This focus has potential benefits:

- Eliminates students browsing fruitlessly through sites that are unrelated, unreliable, or poorly designed.
- In close-reading activities for specific facts within a given site, students can focus their efforts on the reading.
- Ensures that students will work with pages in the target language, when they might be tempted to use ones in their native language, defeating the *process* of the activity in order to reach the perceived objective.

Teacher Preparation

- Choose a website for students, ideally one related to some other class activity, such as a holiday, upcoming field trip, local event or attraction, or writing topic.
- Make up a list of general and specific questions that could be answered with information found on several pages on the site.

Activities

- *Pre-field trip activity.* Before a class field trip, direct students to a site that provides background for the trip (such as a historical or cultural site).
- *Pre-visitor activity.* Before a visitor or speaker to class arrives, direct students to information on the person, topic, or where he or she comes from.
- *Holidays.* Have students research answers to the significance of a holiday in the target culture.
- *Biographies.* Refer students to a specific site that includes biographies of notable people in the target language or culture or a target language encyclopedia. Students find the answers to questions about the life of a particular notable person in history, literature, art, pop culture, etc.

Comparison Shopping

These activities allow students to roam more freely on the Internet and therefore assume a slightly more sophisticated Internet user than for site-specific activities. Students work in pairs on real-world tasks, such as shopping for clothes on a limited budget, finding an apartment, or locating a highly ranked college in a particular field of study. Students can work individually for some activities (shopping, school searching) or pair up for others (apartment hunting).

Teacher Preparation

- Choose one of these activities or a variation.
- Set specific limits for each activity in terms of (play) money available to spend, time for the search, and how their results will be presented to the class.

Clothes shopping

- Set an amount of money that students have to spend online to build a wardrobe appropriate for the season and locale.
- Demonstrate examples of online clothing catalogs with "Shopping Carts," which allow you to collect items you want to purchase with a running total of the cost. (Google has a guide to thousands of online catalogs, *catalogs.google.com*.)
- Go over vocabulary related to clothes (e.g., *active wear, V-neck, inseam, waist*) as well as size conversions with an online converter, such as *www.onlineconversion.com*.
- Students fill a shopping cart with clothes but do *not* Check Out or provide any personal or payment information.
- Students cannot spent over the stated limit, including shipping charges, which are usually calculated at the beginning of the Check Out stage but before payment information is required.
- When all students are finished, they present their wardrobe purchases to the class either from a printout or screen display (with projector) of their shopping cart items.
- Other students evaluate the wardrobe selections for comfort, practicality, and cost.

Finding an apartment

- Set an amount of money that students can pay monthly for an apartment.
- Demonstrate a few apartment listing sites, such as a local paper's online classifieds, a realty office, or the school's housing office.
- Go over vocabulary, issues, and abbreviations related to local housing (*security deposit, cozy, hw floors,* etc.).
- Students decide whether to live by themselves or join others in the search to afford a larger apartment.

- This activity can be extended to having students call the realtor or owner for more details or even visit the apartment.
- Students present the housing they find, either by themselves or with their "roommates" to the rest of the class.
- The class evaluates each situation in terms of its cost, desirability, amenities, proximity to school or transportation, etc.

College searching
- Find a list of degree programs and major fields of study, such as at a college search engine (*www.petersons.com*).

TECHNOTE Printing Web Pages

Students print web pages more often than necessary, perhaps because the printed page seems to carry more credibility and permanence than the same thing on the screen. It's also easier to read printed text. The **CRT,** or "tube" display, offers a flickering image measured by the monitor's **refresh rate** in hertz (Hz), so a 72Hz refresh rate flashes the image 72 times per second. The flat-screen **LCD** display offers a more pleasant viewing experience than the CRT since it illuminates each picture element, or **pixel,** continuously.

Screen resolution, measured in dots per inch **(dpi)** along a line, typically 72 or 96, is much lower than print resolution, typically 300 to 600 for laser printers or 1,200 or more for magazine print. Computers render characters on screen with many individual pixels, not a smooth continuous shape like a marker on a dry erase board. The smooth curves of characters are thus approximated by blurring the edges into the background by a process called **anti-aliasing**, which fills the pixel steps between contrasting colors with intermediate shades. Until we look very closely, this subtle blending of color gradients looks smooth. Since printers can fill these steps with much smaller dots, printed text appears smoother than screen text.

Web pages, unless specifically designed for printing ("printer friendly," see Figure 5.8), are designed for screen display within a web browser window. Consequently, printing web pages can lead to pages that do not fit horizontally on paper, that break at awkward places, that have text obscured by graphics, or that tie up the print queue with graphics-heavy pages that are slow to print and drain toner.

🖨 PRINTER FRIENDLY   ▤ SINGLE-PAGE FORMAT   ✉ E-MAIL TO A FRIEND

Figure 5.8 ■ Many online media articles offer a "printer-friendly" version, where ads, graphics, and site navigation buttons are stripped for an easy-to-print, text-only page.

- Review these fields of study with students and ask them to pick one or two to research further.
- Students compare programs at different colleges. They should consider:
  - costs of tuition
  - cost of living in city where the college is located
  - entrance requirements, such as high school grades and SAT or TOEFL scores
  - desirability of studying in that location (i.e., other attractions)
  - job prospects for a graduate of that program
- Students present their school picks to the class.

Internet References

Learn the Net.com. Online primers on browser basics, surfing, e-mail, downloading files, newsgroups, and more in English, Spanish, and French, *www.learnthenet.com*

Encarta® online encyclopedia, *encarta.msn.com*

Quid. General reference, French atlas, encyclopedia, *www.quid.fr*

United Nations (UN) Cyber School Bus. UN Global Teaching and Learning Project. Site available in six languages (Arabic, Chinese, English, French, Russian, and Spanish), *www.un.org/Pubs/CyberSchoolBus*

Thompson Peterson's. Education resources to help find the right college and financial aid as well as prepare for tests, *www.petersons.com*

CollegeNET. College and financial aid search engine, *www.collegenet.com*

📖 Activity 10 ■ Tour Guide[6]	
	Teacher skills: web browser, tour guide
	Student level: high-beginner to low-advanced
	Content objective: Internet research, conducting a tour
	Software: web browser

Students in this activity use the Internet to research a local attraction, such as a museum, campus, natural attraction, or historical building or site. They then go on a class field trip

---

[6]Dorothy Lynde, at the Center for English Language and Orientation Programs at Boston University, contributed ideas for this activity based on her tour of the Harvard University campus. She reports that tourists and others frequently tag along with her class during the activity, thinking that it's an organized or sanctioned tour. So much the better for an authentic activity.

to that attraction and take turns serving as a tour guide for the rest of the class for different aspects of the attraction. When not serving as a tour guide, the other students play the part of tourists and ask the guide questions.

This activity can be adapted to suit the school's surroundings and student's interests. Students can determine what is important to include in their tour, but teachers might want to establish certain minimum information, such as the name and purpose of buildings, when they were constructed, and so forth.

Pedagogical Rationale

This activity demonstrates how computers can be integrated into other learning activities that rely on more traditional resources and techniques. Students use the computer for background research to prepare them for greater involvement in an out-of-class activity, one that emphasizes speaking in an interesting and natural way in a situation in which they may already be familiar (a tour) or will experience later. Students are expected to read, understand, and remember the information about their tour assignment and present it in an informative way on the tour.

Teacher Preparation

- With the class, decide on a local attraction to tour.
- Assign a building or other feature (a prominent statue, memorial, or location) to each student in advance.
- Spend at least one lab class helping students use Internet resources to research the history, significance, or trivia of their assigned feature.
- Students can take notes while researching their topic, but they should not use them while guiding the tour.
- Determine about how long each student should talk on the tour (minimum and maximum times).
- Make arrangements for the field trip.
- On the day of the tour, lead the class from one tour point to the next and decide which student will start.
- After returning from the tour, discuss with the students what they found most interesting on the tours and what was the hardest aspect of the activity.

Steps for Students

- Read about your assigned topic at the websites of your field trip subject.
- Study the pictures of things you will talk about on the tour.
- Use other websites for information as needed.
- Print out a few pictures of your tour topic and write an outline of your talk beneath them, but do not copy the text verbatim.

- Practice giving your tour talk with a partner in class. Refer to features you discuss in the pictures.

- On the day of the tour, you will give your talk without notes, so be sure you have carefully thought out what you want to say.

- Begin your tour talk by welcoming everyone and introducing what you're going to talk about.

- Tour-goers are there to see what you're talking about more than look at you, so be sure to point frequently to exactly what you're explaining.

- Ask the tour-goers if they have any questions and try to answer them.

Tour Activity Tips:

- Low-level students may benefit from focusing on one specific website, eliminating time on fruitless or confusing Internet searches, while ensuring that students derive information from a reputable source.

- Don't allow students to print out web pages of information and simply read the pages on the tour. Most tour guides do not refer to notes, so a realistic experience would not give students this advantage either.

- Some students may not have been on such a tour themselves and may need the form modeled to them. In advance of this activity, take them on another tour in the area of a similar nature or conduct it yourself, following up with a quiz or reaction activities in class. This preactivity tour reinforces listening while it models the tour form and serves to get students out into the world. Most large colleges offer campus tours, and some may even conduct them in a foreign language.

- To get the ball rolling at the start of the tour, begin with the most confident student, one perhaps likely to talk the longest, thereby setting the tone for other students' talks.

Internet References

Harvard University Virtual Tour, *www.news.harvard.edu/tour*

Freedom Trail, *www.nps.gov/bost/freedom_trail.htm*

6

Audio/Video Activities

❖ How is audio on the computer any different from audio in the tape-based lab?

❖ Besides watching movies, what are good sources and activities for video in the lab? Do I have to digitize my own video?

Stand-Alone Video and Audio

Stand-alone media refers to audio or video clips presented by themselves that are not part of pedantic language software. Presenting a movie on a TV for a class, for example, makes use of stand-alone video as does playing a clip from it on the computer.[1] Language teachers have been using film, television and radio programs, music, and speeches as authentic models of the target language and stimuli for discussion and reaction for as long as these media have been around.

They've also used photographs and illustrations as stimuli for writing and discussion. Computers lend at least three important capabilities to this teaching method: control, access, and integration.

---

[1] Common, **cross-platform** media players capable of playing a wide range of digital audio and video file formats include the QuickTime Player, Windows Media Player, and RealPlayer—all free.

Control

Having audio or video available in a *digital* format (as a computer file) gives each student the ability to individually control its play and replay as needed. Presenting a video to a class with a single TV monitor *broadcasts* the program to all students at the same time and makes no accommodation for differences in listening comprehension or learning styles among students. Controlling digitized audio or video on a computer, on the other hand, gives each student the ability to instantly find a precise location in the file and play it from there with *non-linear* or *random access*, that is, without having to play, fast-forward, or rewind through material along the way. In addition, the elapsed-time indicator (a counter showing the time of play) precisely locates the student in the piece much more accurately than with an arbitrary unit counter on an audio- or videocassette player (see Figure 6.1). Thus, the teacher can refer to parts of the file with the same precision as to a numbered page in a book.

Figure 6.1 ■ The Apple QuickTime Player (available for Macs and PCs) playing an MP3 format audio file from a textbook chapter. On the left of this simple interface, the elapsed-time indicator shows that the playhead (triangle on right of progress bar) is at 5:56. A student can move the playhead to any point in the file to begin playing there.

Access

While access to *analog* (tape-based) audio or video material may be limited to the teacher's audio- or videocassettes, or perhaps those of a local collection, digital material available on Internet news, reference, educational, and other sites opens students up to a much greater quantity and variety of sources.

Integration

Audio, video, and images in a digital format have the flexibility to be integrated into a *multimedia* project or lesson with related and interactive comprehension and reinforcement activities (such as a web page).

Copyright

Converting copyrighted work into a digital format, integrating it into multimedia projects, copying it, or distributing access to it brings up important legal considerations. See Appendix F, Fair Use Guidelines for Educational Multimedia, for a cursory discussion of using copyrighted works, limitations of use by media, and a listing of resources to assist teachers in adhering to the law. It is assumed in this chapter and elsewhere in this book that teachers will comply with copyright law. Individual teachers bear full responsibility for such compliance.

Audio

◈ ACTIVITY 1 ■ Using Textbook Audio	
	Teacher skills: use of audio players or web browser media plug-ins
	Student level: beginning to low-advanced
	Content objective: listening
	Software: media plug-ins or players

Audiocassette tapes have long accompanied language textbooks. Some still do, but many now come with audio CDs instead. In the analog lab, teachers broadcasted or copied this audio out to tape decks built into carrels, where students followed along with the textbooks. (See Chapter 1 for a discussion of *analog* versus *digital* technology.) Having access to such textbook audio was one of the first expectations of language teachers new to CALL. In addition to all of the capabilities unique to the computer lab, delivering textbook audio is a standard and relatively low-tech option.

Pedagogical Rationale

In the labs, audio files are made available to students to use in conjunction with the corresponding textbooks just as they would have used class sets of tapes or a tape broadcast in an analog lab. Because most textbook audio has little, if any, didactic value when separated from the textbook, only students that have the corresponding textbook, either their own or one from a class set owned by the lab, access the audio material.

Listening to textbook audio on the computer may not be the most effective use of computer *class* time, as it is generally more appropriate for

> **TECHNOTE** ■ **One File, Many Users**
>
> Generally, a single computer file, whether it's text, audio, video, or some other type, can only be opened, read, or played by multiple users simultaneously if it was saved as a *template*, *stationary*, or read-only file (see **TECHNOTE: Template** in Chapter 4 on page 35) or resides on a locked server *volume* (hard drive or partition), or whose access is otherwise managed by network *authentication* and document services, such as Windows 200x Server or Novel (PC), or Macintosh Manager or Workgroup Manager (Mac).

homework, whether done in a self-access lab or on the Internet from a student's home computer. Nonetheless, there is some value in using class time once to introduce students to the procedures for accessing the audio material, wherever it's stored, and using the appropriate media players and plug-ins. Some students, for example, might not know that they can stop playing a file at any point and go back and listen to an earlier portion or that the elapsed-time indicator shows them exactly where they are in the audio file in minutes and seconds.

Digitizing Audio

Even though the *nature of use* of digitized textbook audio is no different from that in the analog lab, you need explicit permission from the publishers to digitize their tapes. (See Appendix G, Sample Letter to Secure Publisher Permission.) Publishers also want to know how you plan to *distribute* the audio files or limit *access* to your students, especially if the files will be available on the Internet, such as from a class website or through *courseware*. Only students who have purchased the textbook or are using a lab copy should have access to the files, which is typically restricted with password-protected web pages. In some cases, publishers provide access to textbook audio on their own website to students who have purchased a text or software, access that may require login codes provided with the text or software. At larger institutions that can support a foreign language resource library or digital media library, staff can secure copyright permission to digitize all audio accompanying language texts in use. Faculty simply request access to units as necessary, either through their own website, their courseware site, course pages set up by the lab for use by all students enrolled in the course, or on a department server.

Textbook audio on cassettes can be digitized with practically any computer and then converted into an efficient audio format—one of high *fidelity* (quality) and small file size. Textbook audio on CDs (in CD audio format) is already in a digital format and just needs to be converted into a compressed file format, such as MP3. These resulting files can be distributed to student computers for class use or played or *streamed*[2] from a lab server or web server. (See **TECHNOTE: Recording Sound** on page 101) In most cases, a single audio file on a web or file server can be independently played and controlled by many users simultaneously. (See **TECHNOTE: One File, Many Users** on page 97.)

---

[2] *Streaming* refers to playing audio or video files from a web server without actually *downloading*, or copying, the file to the user's computer. Streaming files begin playing faster than files needing to be completely downloaded first. More important, copyright owners (publishers or broadcasters) like the control they maintain over the distribution of their content through streaming.

Digitizing and Converting Audio

Lab personnel, teachers, or student workers can digitize textbook audio from cassette or convert CD audio.

To digitize from audiocassette:
Play an audiocassette on a tape player while recording it with a sound editor on a connected computer.

- Connect an audio "patch cord" from the player's headphone jack to the computer's analog audio in—usually the microphone jack, a 1/8" or "mini" connector.

Figure 6.2.1 ■ Audiocassette player. Connect an audio patch cord from the headphone jack to a computer's analog audio input (Figure 6.2.2).

- Using the computer's sound control panel, set the sound input to the external microphone.
- Press **Record** in the sound editor application and then **Play** on the tape deck.
- Record an entire side of the tape at a time and save the file in a noncompressed format (e.g., ***WAV, AIFF***). (See **TECHNOTE** on page 101.)
- Using the textbook as a guide, segment this file into small clips, such as lessons, activities, or chapters that correspond to the text.
- Export each of these smaller files to a compressed format or batch convert all of them.

To convert CD audio to MP3:

- To use the tracks on the CD as the individual files, batch convert them.[3]
- If the CD only contains one very long track, then open it with the sound editor, segment it as described previously, and then convert each segment.

Figure 6.2.2 ■ Analog audio input jack on a laptop computer. The symbol for this jack might also be a microphone.

---

[3] Many audio applications will convert audio from a CD into compressed audio files (such as MP3 or other formats). (See **TECHNOTE: Recording Sound.**)

Teacher Preparation

- Prepare audio for students to listen to: digitize and compress it to a format compatible with how students will access it.
- Make the audio files available to students (e.g., class website or shared network folder).
- Instruct students in proper use of audio player application.

📓 ACTIVITY 2 ■ Teacher Recordings	
	Teacher skills: recording audio
	Student level: beginning to low-advanced
	Content objective: listening to customized teacher recordings
	Software: sound editor or voice recorder

Language teachers make constant use of their own voice for modeling, dictation activities, and testing. Whatever can be spoken can likewise be recorded and saved to an audio file that students can access and control individually as they would access local media files or those found on the Internet (such as in Activity 4 in this chapter).

Pedagogical Rationale

Why use computers for routine spoken-word activities in class when you've gotten along fine without them? Since students can play the audio file you save at any time, they do not all need to be engaged in the activity at the same time or begin at the same time. Also, individual control of sound files allows students to work at their own pace.

Teacher Preparation for All Activities

- Record custom audio.
- Compress audio and make available to students.
- Instruct students in proper use of audio player application.

Activity Steps

Dictation. This simple, familiar exercise can be adapted for all levels for the lab.

- Record a passage or sentences in advance.
- Students individually play and replay the file as necessary to type the dictation in a word processor.

- They compare what they've written with a partner, going back to relisten as necessary.
- (Activity extension)
  - Students record the passage from their transcripts and exchange this recording with other groups to verify.
  - They save this recording for the teacher to analyze later.

Scrambled dictation

- Record a passage as described previously but with sentences in a paragraph scrambled (out of order).
- Working in pairs, one student transcribes the sentences while the other assembles them into a logical order.
- (Activity extension) Each student records the assembled passage and exchanges it with other pairs to verify.

Recorded comprehension questions

- Instead of writing comprehension or discussion questions to accompany other stand-alone audio, such as from the Internet, record them.
- Students listen to the content piece and then listen to your recorded questions to respond either in writing or by recording.

Syllable dictation/stress identification

- Record words or sentences for a syllable and stress exercise.
- Students listen to the words, transcribe them, and then identify syllables and stress based on your pronunciation.
- They verify their answers with a partner and relisten to the recording as necessary.

TECHNOTE ■ **Recording Sound**

There are many sound editing applications, or "wave form editors," to record, append, and edit audio files (see Custom-Authored Lessons in Chapter 9 for a sample). *Freeware*, which is freely distributed software, and *shareware*, which is very cheap, are available at software archives on the Internet (see the Internet References on page 108), while commercial software is available at retail sites, campus bookstores, or computer stores and web distributors.

Many of these applications can *encode* your audio recording into a sound file format using a variety of *codecs* (COmpression-DECompression Schemes) to compress them or shrink the file size for network playing. The popular *MP3* format (.mp3) for music retains a high quality for voice recordings in a small file size suitable for playing over a local network, streaming from a website, or e-mailing. Other efficient formats include RealAudio (.ra), Windows Media (.asx), and QuickTime (.mov). Many free media players that come with computers, such as Apple QuickTime or iTunes, Windows Media Player or WinAmp, or RealPlayer, readily play MP3 files. Among these, Apple iTunes can convert many sound formats into MP3.

	ACTIVITY 3 ■ Student Recordings
	Teacher skills: recording audio
	Student level: beginning to low-advanced
	Content objective: voice recording
	Software: sound editor or voice recorder

With all the complexity of computers and variety of programs available, effective CALL activities more often than not make use of simple tools for specific functions. For example, a basic sound recording application (some free or inexpensive) enables students to make brief digital recordings and save, edit, copy, or send them to others. It doesn't have to be an elaborate process or one promising sophisticated feedback or speech analysis, capabilities that computers don't yet possess in practical applications with acceptable reliability. Thus, there continues to be a need for the CALL *teacher*.

The activities in this section—suitable for low-level learners and wide adaptation—emphasize student production and interaction and creative use of the technology by the *teacher* rather than elaborate technical feats by the *software*. Most involve student recordings and recorded teacher feedback.[4]

Pedagogical Rationale

The analog lab excelled at facilitating the listen-repeat-compare routine of the audiolingual method with the two-track audio player-recorders. (See Chapter 1 for a discussion of analog lab technology.) Some commercial software and so-called "turn-key lab systems" (e.g., Tanberg's Divace or Sony's Symphony) offer similar capabilities, but since labs now generally facilitate an *integrative* approach to language learning, the limitations of listen-repeat-compare have less and less appeal in the interactive, creative environment of CALL. Computers did not excel at enabling such audiolingual activities with ease until recently, for a variety of technical reasons. Now these simple activities can be folded with relative ease into the wide range of activities in the CALL lab.

---

[4]Dorothy Lynde and Doug Kohn at the Center for English Language and Orientation Programs at Boston University contributed several ideas for these activities.

Analyzing Pronunciation

This activity emphasizes teacher attention to individual student pronunciation. Although the activity itself is not complicated to set up or perform in class, teachers will need to allot as much time to listening and responding to the recordings as to student writing, a process that will stretch over at least two lab classes.

Activity Steps

- Create a question or brief discussion topic for students or ask them to summarize other listening or reading material.
- Students record their response, review, and rerecord it if necessary.
- Students save their audio files to a location that the teacher can access later.
- After class, the teacher listens to each recording, makes notes of pronunciation problems, and then records comments for the student or appends the student's original recording.
- The student then listens to the teacher's comments and rerecords the passage, trying to correct the errors.
- The teacher listens to the second student recording to see if the noted errors were corrected and then either records comments or discusses them one-on-one with the student.

Strip Story

This activity combines listening comprehension, dictation, and working with a partner to put jumbled sentences in order. Vary the length and complexity of the sentences and story, as appropriate for the level.

Teacher Preparation for All Activities

- Instruct students in the use of the audio recording and playing application(s).
- Establish a location for saving and sharing recorded files in class.

Activity Steps

- Find or write a short passage of several sentences.
- (Variation for higher-level students) Use jumbled paragraphs in a longer text rather than jumbled sentences in one paragraph.
- Divide the class into groups. For a class of 15 students, divide them into three groups of five, where each student in a group is given one sentence of a five-sentence story.

- Each student records his or her sentence individually.
- Group members listen to each other's recorded sentences and transcribe each one.
- The group works together to verify their transcriptions and then puts them in the proper order.
- Each group verifies its story, the words, and order of the sentences with other groups.

Retelling a Story

This activity is an advanced variation on the strip story. Divide the class into the same number of groups as you have parts to a story. A larger class will call for more groups and, therefore, a story divided into more parts. Each part can contain several sentences or several paragraphs. Having students listen to different parts of a story in the lab might also be logistically more practical than physically isolating groups such as by taking them out of the classroom to hear only one part.

Activity Steps

- Find or write a story that can be divided into several parts.
- Prerecord each part and save as separate audio files. Use arbitrary file names that do not indicate order (e.g., *yellow, green, red*).
- Divide the class into groups equal to the number of story parts.
- Each member of a group listens to only one part, so that no one person has heard more than one part of the story.
- Students can take notes on the part they hear but should be discouraged from transcribing it verbatim.
- Group members talk to each other about the meaning of their part until they understand it well.

Saving Sound Files

Ideally, all sound files for students and those saved by students will be saved to a central location, such as a shared folder on a local file server or courseware site. (Lab personnel should establish saving and sharing options for users.) Files to be copied onto removable media or played over a network need to be compressed into an audio format such as MP3.

In small, or non-networked facilities, especially ones with no dedicated lab personnel, students may have to save files to a folder on the computer they are using (i.e., the *local* hard drive). The teacher and other students will have to listen to recordings and respond to them at that same computer. Short recordings (under three minutes) could also be e-mailed as attachments, providing the e-mail accounts used have generous attachment and inbox quotas. (See Appendix B, File Saving and Sharing Options, for a detailed comparison.)

- Students then reorganize into groups made up of members of each of the other groups (representing all parts of the story) and try to piece the whole story together in these new groups.
- (Activity extension)
  - Students each record a summary of the whole story.
  - Distribute the text of the story for groups to verify their recorded reconstruction.

Chain Recording

This activity is a CALL variation on a popular classroom game or icebreaker. Since this activity can be completed as a class much faster *without* computers (by whispering ear-to-ear), consider the following uses for it in a CALL lab, when it will not engage all students at the same time:

- As a *buffer activity* that students work on in between other assignments;
- As a *homework assignment,* where students do their portion in an open lab or at home;
- As a fallback *distance learning activity* in a traditional course that cannot meet on occasion because of the instructor's absence, bad weather, or other reason. Students make a recording on their own and e-mail it to class members in a chain.

Activity Steps

- Record a short passage for students.
- Student A listens (and relistens) to the teacher's recording without taking notes, records what she thinks she heard, and then saves this file.
- Student B listens to student A's recording and records what he thinks she said.
- Repeat until the last student records the passage.
- To verify the sentence, students work backward toward A, thus student O verifies and corrects his sentence with N who verifies and corrects with M, etc. If this is not practical, discuss as a class the evolution of the original passage to the final student recording.

Answering Machine Message

Students write the outgoing message for an answering machine for different purposes, such as a home, small office, plumber's or electrician's business, divorce attorney, etc.

Activity Steps

- Assign the types of message students are to record and what information they need to provide.

- Students record their message(s).

- Other students listen to the messages and record a caller message to leave for that person or business.

- (Activity extension) Students label their message recordings with their names but not whether it's an outgoing message or a caller message. Students listen to all of the outgoing and caller messages and try to match them without asking other students which recordings they did.

Record Movie Show Times

This activity is a short, fun, creative recording exercise that introduces students to the form and vocabulary of recorded movie listings. A newspaper or online movie listing can be used to provide titles, times, and theaters.

Activity Steps

- If students are unfamiliar with the form of the "movie phone" recording, they can call a local one to hear it modeled, or the teacher can create a movie phone recording for the same purpose.

- Students record movie show times with theater name, titles, times, and short descriptions of the films, either real or imagined.

- (Activity extension) Students listen to the movie information recordings of other students and compile a movie show time listing, which can then be verified with what other students have written.

Summarize Lectures or Programs

This activity reinforces note-taking and summarizing skills.

Activity Steps

- Students listen to a live lecture or a recorded audio or video program and take notes.

- Students record a summary of the lecture or program from their notes.

- Working in pairs, students listen to their partner's recording, discuss corrections and additions, and rerecord.

- (Variation) Assign each student a different prerecorded lecture or program to listen to and record a summary. Have the other students listen to the summaries and try to match them up with a list of the program or lecture titles.

📓 Activity 4 ▪ Online Broadcasts	
	Teacher skills: web browsing, using media plug-ins
	Student level: intermediate to advanced
	Content objective: accessing online audio news broadcasts
	Software: web browser, media plug-ins

Many talk or news radio stations or programs make some or all of their programming available online, a good amount for free. In addition to the popular NPR site for ESL, well-known multilingual sites for audio include the BBC, CNN, and VOA (Voice of America). Audio or video on these sites can be used to facilitate a variety of comprehension activities. (See Activity 8, Media News, in Chapter 5 for detailed activities and discussion of sources.)

Teacher Preparation for All Activities

- Find appropriate media sites and *bookmark* them (see the **Bookmarking a Site** sidebar in Chapter 5 on page 62).
- Verify that students can access all media to be used in class.

Activity Steps

Listening comprehension

- Create cloze exercises, comprehension questions, or discussion activities for authentic audio or video.
- Students work alone or in pairs to answer questions on paper or from a distributed text file.

Supplementary materials

- Search broadcast media sites for teaching materials that are ready to print or be used online by students.

> **Activity Tip: To Bookmark or Not?**
>
> You can refer directly to a media file's *URL* without launching the web browser at all. That is, URLs are not just for web pages (.html files), but for any accessible file on a web server (e.g., images, *PDFs*), including the media files (e.g., a RealPlayer audio file) linked on web pages. (See **Bookmarking a Site** sidebar in Chapter 5 on page 62.) But in contrast to this direct route, consider showing students how to navigate the site themselves using the main navigation menus or the "search" function, which most large websites offer on every page. Teaching students how to navigate the site themselves empowers them to return to it on their own and use it as a resource.

■ Many U.S. media sites that offer educational materials gear the site to K–8 students, but the language may be accessible to adult ESL students.

Work with transcripts

■ Combine online audio with transcripts available through the same media outlet (such as CNN) or through the full-text LexisNexis database, if your institution subscribes. (See Chapter 8, Text-Based Activities, for a discussion of LexisNexis.)

Internet References

Plantronics® USB headsets, *www.plantronics.com*

Telex® USB headsets, *www.telex.com*

c/net. Shareware, freeware, and demo software archive for all operating systems. Search for the type of program you're looking for or browse through the categories and then read the program descriptions, *download.com*

TuCows Software Library. Similar to c/net in title range but with an original focus on communications software, *tucows.com*

Apple iTunes. (Mac and PC) Free music player, collection organizer, CD burner, and MP3 converter, *www.apple.com*

Video

	ACTIVITY 5 ■ Scenes from TV or Film
	Teacher skills: digitizing and basic editing of video, use of video players
	Student level: intermediate to advanced
	Content objective: listening, interpreting scenes
	Software/equipment: VCR, video editor and media converter or video card for digitizing, voice recording program

In this activity's simplest form, students watch short scenes (three to five minutes) taken from movies or TV programs and then, working alone or in pairs, complete comprehension tasks from a separate worksheet. It doesn't need to be more elaborate than that, because the lab primarily facilitates individual control over viewing the material—though the activities here offer more involved variations. While digitizing and editing video has become easier than ever, you may want lab personnel or experienced CALL teachers to prepare your video scenes for use in the lab.

Pedagogical Rationale

A scene most amenable to this kind of intense language and situation analysis might include some of the following characteristics.

Ideal video scene

- It stands on its own and has meaning outside the larger context or plot of the program as a whole.

- The interplay among characters leaves room for questions, such as who they are and what their relationships and histories are.

- The action or dialogue gives some clues as to what might have happened before this scene or what might happen after, though without certainty.

- A scene taken from something that students will later view in its entirety (though probably not on the computer) sets up an opportunity for them to recognize this scene and make a connection to the larger context.

- A scene taken from a popular, current film or program might more naturally strike students' interest.

- A scene taken from an obscure work might expose students to something that they normally wouldn't see, such as a classic, art house, or independent film.

| TECHNOTE | ■ **Media Players and Viewers** |

Stand-alone audio, video, and graphics can be played or viewed on Macs and PCs with free software.

- Most video used in this manner will be **encoded** (compressed after digitizing) into one of four formats: QuickTime (.mov), RealVideo (.rm), Windows Media (.asf)—played by players of the same name—or **MPEG** (.mpg), which can be played by all of these players.

- Most audio will be encoded into one of four formats: QuickTime (.mov), RealAudio (.ra), Windows Media (.asx)—also played by players of the same name—and MP3 (.mp3), which can be played by all of these players. Common **uncompressed** audio formats include **AIFF** and **WAV**, neither of which is effective for long clips played over networks, because the file size is too large.

- Graphic file formats common on the Internet, **JPEG** (for photos), **GIF** (for drawings), and **PNG** (any image), can be viewed in a web browser, the Windows Picture and Fax Viewer (PC), QuickTime Picture Viewer (Mac and PC), or Preview (Mac OS X).

Working with short video clips allows each student to view the material at his or her own pace and intensively analyze the language of the dialogue or the interplay among characters, whereas watching a film or TV program in its entirety leaves students struggling to understand the plot—a more general analysis. Repeated viewing combined with verification of answers with other students de-emphasizes the teacher as an answer key. The range of material available in this tailored activity, furthermore, holds greater promise of tapping into student interests than the narrow offerings of contrived scenes in pedantic video material.

Teacher Preparation for All Activities

- Find an appropriate scene of about three minutes from a movie or TV program.[5]
- Digitize the clip and make it available for students to view individually on lab computers.
- Distribute the related worksheets to each pair working together.
- Demonstrate how to use the media player on the computer, including adjusting volume, pausing, and moving back and forth along the timeline.

Activities[6]

Vocabulary

- As a pre-viewing activity, write the key vocabulary from the scene on the board or a handout without definitions.
- Students watch the scene and try to infer the meaning of the vocabulary items from their use and context.
- After viewing, discuss the vocabulary items.
- Students include the vocabulary items in written or recorded summaries of the scene.

Close listening

- Write comprehension questions about themes or details from the scene.
- Students watch the scene to answer the questions.
- Students verify their answers with a partner and then with other groups.

---

[5] Three minutes or less would fall within fair use allowance for motion media (see Appendix F).

[6] Doug Kohn, senior lecturer in the Center for English Language and Orientation Programs at Boston University, contributed to the video activity ideas in this section.

Finish the story

- Students work with a scene to gain a good understanding of it, such as with the previous close listening activity.

- Then they work in pairs or groups of three to write a plausible continuation of the dialogue in the scene or one that might precede it.

Transcription and acting

- Divide students into groups whose members equal the number of speaking characters in the scene.

- Each student in a group picks a character and transcribes his or her dialogue in the scene.

- Each group then acts out the scene, based on these written transcripts, either within groups or in front of the class.

- (Activity extension) Other groups comment on and verify the accuracy of the dialogue and faithfulness of the reenactment.

Summarize and assemble

- Find several short scenes from the same movie or TV program and create a separate file for each.

- Divide students into groups whose members equal the number of scenes.

- Each group watches only one scene and then writes or records a summary of it.

- Groups then read or listen to the recorded scene summaries of the other groups and try to piece the scenes together chronologically.

- Groups discuss and verify their order with other groups.

Follow-up

- Students work with a scene to gain a good understanding of it, such as with the *close listening* activity described earlier.

- They then use the Internet to research answers to questions about the subject or larger historical or cultural context—questions that cannot be answered in the scene alone. Lower-level students could be given a specific website to find the answers.

DVD extras

Movies on **DVD** often include supplemental materials that delve deeper into the making of a film or its subject. These materials might include interviews with the directors, actors, or real-life persons depicted on-screen, biographical summaries, historical time-lines, maps, and director voice-overs of the film describing behind-the-scenes details.

- Devise comprehension questions to be answered with these DVD extras, such as why the director set up a particular scene as he or she did.

- Each student or group will need access to the DVD and a computer with a DVD player to view it, thus they may have to take turns completing this activity.

TECHNOTE ▪ **Digitizing Video**

In many cases, lab personnel rather than individual teachers will digitize material and make it available to students in a class. So the following needn't discourage those without technical experience.

Programs on TV can be recorded with a home VCR onto a videocassette tape. Use the "SP" or standard play recording speed for best quality. The tape can then be played on a VCR connected to a computer with a video input *card* installed or through a media converter, much as we digitized audio (see the **Digitizing and Converting Audio** sidebar, page 99). These cards or converters digitize the analog audio and video signal from the tape and convert them to a digital video file on the computer using any of a variety of programs.

The media converter, a small, inexpensive device (see Figure 6.3), connects to the computer through a high-speed port such as **USB** 2.0 or **FireWire**® (IEEE 1394). Free video editing programs, such as iMovie® (Mac) or Windows Movie Maker (PC), can import the **DV** stream in real time into the computer from the converter box as the VCR is playing it.

After importing, editing, and cropping the video, save it in a common video file format (such as MPEG) that can be copied to a lab

file server or web server. DVDs, unlike video-cassettes, are already in a digital format, but they restrict direct lifting of its video through copy-protection technology.

Home DVD recorders can record broadcast programs directly to a digital format. On a computer, copy these files to the hard drive to edit.

Figure 6.3 ▪ Media converter, which takes an analog audio or video input (e.g., from audio cassette player or VCR) and converts the signal to digital, which can be saved and played on the computer.

🖎 ACTIVITY 6 ■ TV Ads	
	Teacher skills: digitizing and basic editing of video, use of video players
	Student level: intermediate to advanced
	Content objective: listening, interpreting ad messages
	Software/equiptment: VCR, video editor and media converter or video card for digitizing, voice recording program

Many language teachers analyze television and print ads with their students and use them for creative activities. They're short, omnipresent, have high production values, reflect the culture, and are often amusing. Activities with TV ads have the same software, equipment, and skill requirements as the TV and movie scene activities described previously, except that some TV ads may also be found on the Internet ready to use.

Pedagogical Rationale

In addition to providing models of the target language, ads provide opportunities for creative, interactive activities. As students are ad consumers, either in their first language or the target language, they can naturally relate to the format and concepts, perhaps to particular campaigns. Recent ads, then, provide familiar and relevant content to students, and by analyzing them students may even begin to appreciate common advertiser ploys and marketing concepts.

Where to find ads

- **Taped from TV.** Since ads aren't scheduled like TV programs, you'll have to tape an hour or two of programming and review the tape later (or while watching) for promising ads to use in class. Just digitize the ad or ads that you need from the tape.

- **Company websites.** For ads already in a digital format, look online. Many companies feature their own current TV ads on their corporate websites. Go to the site of a company of interest, perhaps one that has run interesting or high-profile ads in the past, and use the site's search tool to look for TV Ad. Apple demonstrates the quality of its QuickTime streaming video with some of its TV ads online as well as movie trailers, music videos, and other video content (their foreign sites offer ads in other languages). Other large, concept companies also feature some of their TV spots on their sites: BMW, FedEx®, Microsoft, Pepsi®, Coke® (the Library of Congress even archives vintage Coke ads). Many international brands maintain sites in multiple languages. Search for "TV ads" on these sites or look for the Corporate Information link. Once you find an ad online, download it as soon as possible as these ads frequently change and may not be available on a company's website for long.

- **Political and issue campaigns.** Go to a particular candidate issue or party site (e.g., stop smoking) and search for "TV ads."

- **Advertiser trade publications.** Some sites (such as *adweek.com* and *adage.com*) make a variety of commercial, issue, and political ads available for criticism.

- **Awards programs.** The Clio Awards, among other awards, annually recognizes funny, creative, or effective advertising from many countries in their original language.

TECHNOTE ■ **Downloading Online Video**

Some video found online can be downloaded, and some can't. If there is a saving option in the media player used for the video, then you might be able to save it. When you click on a video link, the appropriate media player (e.g., QuickTime Player) will launch and begin playing the clip, usually after it has **buffered** a certain percentage of the clip. By buffering, some of the clip downloads to memory before it begins playing as a buffer for continuous play when connection slowdowns occur. If a clip is downloadable at all, it is only after it has buffered 100 percent. More and more audio and video, however, is **streamed**, meaning that it plays as it's received, like a radio or TV broadcast, and does not download a file that can be saved locally. See Figure 6.4.

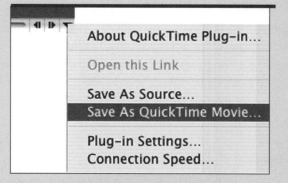

Figure 6.4 ■ Some video available online, such as movie trailers from Apple's QuickTime site, can be downloaded and saved with the QuickTime Player Pro.

Activities

Vocabulary and listening comprehension

- Use ads in place of scenes from TV or film in the vocabulary and close listening activities described previously.

Write the dialogue

- In pairs, students watch the video without sound (leave headsets on the desk).

- They write the dialogue or voice-over narration for it (plausible or silly, as long as it's creative and related to the video).

- They play the ad video and speak the dialogue they've written. For large classes, use a projector to display each ad while each team provides the audio—sort of a video karaoke.

- Compare the actual audio on the video with the students' versions.

Stand-Alone Images

Language teachers have long used photographs or illustrations in books, paintings in museums, and ads from magazines, billboards, and other sources to stimulate student written or oral response. Computers facilitate *access* to images of all kinds and *delivery* of high-quality full-color representations of such work. Present images to students via

- word processing document
- slide show presentation
- web page
- individual image files saved to a shared network volume or e-mailed as attachments

However the images are delivered, students view and respond to them in activities of description, matching, or comparison. (For a discussion of saving web images, see Web Projects in Chapter 7, **TECHNOTE: Saving Web Images**, page 128.)

Internet References

Dazzle Hollywood DV-Bridge (analog-to-DV media converter), *www.dazzle.com*

The Video Vault. Dozens of downloadable video clips from funny TV ads and ad spoofs from around the world, *www.giesbers.net*

AdCritic provides access to hundreds of video ads, commercial, political, and public service but only on a subscription basis. Access was initially free, but the overwhelming response exceeded its capacity to stream online video, *www.adcritic.com*

Clio Awards, *www.clioawards.com*

The Library of Congress, American Memory (Coca-Cola Advertisements), *memory.loc.gov/*

Companies Providing Their Ads Online

Apple ads, *www.apple.com/quicktime*

Advertising Age, *www.adage.com*

ADWEEK, *www.adweek.com*

BMW produces short films featuring their cars, available for downloading from its site, *www.bmw.com*

FedEx, *www.fedex.com*

Microsoft, *www.microsoft.com*

Pepsi ads, *www.pepsi.com*

7

Project Activities

❖ I'm tired of my students searching endlessly on the web. What's a more complex and structured web-searching activity they can do?

❖ PowerPoint seems to make my students' presentations worse. What can I do?

❖ I want my students to create something interesting and engaging that they can take home with them. What are my options?

The power of the computer in language learning shines in project-oriented activities. They give rise to student interaction, discovery, and creativity combined with acquisition of content knowledge, computing, and other skills in a process they feel ownership of and with a tangible product to show for it. Projects take a great variety of forms and can be adapted for different languages, environments, levels, and purposes. While project activities hold out the prospect of being more rewarding for a class than many exercise-based activities, they also require more careful teacher planning, preparation, involvement, and follow-up.

117

As with many new classroom activities, computer projects tend to get better as they are refined over time with repeated implementation, bringing greater teacher expertise and confidence.

Project Planning Considerations

- *Pairing or grouping students:* Pairing unlike L1s is ideal (though only likely in a second language environment), but also consider pairing by complementary work habits and technical skills (i.e., the neophyte with the know-it-all).

- *Teacher familiarity with tools:* Don't try to teach what you don't know; work through the projects in advance to test the feasibility of the activity and prepare for trouble spots.

- *Orienting students to tools:* Invest time up front in showing students how to use applications effectively.

- *Scheduling*: Establish a schedule with clear goals, and enforce deadlines.

- *Divide and conquer:* Segment the project into manageable stages and activities to mark student progress and keep groups from getting too far ahead or behind the rest of the class.

- *The process is the thing:* Invest at least as much in evaluating and assisting students with the process of the project as evaluating their final product.

Web Projects

Everyone wants to make a web page. Why not? For information sharing, especially in education, it's becoming as commonplace as creating text documents. There are many approaches to having students create web pages, but an essential choice boils down to three options:

1. creating them from scratch (i.e., from a blank HTML page)
2. using a *wizard* or *template*
3. exporting *HTML* from another application, such as a word processor or slide show application

Teachers or students who want to proceed directly to web page creation might prefer options 2 or 3 (see Activity 4 in this chapter). These approaches—especially number 3, which converts one document type into another automatically—spares students the knuckle-skinning process of creating pages manually but also leaves them unaware of how things work under the hood. If a page breaks down, such as with problems of layout or functionality, then they don't have the know-how to fix it. Moreover, students need background information to put the activity into context, understand the relevant *concepts* not just the specific *procedures,* and make it a meaningful series of projects.

Pedagogical Rationale

Challenging, interesting projects require following written and spoken directions, reading, writing, and collaborating with other students in pairs. Students learn a valuable skill while practicing the target language and expanding their vocabulary. Web-authoring projects take advantage of enthusiasm students may have (or soon develop) to learn how to create web pages for personal, academic, or professional purposes. Students take ownership pride in the pages they produce and have a stake in completing them as their peers evaluate their work. Pages shared via a class website offer family and friends back home a glimpse of what students are working on, and the program can link to these pages as examples of student work.

Elements of web projects

- browser basics (see Appendix D, Web Browser Basics)
- basic principles of good web page/site design
- structure and components of a web page
- planning and design of site
- copyright considerations for borrowed work (see Appendix F, Fair Use Guidelines for Educational Multimedia)
- HTML basics
- using a *WYSIWYG* HTML editor (WYSIWYG = what you see is what you get)
- *local* vs. remote file management

The knowledge and techniques acquired in the activities in this section build in a cumulative fashion, though any one can be singled out and adapted for a class activity given the coverage of prerequisite information elsewhere.

📖 ACTIVITY 1 ■ Evaluating Websites	
	Teacher skills: web browsing, understanding good site design and domain categories
	Student level: intermediate to advanced
	Content objective: recognizing site purpose, effectiveness, and good design
	Software: web browser

What makes for a good website? Visual appeal, originality, interactivity, ease of navigation, quality of content? Some measures are largely subjective, but experienced web users and designers would be inclined to agree on certain practical elements of functionality and how a site's design should reflect its primary purpose (entertainment, information, communication, etc.) and respect its primary audience. Before students can begin to build their own pages, they should have an idea of what designs and features work for a particular purpose and why. This activity gets them thinking about pages critically according to a set of criteria—the way they will need to think about their own pages later. Adapt this activity for higher-level students with more sophisticated criteria.

Pedagogical Rationale

Before students write, they read. They read what experienced writers have written much more than they will ever write themselves. From a wide range of reading they glean a great deal—vocabulary, structure, idioms, usage, rhetorical patterns, use of creative metaphors, and so forth. Likewise with creating web pages, students need to have seen a great many examples of layout, graphic and typographic design, functionality, organization, and so forth, in order to begin to produce their own web pages. As writers are lifelong readers, a web page creator must continue to compare his or her designs with the work of professionals.

Teacher Preparation

- Find at least three different websites for students to evaluate, ones from different "top-level" *domain* categories:
  - .gov (official U.S. government site, e.g., *www.immigration.gov*)
  - .com (commercial site, e.g., *www.cnn.com*)
  - .edu (educational site, e.g., *www.bu.edu*)
- Use other domain examples (.net, .mil, .org, etc.) as desired.
- For foreign language sites, choose sites that represent these different categories (government, commercial, educational, etc.).
- Low-level students or those with little web browsing experience might need the following site evaluation steps demonstrated on one example site, especially to deal with new vocabulary issues (e.g., *horizontal scrolling, contrast, navigate, dead link*).

Steps for Students

- Go to websites the teacher has chosen to represent different categories.
- Evaluate each site by answering the following questions.

About content

1. What's the **purpose** of the site (e.g., to sell, entertain, inform, educate)?
2. Is there an **appropriate amount** of material (text, links, graphics) on each page (too much or too little)?

3. Is any of the language on the site **unclear** to you?
4. Are the **graphics helpful** to understanding content or confusing?
5. Are there any **dead links** (links to other pages not found)?
6. Are the **links** helpful? Are any missing?

About format and appearance

7. Are the pages **attractive?**
8. Is the text on the pages **easy to read?**
9. Is the **contrast** (combination of text and background color or image) effective?
10. Do any pages require horizontal **scrolling** (sideways to the right) to view all of the content?
11. Can you easily **navigate** the pages within the site without getting lost? Is there a navigation bar on each page?
12. Is each page **titled** and clearly a part of the same site (e.g., using a consistent design)?
13. Do any page components **not work** (e.g., pictures not loading or text appearing scrambled)?
14. Are you **unable to view** some of the site because of
    - the web **browser** you're using (incompatible)?
    - the computer *platform* you're on (Mac or PC)?
    - your **connection** speed (too slow for large images, audio, or video)?
    - missing media player *plug-ins* (QuickTime, RealPlayer, Flash, Shockwave, etc.)?

🖹 ACTIVITY 2 ■ Purpose and Audience	
	Teacher skills: web browsing, understanding good site design and domain categories
	Student level: high-intermediate to advanced
	Content objective: understanding site design and purpose by category
	Software: web browser

This activity builds on the critical evaluation of website design in Activity 1. Students will focus on the purpose of various sites and the intended audiences. The sites in this activity demonstrate various types or categories of websites with different purposes and designs.

Pedagogical Rationale

No one website design or approach will satisfy the needs of all content, purposes, and audiences. Even student-designed sites should reflect the needs and expectations of the intended audience and follow a design consistent with the nature of the content.

Teacher Preparation

- For foreign language study, replace the sites in Table 7.1 with similar examples of sites in the target language.
- Address the vocabulary issues in the category labels in the table (e.g., *auction, informational, small business*).

Steps for Students

- What's the **purpose** of the sites in each category in Table 7.1?
- Who is the audience for each?
- Is it clear and **easy to understand** the purpose and intended audience from the home pages of the example sites?
- What design elements do sites within a category have in common?
- Find at least one other website to add as an example to each category.

TECHNOTE ■ HTTP, FTP, HTML

HTTP (hypertext transfer protocol): A **protocol** is a standard of communication. HTTP defines how files are transmitted from an HTTP server (i.e., web server) to a computer running a web browser. HTTPS is a secure web server using encrypted transmission of data, usually for transactions and personal data.

FTP (file transfer protocol): Unlike HTTP, which is a one-way transfer, FTP defines two-way file transfer—*uploading* to a server and *downloading* from it. Also unlike HTTP servers, FTP servers usually require a log-in (sometime "anonymous"). After you create web pages, you upload them to a web server, or *host,* with an FTP program, or *client,* such as Fetch (Mac) and WS FTP (PC). Some HTML editors have this FTP capacity built-in, so no separate client is needed.

HTML (hypertext markup language): Not technically a computer language, HTML defines how a page will display in a web browser, which interprets HTML. An HTML document is simply the code, in plain text, describing a web page. Any word processor or text editor can open HTML, though only with an HTML editor, such as Mozilla Composer or Macromedia® Dreamweaver, can you modify the page visually (i.e., without typing HTML code).

TABLE 7.1 ■ Website Types

Category	Example sites
Corporate	Ford, *www.ford.com* Amazon, *www.amazon.com* Apple, *www.apple.com*
News/Information	Weather Channel, *www.weather.com* WBUR Radio, *www.wbur.org* *Boston Globe* newspaper, *www.boston.com/globe*
Small Business	Select Design, *www.selectdesign.com* Angora Cafe, *www.angoracafe.com*
Informational/Educational (nonprofit)	How Stuff Works, *www.howstuffworks.com* PBS TV, *www.pbs.org*
Government	Town of Sharon, *www.state.ma.us/cc/sharon.html* Bureau of Citizenship and Immigration Services, *www.immigration.gov*
Auction	eBay, *www.ebay.com* uBid, *www.ubid.com*
Biographical	A&E Biography.com, *www.biography.com* Encyclopedia.com, *www.encyclopedia.com*
Scientific	Astrophysics Research, *heasarc.gsfc.nasa.gov* CERN, *www.cern.ch*
Travel	Orbitz (travel booking service), *www.orbitz.com* Massachusetts Tourism, *www.massvacation.com*
Class	French 104 (Univ. of Illinois), *www.french.uiuc.edu/FR104* StudyCom, *www.study.com*
Instructional/Reference	W3Schools (web development), *www.w3schools.com* Web Monkey Reference, *webmonkey.wired.com/webmonkey*
Entertainment	Barney (children's TV character), *www.hitentertainment.com/barney* Miramax Pictures, *www.miramax.com*

📖 ACTIVITY 3 ▪ Web Page Anatomy	
	Teacher skills: web browsing, basic web page authoring
	Student level: intermediate to advanced
	Content objective: identifying web page components
	Software: web browser

This web activity begins to delve into the *mechanics* of a web page, in particular, its component pieces. A concise primer on these components precedes the activity and can be used as a reference for later web activities.

Pedagogical Rationale

To further prepare students to create their own web pages, they will learn how to identify major components of a page, such as text, graphics, links, as well as some of their characteristics.

Components of a Basic Web Page: A Primer

A web page is different from a word-processing document. In addition to text, it includes *references* to other separate files (inserted graphics, sounds, videos), *hyperlinks* to other pages and files, form objects, and other code that affects its functionality. These elements appear to come together as a web page when viewed by the web browser. Major visible components of a simple web page are briefly defined here.

Text

Unlike graphics, text is *part* of the web page; it's contained within the HTML file. Text is typed directly into a web page or pasted from a word processor and then formatted in the same way.

Normal HTML text comes in seven sizes (1–7), with 3 being "normal" or the *default*. Any text can link to something else (a hyperlink).

Graphics

Graphics are not a part of the web page itself but exist as separate image files. The HTML code of the web page includes instructions for where to find graphics within the site or elsewhere (the *path*) and where to place them in the web page (i.e., it *refers* the browser to the graphics files). Graphics inserted in a page can also be hyperlinks. The three basic file formats used for images on the web are GIF, JPEG, and PNG. Flash provides fancy animations.

- **GIF** (Graphics Interchange Format—usually pronounced with a hard /g/) images support only a small number of colors and cannot represent many subtle gradations of the same color, such as in a photograph. It supports 256 colors but actually only 216 "web-safe colors," which appear the same on different kinds of computers. Sketches, cartoons, line art, and text work well as GIFs and result in a small file. GIFs also support transparency of one color, where you pick a color in an image to be invisible. An image background color can be set to transparent so that it blends in with the same underlying color on the web page and the image does not appear as a box.

- An **animated GIF** (GIF89a), a special type of image used in many banner ads, cycles through a series of frames contained within an image to give the appearance of movement. A special utility or graphics editor creates an animated GIF from many individual images.

- **JPEG** (Joint Photographic Experts Group) images support millions of colors, thereby representing photographs or images with many subtle shades of a color well. It can be compressed at varying qualities: the higher the compression, the smaller the file size but lower the quality. It does not support transparency and is generally ill-suited for line art and text.

- **PNG** (Portable Network Graphic) images combine some of the features of GIFs and JPEGs (transparencies and support for true color) but tend to result in larger files than GIF or JPEG.

- An image that a web page uses for its **background** is *tiled,* or repeated across and down the page, to fill the background of the page instead of a solid color. Background images may provide an underlying design for the page or set off a vertical column on the left of a page for navigation links, separating it from the body of the page containing the main content.

Links

A link, or hyperlink, is a connection to another web page, image, file, or action.

- **Text.** Hyperlinked text used to be consistently identifiable by its blue color and underlining. With the wide use of Cascading Style Sheets *(CSS),* especially on large or carefully designed sites, this convention has waned. Now we find linked text any color and rarely underlined. To know if such text is linked, pass the pointer over it. The pointer changes to a hand over links, and the linked file's URL appears on the bottom of the browser window in the *status bar.*

- **Images.** Any image on a page, except for the background image, can be a hyperlink.

- **Internal** links refer to pages or files within the same website and are usually expressed as *relative paths* (e.g., students/saito.html).
- **External** links refer to pages or files outside the current website and are expressed as *absolute paths* (complete URLs, e.g., *http://celop.bu.edu/students/saito.html*).
- **New window.** A link can open in a new browser window (i.e., not the current window, where the link is), an option used for external links so that the visitor still has the referring (original) page open underneath the new window.
- **Mailto.** A text or image link that invokes a new e-mail message.

Color

Several elements of a web page can be assigned a solid color: the text, page background, and table cells. *Contrast* figures highly in the readability of a page. Dark text on a light background—what we're accustomed to on paper—offers the highest contrast and greatest readability on-screen.

Form Objects

Forms accept user input. *Form objects*—check boxes or buttons, text fields (boxes to type text into), scrollable lists, *pop-up* (or "jump") *menus*—are used on quizzes, surveys, order forms, or search tools. The web server acts on the input and responds.

Table

An HTML table is similar to one used in a word processor, such as Word, with rows and columns. A table can have visible or invisible borders. As a structural device, usually without visible borders, a table helps with the layout of text and graphics on a grid, ensuring spacing consistency when viewed in different browsers.

Frames

Frames are a structural option in more complex web page authoring, where two or three web pages appear within a single browser window, often seamlessly with no visible borders. You know you're on a web page employing frames if you scroll down and one side doesn't move, usually the left or top with the navigation bar.

Identifying Web Page Components Activity

Practically any web page can be used for this activity where students identify text, images, and links. Pick several conventional pages that don't employ Flash or other special types of graphics.

Steps for Students

- Go to the assigned web pages and answer the following questions about each.
  1. What text is HTML, and what is in the form of a graphic?
  2. Which are the stand-alone graphics on the page and what format were they likely saved in (JPEG or GIF) based on the nature of the image?
  3. How many links are on the page? Which are external, internal, or mailto?
  4. What's the page background, an image or solid HTML color?

| TECHNOTE | ■ **Saving Text and Whole Web Pages**

Most text found on web pages can be selected, copied, and pasted into a word-processing or HTML document. If you cannot select the text on the web page, save the page as *text-only* or *source* (**File > Save As...**). The text-only file format, which any word processor can read, saves only the text content on a web page. Saving as source saves the page intact with text, pictures, and links, such as for *off-line* viewing with a web browser. These options will not work with all web pages, such as **dynamic** pages that refer to other pages for content. Also, some text on web pages, especially highly stylized text, such as logos, takes the form of graphics. You can only save these as images.

Determining Answers

1. If you can select it like text in a word processor, then it's HTML text, not a graphic.
2. See information on image formats as discussed. To confirm, click the mouse button and hold (Mac) or right-click (PC) to save the image file (choose **Save Image...**) and note the extension in the filename (.jpg, .gif, or .png).
3. *Mouseover* a link and look in the status bar in the bottom of the browser window for the resulting URL—where that link will go.
4. Look in the HTML code (**View > Source**) in the line that begins <BODY> (known as the "BODY tag") for a background image. For example, <BODY background="i/back.gif"> indicates that a background image is used, "back.gif" (a GIF image), not a solid background color rendered by the browser.

TECHNOTE ■ Saving Web Images

Most images found on web pages can be copied to your computer (see Appendix F, Fair Use Guidelines).

- (Mac) Click and hold the mouse button on the image until a pop-up menu appears (see Figure 7.1). Select the save or download image option.

```
Open Link in New Window
Download Link to Disk
Copy Link to Clipboard
Add Link to Favorites

Open Image in New Window
Download Image to Disk
Copy Image
Reload Image
```

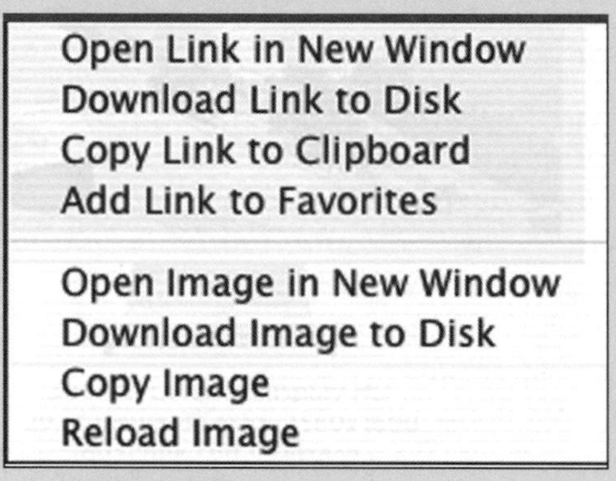

Figure 7.1 ■ The pop-up menu that appears when you click on a web image.

- (PC) Click the right mouse button on an image. From the pop-up menu, select the save or download image option.
- Save the image file to your web project folder and give it a descriptive name, but keep the *file extension* (.gif, .jpg, or .png).
- This image is already in a compatible format to insert into your web page.

Save a page background image by first determining its location in the <BODY> tag of the page's HTML source code and loading the image by itself in a new browser window. Some graphics, such as Flash movies or Java applets, can only be saved using the computer's *screen capture* utility, which copies anything appearing on your screen.

- (Mac) Trigger the built-in screen capture by pressing **Apple-Shift-3** (**Apple-Shift-4** gives you crosshairs to select only the desired area to capture). The picture is saved to the Finder desktop as a PDF (OS X) or the hard drive as a PICT (OS 8, 9).
- (PC) Press the **Print Screen** key. The picture is saved in memory to the Clipboard (short-term memory) and needs to be pasted into a graphics editor.
- Open the image in a graphics editor to modify as needed.

Shortcuts

There are four ways to access the same common commands in Composer and most applications:

- *Menu:* (top of screen) Click on a menu and select item, e.g., **Insert > Image...**
- *Toolbar:* (top of application window) Click **Image** button to insert image.
- *Mouse click*: Click right mouse button (PC) or **Ctrl**-click (Mac) to access commands that vary by context, e.g. click in table cell for **Table Cell Properties**.
- *Object*. Double-click left mouse button on object already inserted, such as image, table, horizontal line, to modify properties.

	ACTIVITY 4 ■ Authoring Mechanics—Recreating a Demo Page
	Teacher skills: basic web page authoring and file management, simple image editing
	Student level: intermediate to advanced
	Content objective: re-assembling a simple web page
	Software: web browser, WYSIWYG HTML editor

This activity is a first attempt at web authoring, one that focuses only on the *mechanics* of using a WYSIWYG HTML editor to reconstruct a simple demo web page that the teacher has already made and demonstrated. The hands-on exercise introduces and reinforces the fundamental components and principles of constructing a page, building on what was learned previously in this chapter. Students each re-assemble the sample page but help each other as needed.

Pedagogical Rationale

As in other activities where we divide and conquer, we avoid cognitive overload by separating the *content creation* aspect of page authoring from the *mechanics* of how the pieces go together, focusing at this point only on the latter. Think of this task as trying to reconstruct the model on the Tinker Toy barrel: the pieces are ready to put together and you know what the result should look like. Once students learn the mechanics, they can move on to their own content, their own creations, and face fewer simultaneous challenges by calling on what they learned in this activity.

Teacher Preparation

You need not be a tech guru, but ideally, you should understand how to make a very basic web page—including naming, organizing, and uploading files and creating or editing simple graphics. A non-technical teacher can learn what he or she needs to know by building his or her own simple personal, professional, or course site. Alternatively, for teachers with no experience but an eagerness to get started, the student steps may guide a first foray into making a web page. The image editing skills could be replaced by finding existing graphics on the web or elsewhere. (See **TECHNOTE: Saving Web Images** on page 128.)

- Construct a simple web page with a few graphics, some text, links, and a background color (see example, Fig. 7.1). This page will serve as the example to demonstrate and later for students to reconstruct. The page could be about anything, but a comparison of two things provides an opportunity to use a simple two-column table.
- Create a folder, "sampleWP," and save the source files in it.
- For the sample page in Fig. 7.1, we have the following files:
  - **text.txt**—The text for your demo web page: a short introduction and two lists representing points in a comparison of two things (a laptop vs. a desktop computer in the example). Students will copy and paste this text into their pages. Save this word processing document in the **text-only** (.txt) format to exclude formatting and characters not supported by HTML without special coding, i.e., characters that may not appear on a web page as they do in a text format like Word.
  - **banner.gif**—banner graphic to appear across the top of the page
  - **laptop.jpg**—image of laptop computer for comparison
  - **desktop.jpg**—image of desktop computer for comparison
- Distribute this folder, which does not include the finished HTML file, to each student (see Appendix B, File Saving and Sharing Options).
- Preview the vocabulary from the student steps (e.g., *prompt, assign, arrange, align*).

Steps for Students[1]

- Launch the HTML editor and open a new document (**File > New**).
- Save the file (**File > Save**) into the web folder, "sampleWP," where all the other files are located, with the file name "index.html."

---

[1] The steps in Activities 4 and 5 refer to Mozilla 1.7 on Windows XP but will apply to many HTML editors generally.

- The first time you save, you might be prompted to give a *page title* (different from the *file name*), which will eventually appear in the top title bar of the browser window. For the title, type "Desktop or Laptop?" If the Save command does not prompt for a page title, then go to **Format > Page Title and Properties:** Title.

- Assign the background color: **Format > Page Colors and Background.** For background, select white or type the code for white, #ffffff.

- Insert a *table* to hold and arrange your content: **Insert > Table:** rows=4, columns=2, width=600 *pixels,* cell padding=10, border=0.

- Align text and graphics horizontally across rows. Select all cells in the table by clicking in the top left cell and dragging the pointer diagonally to the bottom right cell. Select **Format > Table Properties:** cell: vertical alignment=top.

- Merge the first two cells. Click the mouse in the first cell, column 1, row 1 (top left). Drag the mouse to the right to select the adjacent cell (column 2, row 1). Select **Table > Join selected cells.**

- Insert the banner. Click in the newly merged cell. Select **Insert > Image... > Choose file...** and *browse* (look) for "banner.gif" in the web folder.

- In the top cell, click to the right of the banner, then hit the **enter/return** key twice to add two line breaks (paragraph returns).

- Open the file "text.txt." Select and copy the introduction text, and paste it two lines beneath the banner image on the web page (in the same cell).

- Add more images. Click in the cell at column 1, row 2. Select **Insert > Image...**, and browse for "laptop.jpg" from the web folder. Click in the next cell (column 2, row 2), and insert "desktop.jpg".

- Add bulleted lists. From the "text.txt" file, copy the laptop information and paste it in the cell beneath the "laptop.jpg" image (column 1, row 3). Copy and paste the desktop information text beneath the "desktop.jpg" image (column 2, row 3).

- Format text. Select the Introduction text on the web page. Select **Format > Font > Arial, Helvetica** (an easily readable *sans serif* font). Repeat **Format > Size > small** (or **2**). Repeat **Format > Text color >** *choose any dark color.* Alternatively, use the toolbar buttons for text formatting.

- Make the lists bullet style. Select the text under one of the pictures. Format it as described for typeface, size, and color. Click on the bulleted text formatting icon on the toolbar. As in a word processor, the bullets repeat each time you hit the **enter/return** key. Be sure that each point is on its own bulleted line. Repeat for the other list.

- Make hyperlinks. From the "text.txt" file, copy the URL for the example laptop. On the web page, select the picture of the laptop and then **Format > Image:** Link (or **Insert > Link**). Paste the URL into the box for the link. Repeat for the desktop computer.

- Repeat the links described except first select the text headings for each of the pictures (e.g., Laptop Computer) and then establish the links, **Insert > Link.**

- Create a (external) link to the class or teacher's main web page. Click in the bottom right cell (column 2, row 4). Type the name of the class or teacher. Select this text and then click on the right text alignment button on the toolbar. With the text still selected, go to **Insert > Link** and type the URL for the teacher's, class's, or department's home page.

- Check the page in the web browser. Select **File > Browse** page to see how the page will actually *render* (appear) in a web browser.

- Return to the HTML editor to fix problems. You may need to add extra line breaks after text or pictures for a more spacious look or align the text or images within cells. To align cell content, select the cell(s), **Table > Properties:** cell: alignment=top, bottom, right, or left.

We've reconstructed the demo page *locally*: It exists only on our computer. To make it available on the Internet, we would need to upload our "sampleWP" folder to a web host (see the **Web Host** sidebar on page 136).

Activity Tips

- Activities 4 and 5 in this chapter refer to commands used in Composer, the free *WYSIWYG* HTML editor bundled with Mozilla for Macs, PCs, and Linux. The *concepts* of building a page in one editor transfer readily to others, though the exact *procedures* may differ slightly (e.g., the exact name of and menu a particular command is found in or the wording and placement of options in dialog boxes).
- *Any* WYSIWYG HTML editor will do as long as the teacher is familiar with it, and the students have access to it.
- Web authoring requires organization. Keep all files in the same folder (in this activity, "sampleWP").
- Many common commands and formatting can be performed faster using toolbar buttons than menus (e.g., text formatting, linking, inserting images and tables). These toolbars work just like ones in word processors. Mouseover the toolbar buttons to see their bubble descriptions.

🎓 ACTIVITY 5 ■ Using Website Wizards, Templates, and HTML Export	
	Teacher skills: basic web page authoring, use of wizards or templates, word processing
	Student level: intermediate to advanced
	Content objective: creating web pages using helper utilities
	Software: web browser, *WYSIWYG* HTML editor or word processor with web features

In addition to creating web pages from scratch, there are other means of putting information in a web form: **wizards, templates,** and HTML export. Some HTML editors, such as Microsoft FrontPage®, as well as word processors, such as Word, AppleWorks, and WordPerfect, all offer some assistance in creating web pages for those with little or no knowledge of HTML or time to learn.

Pedagogical Rationale

Wizards, templates, and HTML export work best in a class not undertaking web authoring in-depth, that is, a class that does not have it as a learning objective. In addition to being a means to quickly put information in a web form, good wizards and templates can demonstrate examples of different designs for different purposes. A relatively uncomplicated assignment, such as a personal or "bio" page, can serve as a precursor to a more professional online resume.

Wizards

Built into many applications, wizards assist the user in completing a task by offering a limited set of choices in step-by-step procedures. Website wizards usually go through four or five self-explanatory steps, having the user choose a basic layout design (personal, corporate, frames), background or color scheme, and number of pages and links (see Figure 7.2). The wizard creates the site (a few linked pages with navigation) with placeholder text that the user replaces with his or her own text.

Figure 7.2 ▪ The website wizard in MS Word, which builds a site struture based on responses to a few questions.

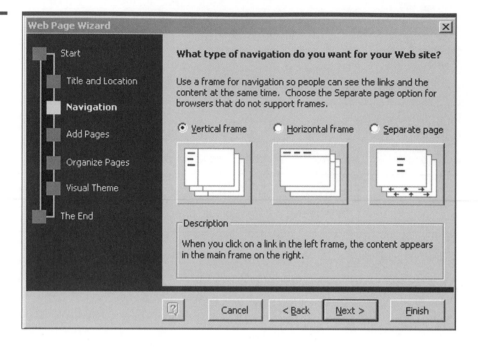

In addition, some web hosts also offer online versions of a website wizard, with added features to automatically update and appear in a page, such as weather for a selected city and selected stock quotes and news categories. The online wizards function entirely through a web browser.

Teacher Preparation

Students should be able to complete a personal page about themselves with no outside research, and pictures of each student could be taken in class.

- Find a word processor or HTML editor that includes web wizards or templates.
- If available, wizards or templates can generally be found in the new file dialog (**File** > **New** > *from wizard or template*).

Drawbacks to Using Wizards, Templates, and HTML Export

- With limited choices, it's unlikely that you will wind up with a design that exactly fits your purpose.
- They hide the process of page building, substituting simplified, generic selections.
- They don't explain some of the page elements in which the user is supposed to make choices, possibly leading to undesired results and confusion.
- They don't produce pages ready to publish: The placeholder text needs to be edited, links and graphics added, additional pages added, a web host found, and files uploaded.

Personal web page outline

- [student's picture]
- name
- school affiliation
- e-mail
- personal, academic, or professional interests
- schools attended
- work experience
- links to separate pages with samples of student writing, slide show projects, or artwork
- related web resources (links)

Steps for Students

- Sketch your web pages on paper.
- Determine how many separate pages you need in your site (1–5).
- Create a folder to save all HTML and image files.
- Collect the image(s) for your page(s).
- Choose **File** > **New** > *from wizard.* Some programs take you to dialog boxes with all templates and wizards.
- Make choices in all of the categories presented: style, design, number of pages and links.
- After the wizard builds the site, open each page with an HTML editor and edit the placeholder text on each page, customizing text and adding links and images.
- Experiment putting the same content into several different designs and compare the results.

TECHNOTE ■ **WYSIWYG**

"What You See Is What You Get," an important advance in the usability of computers brought about by the graphical user interface (*GUI*—as opposed to a command line interface, such as DOS). A WYSIWYG HTML editor (e.g., Mozilla* Composer, Macromedia Dreamweaver, Microsoft FrontPage) allows you to create web pages by laying out text and graphics visually, with no knowledge of or contact with the underlying HTML code; however, being able to edit even a little HTML code will prove invaluable in fixing problems. Free, consumer-level WYSIWYG HTML editors include Composer; professional-grade products include Macromedia Dreamweaver.

*Mozilla, the original name of the Netscape web browser, is the nonprofit organization that manages the *open-source* development of the Netscape browser. Open-source software describes programs whose source code is publicly available free of charge, so programmers can collaborate on improving and sharing them. The Netscape browser, in the form of Mozilla, has thus improved.

Web Host

You create web pages *locally* (saving them to your hard drive or inserted disk). When you are ready to share them with the world, you find a *web host*: a web server that you can upload your HTML and image files to. Many large schools allocate space on the school's web server to faculty, staff, and even students. In addition, they may make available certain other capabilities, such as restricting access to your site, processing forms, and providing a secure server (HTTPS) for sensitive information. Commercial Internet service providers (*ISPs*—whom you pay for access to the Internet if you don't have it otherwise) and specialized web space hosting services perform the same functions (usually throwing in a few e-mail accounts as well) for a monthly fee. Some advertiser-driven web hosts offer *free* web accounts, but their low performance and practice of tacking ads to your site make them a poor choice for anyone serious about maintaining a website. With any host, you *upload* (transfer from your computer to another) your website files via an FTP *client* (see **TECHNOTE: HTTP, FTP, HTML** on page 122) or HTML editor with built-in file transfer capability (Figure 7.3). Your web host then shares your site with the world. Subsequently, upload any changed files as needed.

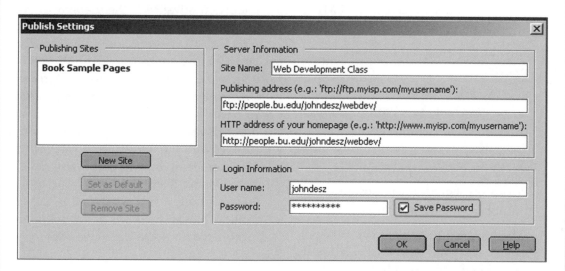

Figure 7.3 ■ Most WYSIWYG HTML editors have a build-in FTP client used to upload web pages and other files you create on your computer to a web server. In Composer, above, we configure connection settings for this website, then simply click the Publish button on the Composer toolbar for any finished page.

Templates

A feature supported by more HTML editors is the template (called "stationary" in some programs): stock documents or ones built into the HTML editor with ready-made designs. The user picks a template design and replaces placeholder text and links with his or her own content.

While an experienced web developer would not use wizards, he or she would definitely use templates, mostly custom documents of his or her own design saved and reused on other pages. Sophisticated HTML editors, such as Dreamweaver, dynamically associate pages based on a custom template with the template file itself, so that when the template is modified in any way, those changes are then made on all of the pages based on that template, ensuring consistency and ease of maintenance for large sites.

Steps for Students

- Find a word processor or HTML editor that offers web templates.
- Create the personal page as in the web wizard activity outlined previously.
- Choose a template design.
- Save each page needed for the site with a different file name.
- Edit each page with your personal information, replacing the placeholder text.
- Unlike a wizard, templates will not create links among pages automatically, as with a navigation bar. See instructions in Activity 4 in this chapter for adding navigation links on each page to the other pages.

Exporting HTML from Word Processors

Many word processors, including Word, AppleWorks, WordPerfect, and Nisus Writer, save (or "export") a word-processing file as HTML, quickly creating a web version of the document. Although not perfect, the option generally reproduces the formatting in the word-processing document reasonably well for the web, including text, links, and inserted images, and packages the HTML file and images into a web folder. This HTML page can then be opened in an HTML editor and fine-tuned, as needed, before uploading to a web host. For text documents with numerous special characters (accented letters, em-dashes, copyright symbols, smart quotes), exporting as HTML can be a faster and surer way to include these characters as intended. Copying text from a word-processing document and pasting into an HTML document, on the other hand, may strip some of those characters of the formatting they need to appear on a web page the same way.

Steps for Students

- Find a word processor that saves files as web pages (**File > Save As > HTML** or **File > Export to HTML** or **Web**).

- Create the same personal page as in the wizard and template activities but use only the word processor.

- Type and format your text and insert your pictures into a word-processing document. Use color for text and background as needed. (In Word, for example, to add a colored background, choose **Format > Background** and choose fill color.)

- Hyperlink text and images. (In Word, highlight a word or image to link, then **Insert > Hyperlink...**).

- Follow instructions in Activity 4 for adding navigation links on each page to the other pages.

- Export the page as HTML (be sure to add .html to the file name) and check it in a web browser.

Internet References

HTML EDITORS

Mozilla (PC, Mac, free), the Mozilla Organization, *www.mozilla.org*

Macromedia Dreamweaver HTML editor (PC, Mac), *www.macromedia.com*

Adobe GoLive HTML editor (PC, Mac), *www.adobe.com*

Microsoft FrontPage HTML editor (PC), *www.microsoft.com*

List of free programs, including HTML editors, *www.thefreecountry.com*

FTP CLIENTS

WS_FTP FTP client (PC), Ipswitch Software, *www.ipswitch.com*

Fetch FTP client (Mac), Fetch Softworks, *fetchsoftworks.com*

Desktop Publishing Projects

✎ ACTIVITY 6 ■ Class Books	
	Teacher skills: basic print design/layout, using images with text
	Student level: high-beginner to low-advanced
	Content objective: basic print layout and typography concepts, book design and collaboration
	Software: word processor, camera, graphics editor, desktop publishing program (optional), portable tape recorder (optional)

A class book resembles a student yearbook but is somewhat narrower in scope as it pertains primarily to a single class in one semester. It describes the class, its members, activities, and environment in a way that reflects the experience of a group of students studying language in a particular place or school. When finished, it's printed, bound, and distributed to all students in the class.

Such tangible projects serve other purposes as well. A class book provides a memento of a student's language learning experience—especially poignant for the students in a short-term study-abroad program—and encouragement for keeping in touch with classmates after the course. Serving the marketing needs of language programs, the books also find their way deep into their target market—passed around among friends, family, and colleagues of former students—revealing more about the actual experience of the program than a brochure.

Pedagogical Rationale

Class books offer an opportunity for a cooperative, production-oriented class activity that can be adapted to any level. Visions of the end product provide a spur for research, writing, and interviewing, while the process encourages cooperation, creative deliberation, and critical review of each other's work. The approach to planning and assigning the content resembles the process at a small newspaper: Writers discuss the makeup of the content with the editor (the teacher), who assigns responsibility for different parts, guides students in their fieldwork and writing, and hounds them about deadlines. Together they discuss how the components will go together.

Taking Good Pictures

A good photograph takes careful composing and setup.

Composition: Consider the entirety of the picture: What's in it, what's cut off, how the subject features relative to everything else in the frame, and how the major objects are balanced relative to one another.

Orientation: Is the subject oriented horizontally or vertically? Rotate the camera accordingly.

Subject proximity: Pictures of people are often taken too far away. Unless you must also frame a large backdrop, get closer. Details attract greater interest.

Background: In the two-dimensionality of a flat image, the background can blend in with the subject in a distracting or absurd way, like a tree behind the subject appearing to be growing out of the subject's head. Avoid busy backgrounds.

Backlighting: Avoid backlighting. If your subject is in front of the main light source (such as a window), the camera may adjust for this brightness, leaving the subject underexposed and dark. Be sure the main lighting source faces your subject, or force the flash ("fill in" mode) on the camera.

Flash hot spots: The flash may produce intense light reflections on shiny surfaces (such as glass or sweaty skin). Shoot these surfaces at an angle so the flash bounces off in a direction other than the camera's.

Originality: Try perspectives offering atypical angles or interesting juxtapositions of subjects and background.

Teacher Preparation

- **Layout.** Low-requirement projects can get by with a capable word processor, which manages inserted graphics and other simple layout features reasonably well. Collect printed pages of content from students, photocopy images, and then photocopy and staple everything. More complicated projects, or ones with a more professional look, could benefit from laying out text and images digitally in a desktop publishing program, such as Adobe InDesign® or PageMaker®, or QuarkXPress, and then sending the files to a print shop for printing and binding.

- **Distribution.** In addition to distributing printed copies of the finished book, electronic color copies could be distributed at little or no cost. The portable document format *(PDF)* reproduces print documents—including text, images, line art, color, and hyperlinks—more faithfully than any other print format, creating a complex document that appears exactly the same on any computer. PDF files can be e-mailed as attachments or made available on a class website as downloadable documents. Adobe Acrobat® is required to create a PDF, and the free Acrobat Reader® is required to view one. (Mac OS X comes with a built-in ability to easily save any document as a PDF and read PDFs with the built-in program Preview.)

Creating a web (HTML) version of the book could make for an interesting web project in itself, perhaps as an extension of the class book project. A book produced entirely in Microsoft Word or AppleWorks as multiple documents, for example, could be exported to HTML, and the resulting files fine-tuned and formatted for a web layout using an HTML editor.[2]

Possible elements of a class book

- Student biographies
  - Pairs interview each other and then write short biographies or interviews using direct quotes or reported speech.
  - Students exchange and correct each other's written interviews.
  - Students take each other's pictures to insert into their interview documents.
- Articles reflecting on differences between the target language or culture and first language or culture
  - What was the first odd difference you noticed (custom, habit, appearance)?
  - What word or phrase puzzled you the most in your first contact with the language outside of class?
  - What element of the host culture (food, manners, customs, law, housing) would you like to see adopted by your culture and why?
  - How do you think student life differs?
  - How do clothing fashions differ?
- Accounts of class field trips or other outings
- Profiles of the cities or countries class members come from
- Interviews
  - Interviews with program staff, faculty, and students.
  - Brief "man-on-the-street" interviews in a popular (safe) area of town with a narrow, specific focus.
  - Surveys on a specific topic (e.g., relating to a close holiday, current news event, personal preference, issue of interest to this student population), with the results displayed in graphs.
- Photography and artwork by class members
- Advice column for common student questions and concerns

---

[2] A web version would need to be scrutinized more closely for personal and contact information that you might not want widely available as well as copyrighted works (text, pictures) that cannot be made available on the web without permission.

- Reviews of local attractions: neighborhoods, restaurants, clubs, theater, museums, sporting events, historic sites, tours, parks, recreation, natural attractions, etc.
- Reviews of popular movies, songs, or TV shows currently playing
- Ads for local businesses that students frequent (donations could help fund printing)
- Trivia quiz about class members, the school, the host city, or pop culture
- Language quiz by students about the target language
- Contact list of all class members, including e-mail and mailing addresses
- Directory of helpful resources for students related to living in the host culture: people, offices, services, stores, tourism, housing, etc.

Book layout considerations

Text (see Figure 7.4)

- To give the pages more of a magazine feel, use two columns for text and $1\frac{1}{2}$ line spacing. Most word processors can create columns with the **Format** menu.
- Any *font* available on the computer can be used in the document, but these fonts must also be available on the computer that prints the document.
- Use text boxes (usually available in the **Insert** menu or the drawing tools) for image captions and short pieces, the latter set off with a border or shading (like the **TECHNOTE** at right).
- Use a "drop cap" for the first letter of articles (e.g., available in Word under **Format > Drop Cap....**).
- Use "text pullouts" for interesting quotes from an article as a teaser to use up extra space and to provide more of a magazine look. Copy a sentence from the article and paste it into a free-floating text box with *text wrap* enabled (see **TECHNOTE: Text Wrap**).

TECHNOTE ■ **Text Wrap**

Text wrap refers to lines of text accommodating or *wrapping around* an object in the same horizontal space, such as an image or text box (such as this **TECHNOTE** or the pullout quote in Figure 7.4). Text wrap is found in the properties of the object, not in the text doing the wrapping. In Word, for example, right-click (PC) or Control-click (Mac) on an image to **Show Picture Toolbar**, which includes a text wrap button. Text-wrapping options concern (1) the gap between the text and the object and (2) whether the wrap should accommodate a square object, such as a photograph, or an irregularly shaped object, such as clip art. Without text wrap, objects could not be positioned alongside text but would have to go completely above or below the lines of text or the object would cover or be covered by the text. When we intentionally place text on top of an image, such as a label, that text box is in a separate *layer* on top of the image.

Figure 7.4 ■
Example page from a class book, showing some layout features possible with some word processors that can jazz up the look of pages, such as multiple columns, images, text wrap-around images, image captions, drop caps (large first letter of first paragraph), text pullouts (quote from text pulled out and enlarged in text box).

The Presidential Race in Boston

by János Széchenyi

Boston was an exciting place to be during the 2004 U.S. presidential campaign. The Democratic Party candidate, John Kerry, is the U.S. Senator from Massachusetts, with a home on Beacon Hill in Boston. Kerry did not have to campaign in most of New England because all six states, except for New Hampshire, vote solidly for Democratic presidential candidates. This year, even New Hampshire did.

The election was held Tuesday, November 2. The Democratic National Committee decided to use Copley Square in Boston as the setting for what they hoped would be Kerry's victory speech and celebration. Beginning a week before the election, the area bounded by the Boston Public Library, Copley Plaza Hotel, the John Hancock Tower, Trinity Church, and Boylston Street was taken over by staging and the media.

Huge satellite TV transmission trucks and other media vehicles filled the streets around Copley. Elaborate staging, with banners and flags draped across it, was constructed in front of the library looking out on the Square. Traffic was rerouted around the Square and pedestrians had to walk in front of Trinity Church to get through.

By the night of the election, thousands, mostly Kerry supporters and college students, began pouring into the area, waiting for a scheduled appearance later in the night by the candidate himself, Kerry. In the meantime, people waited for singers, all Kerry supporters, who performed free concerts. The party went on long after all of the polls in the U.S. had closed. By midnight, there was still no definitive results

By the night of the election thousands, mostly Kerry supporters and college students, began pouring into the area, waiting for a scheduled appearance by Kerry.

from polls in some of the important "swing" states, particularly Ohio. At about 2:30am, with a crowd still filling Copley, Kerry's running mate, candidate for vice president John Edwards, came onstage and spoke briefly to supporters, saying that they were going to wait until every vote was counted. But Kerry never appeared. He remained in his Beacon Hill residence with his political advisors.

It wasn't until early the next day that it became clear that the Ohio vote would go for the Republican Party candidate, President Bush, giving him the numbers he needed in the Electoral College to win the presidency for a second term. Much of New England was deeply distressed by a Bush victory, especially Boston, not just because it is the home of Kerry but because it is the home of many of the liberal ideas espoused by the Democratic Party.

Massachusetts voted for Kerry overwhelmingly over Bush, 62% for Kerry to Bush's 37%. Bush garnered 51% of the popular vote in the U.S. Thus began much talk and writing about the difference between "red" American (those states voting Republican) versus "blue" America (those states voting Democratic).

Staging goes up in front of the library (left). On election night, thousands gather in the Square (right).

10   CELOP SEMESTER BOOK | FALL 2004

Images

- Images must be in a digital format for insertion into the word-processing or desktop publishing document. If using a film camera, scan the prints chosen for the book and save them in a compatible image file format for the program used for layout (TIFF, JPEG, PICT, or bitmap). Most film-developing services can also process film as JPEG files to floppy disk, CD, or a website for customer downloading. Most digital cameras can save pictures in the JPEG or TIFF format, but some word processors can't import TIFF images (a noncompressed, high-quality format used for professional print publications).

- Add an image to a document in most word processors by using the **Insert > Picture > From File** command or by copying it in an image editor and pasting it directly from the clipboard memory.

- Use an image editor to *scale* images to the desired size and then insert the image file or paste it directly into the document. Otherwise, resize the image in the text document with the resizing handle on the lower right corner of the picture holder (use the **Shift** key, if necessary, while resizing to *constrain* the scale to the original proportions and avoid distorting the image shape).

- Apply the text wrap feature to images that are no wider than about half the width of the text on the page. Wrapping lets the text flow around the image. Double-click on an inserted image or look in the picture toolbar or properties for text wrap (see Figure 7.5).

TECHNOTE ■ Typography

Teachers and students engaged in elaborate print projects will benefit from understanding certain type and layout characteristics.

- **Font:** "Font" is often used interchangeably with "typeface." As far as most users are concerned, they're the same. Technically the *typeface* describes the *design* of the characters in a set, whereas *font* is the final appearance at a specific size when attributes such as bold and italic are added. So typeface is the name, like Arial, but font is the combination of other settings, including size and style.

- **Serif:** Standard, nonornamental typefaces are broadly classified as *serif* or *sans serif* (without serif). A serif font has the small decorative embellishments at the ends of the lines of a character (sometimes called "feet" when they occur on the bottom), as seen in the tops and bottoms of the lines in a Times New Roman **H**). Sans serif fonts, such as Arial in this sentence, have members of consistent thickness for a clean, plain look: **H**. Sans serif fonts are more readable in small print sizes or for a web page.

Figure 7.5 ■
Double-click on an image in Word to get the Format Picture tools. Add color or a border to a picture box, make the image semi-transparent, or, using the Advanced features in Layout, specify word wrapping.

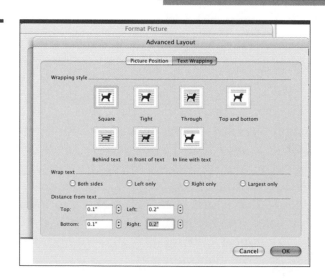

- Unlike images used on web pages, images for print can have varying resolutions. Generally, the higher the *dpi*, the sharper and more detailed the image.

- Images generally print darker than they appear on screen, especially grayscale. Be sure photos and illustrations are bright. The image editor built into Word can brighten inserted images (with the Picture Controls toolbar).

- Take pictures of individuals or groups close enough to identify their faces clearly when printed.

Formatting

- Combine all of the texts that students write (by copying and pasting) into one file to format consistently and paginate. Use the same typeface and size for all articles, and establish a standard formatting for titles, bylines, picture captions, etc.

- Use a header or footer with the name of the book, semester, and page number.

- Unlike web page text, printed text usually employs serif typefaces (e.g., Times New Roman, New York, Palatino).

- Let students know if the book will be printed in grayscale (using black ink only) or color before starting the book. Because of the cost of high-quality color printing, you might only be able to afford to print the cover in color.

Internet References

Basic principles of journalism, Family Education Network, *www.teachervision.fen.com*

The Journalist's Toolbox, American Press Institute, *www.journaliststoolbox.com*

Popular Photography & Imaging Magazine online (see "How to" section), *www.popphoto.com*

Graphic design tutorials, About.com, *desktoppub.about.com/cs/tutorials*

Adobe Acrobat, PageMaker, InDesign, *www.adobe.com*

QuarkXPress, *www.quark.com*

Video Projects

Video projects can be approached from many different angles. A project that begins with students shooting video could also include a focus on the fundamentals of camera work, composition, lighting, and sound, whereas a project that uses only still images or existing video files to stitch together into an original work would focus on developing a story line and editing techniques. (For shooting tips, see the sidebar **Shooting Good Video** on page 152.)

Editing video projects involves piecing together video and audio and synchronizing them. Productions based on voiceover narration are often edited by recording the narration first and then laying the video and still images on top of the audio track. Productions based on video with *ambient* audio (sound captured in-camera with the video) often have additional audio tracks (voiceover narration, music, sound effects) added after the video footage is pieced together in editing. Thus, how the video is edited will depend largely on whether the project is driven by video shot in-camera or a story script read as narration.

In any case, students need instruction and practice with the equipment and software and need to be effective at sharing duties in group work. The following activities assume that the teacher has taken the time to acquaint him- or herself with both beforehand or other faculty or lab personnel will assist.[3]

Pedagogical Rationale

A video written, acted, shot, and edited by students is perhaps the ultimate multimedia CALL project activity. It demands creativity, close cooperation, planning, writing, speaking clearly in acted scenes, and learning at least the concepts of a valuable skill, video editing—all while producing a tangible product that can be presented to others and saved for posterity. Language teachers have long used video cameras for class activities, but computers give students full access to another creative stage: editing.

Students' facility with the technology of shooting and editing video presents somewhat of a dilemma: A lack of skill can lead to unappealing projects, both to the producers and viewers, but a fixation on the technical aspects, especially in editing, may be at the cost of the language value of the project as an interactive activity.

Teacher Preparation for All Video Projects

■ Clearly establish project parameters at the start to keep students' work on track.

   If shooting video with a camera

   • location: confined to class, campus, or check the camera out and shoot anywhere?

   • set: create a custom set with scenery or use existing location setting only?

   • lighting: use ambient lighting only (sunlight or room lights), on-camera lights, or additional lighting?

   • audio: use camera's built-in mic or external mic?

   • total time available for shooting

---

[3] Some approaches to video projects in this section were refined by input from Doug Kohn at the Center for English Language and Orientation Programs at Boston University, who uses video projects in ESL classes as a way to get students to think critically about films viewed for class—a way to connect lab work with the classroom curriculum.

Editing project parameters
- minimum and maximum program length
- effects that can be used, if any (e.g., clip transitions, picture effects)
- the use of voiceover narration, music, or other audio
- material sources: from students' own video and stills or external sources, such as videotape, *DVD*, or the Internet?

■ Assign jobs to group members or have them decide. Include a director—someone with initiative and ability to lead others so that work on various stages is coordinated and doesn't stall.

■ Discuss process for script writing by individuals or groups. It mirrors other process writing and peer reviewing.

■ Have students do a short demo program before tackling a more complex project. Critique this first program so students can apply the lessons learned to the second.

Topics for video projects

■ **Make a movie trailer.** A *trailer* is an ad for a movie or TV program composed of clips from the work and a voiceover introducing it in order to draw viewers. Students take short clips of work viewed and discussed in the course and string them together with a voiceover narration and titles to promote the work. Examples of trailers can be found on websites promoting new movies.

■ **Critically review a work.** Review a film or TV program viewed in the course. Focus on a theme or subtext, such as the work's violence; its treatment of a character's actions or background; or its depiction of an era, place, or event, etc. Use clips to support the interpretation as well as on-camera commentary. Two people could provide opposing takes on the same film and face off in the on-camera commentary.

■ **Create a movie from clips.** A longer, more advanced project has students choose scenes from separate films to weave together into a new narrative creation that makes sense.

■ **Choose a topic by genre:**
- instructional
- documentary
- news program, current events, point-counterpoint
- talk or game show
- commercial
- drama or comedy

✦ ACTIVITY 7 ■ Creating a Video Program with Stock Content	
	Teacher skills: basic video shooting and digital editing
	Student level: high-intermediate to advanced
	Content objective: creating video messages and stories, shooting and editing video
	Software: video editing software; optional depending on activity: graphics editor, sound editor, analog or digital video camera, analog-digital video converter

Most students have been passive viewers of TV and movies since childhood. Accustomed to the high production values of these programs, they may carry unrealistic expectations into their own projects. While an entire semester would need to be devoted to video production techniques to begin to bridge this gap between their expectations and abilities, an activity focusing on the mechanics may at least remove some of the mystery of the process. Just as we do for the web authoring and slide show presentation projects, we separate the mechanics of using the application from the content creation aspect. This activity gives students a chance to take stock media files and practice assembling and manipulating them in the video editor without necessarily thinking about constructing meaningful content.

Teacher Preparation

The teacher will need to know the basics of using the video editor chosen for class (see Internet References at the end of this activity); how to collect media files to use, import, and manipulate; and how to export the project to a video format that can be efficiently played over a network or saved to *CD* (such as *MPEG* file) or to DVD. Prepare a folder of media items for students to practice importing and manipulating using the video editor. Put several samples of each media type in its own folder:

- video clips
- audio files
- image files

Steps for Students

- Open a new video project.
- Import at least one of each type of media from the samples folder.
- Assemble a video track that includes
  - opening title
  - at least one video clip
  - at least one still image
  - closing credits
- Assemble audio tracks that include
  - background music over titles, credits, or video
  - voiceover narration recorded in the editor or imported from a separate, prerecorded audio file

Figure 7.6 ■ Apple's iMovie video editing program, a fast and easy editor for simple to moderately complex projects for beginners.

TECHNOTE   ▪ **Using Stills in Video**

A *still* is a single image, such as a photograph, used in a video or film. In order to fill a video screen with a still, its size (in pixels) and proportions, or *aspect ratio*, must be the same as video, 4:3, meaning 4 units in width for every 3 units of height. Standard computer screens fit this proportion, and their screen resolutions are expressed in 4:3 ratios, such as 640 x 480 and 1024 x 768.

If you import an image into your video editing software smaller than the program's workspace resolution, then the image will be surrounded by an area of black to fill the difference (see Figure 7.7). Unless your video editor can *scale* imported stills, use an image editor to resize before importing. Pictures not in the 4:3 ratio can only be maximized along the longer axis.

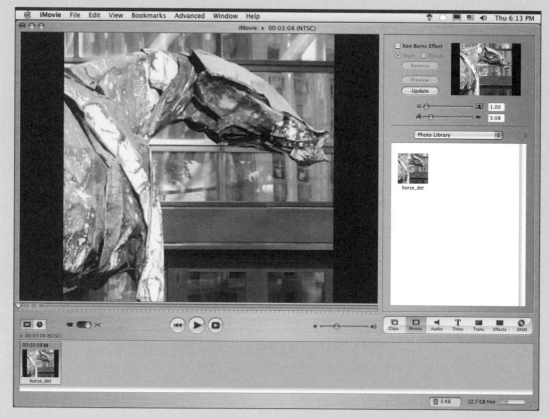

Figure 7.7 ▪ An image that does not conform to video's 4:3 aspect ratio will not fill the screen when imported into a video editor. Apple iMovie can, however, scale still images (zoom in) to fill the screen.

📖 ACTIVITY 8 ■ Creating a Video Program and Shooting Video	
	Teacher skills: basic video shooting and digital editing
	Student level: high-intermediate to advanced
	Content objective: script writing, shooting video, editing
	Software: analog or digital video camera, analog-digital video converter, video editing software; optional depending on activity: graphics editor, sound editor

As with many other projects covered in this chapter, *preparation* to use the applications or equipment is at least as important as actually using them. While a video camera and editing software provide motivation for student involvement in this project, they can also distract students, like desserts before the entrée, from learning what they need to know to understand the full context of their undertaking. In video production one formulates clear ideas and detailed plans for shooting and editing first, which are then realized with the camera and editing later.

Teacher Preparation

- Establish the parameters of the project both for the video shooting stage and editing (see Activity 6).

Student Steps

Create script

- Brainstorm topics or ideas or choose from teacher's options.
- Write a script with stage directions (what actors *do*), camera placement, or "point of view" (POV). Follow process-writing steps in Activity 6.
- Create a "storyboard," where main scenes are depicted in sketches, to establish shooting requirements—location, setting, props.
- Assign jobs to each group member: director, actor, videographer, scenery and props.
- Act out the script in rehearsal; modify it as necessary.

Shoot video

- Learn how to use the camera and practice shooting (see sidebar on **Shooting Good Video** on page 152).

- Set up each scene (setting, props, camera, lighting, sound, actors).
- Shoot each scene multiple times (known as *takes*) if possible to have a choice of the best take in editing.

Edit

- Collect supplementary content that will be used in editing: information for titles, subtitles, credits; images; and music or other audio.
- Learn how to use the video editing software. Study primers and tutorials that come with the software or ones available on the Internet. Explore the program before starting to work with your project content.

Shooting Good Video

Whether you use an analog video camera (VHS, 8mm) or a digital one *(DV)*, the video you edit on the computer will only be as good as the video you shoot with the camera. Observe the basics:

Steady camera. Nothing makes compressing digital video more difficult and inefficient than unnecessary picture movement. Either use a tripod for all shots or, for hand-held shots, leave the lens zoom setting all the way out (wide). Zooming in magnifies camera movement.

Sound. Most built-in video camera microphones have a very limited sound pickup range. Beyond a few meters, the *ambient* noise may interfere with the subject. Either keep the camera close to the subject or use a remote microphone on or near the source of the audio.

Lighting. Built-in video camera lights provide extra lighting to the front of a close subject but cannot completely illuminate a scene or have much effect beyond a couple meters. Shoot in well-lit areas but avoid *backlighting*, where the light source is behind the subject, as this leads to an underexposed subject.

Panning and zooming. Panning, moving the camera side-to-side to follow a subject or take in a wide field of view, may lead to unwatchable video. Shoot separate shots of a wide field, instead, or use a good tripod with a slow, smooth action. Zooming makes the viewer aware of the camera, distracting him or her from the subject. Use it only in small increments and slowly.

Composition. Compose what's in your field of view purposely; don't simply accept what you get in the viewfinder. Avoid distractions in the background by getting closer to the subject, have it fill the screen and keep the view as focused on the subject as possible.

Continuity. Watch for changes in scenes, especially objects in the background. They may make for awkward cuts later in editing, when footage shot over time is compressed into clips from selected takes.

- Digitize analog video or import digital video (DV) from the video shoot into the video editing program. DV files are very large. Use only the scenes that will be used.

- Edit the video, and have the teacher review and critique it.

- Save it in a format compatible with what you want to do with it (burn it to CD or DVD, leave it on a computer or server, or upload it to a website).

- Screen the videos individually or as a group.

  - **Individual.** Run projects on individual computers (such as where they were edited), and have students walk around the lab to view each one (like kiosks). By viewing each video individually, students can control the playback and watch again if needed. They can also be prompted to comment on each work in a word-processing document open like a journal on the same computer or in an electronic chat environment.

  - **Group.** Project one video at a time before the entire class in a screening. Have "producers" introduce their work and answer questions about it afterward.

Presentation Projects

The use of slide show or presentation software—predominantly Microsoft PowerPoint—is ubiquitous in corporate meetings, sales, training, education, and just about anywhere else a presenter stands before an audience to train, educate, inform, persuade, or sell with the help of a computer and projector. Presentation programs, also known as **slideware,** present text and graphics in a consistent format on a series of slides to display on a computer. When projected for an audience, they must also be readable at a distance.

Pedagogical Rationale

Students use slideware more and more to update chalkboard or flipchart presentations with expanded capabilities of color graphics, video, sound, and hyperlinks. In so doing, they are preparing themselves for future expectations in education or work to use such technology with effective techniques. For language students in particular, the lure of computer technology may also make an otherwise petrifying task—presenting in front of people in your second language—appealing.

Largely absent in the stampede to jump on the slideware bandwagon, however, is careful consideration of the *effectiveness* of this media, as popularly employed, for the purpose of education and language learning. Like computers in general, slideware is a tool that can be used wisely to advantage or unwisely for a waste of time. So before we jump into a slideware activity, let's take a critical look at what slides do and shouldn't do when accompanying a presentation.

PowerPoint: A Primer

Use the Tool; Don't Let It Use You

Though supposedly designed to present content, PowerPoint is preoccupied with format. We can't assume, therefore, that students can use it to create a meaningful presentation without instruction, guidance, and critical feedback on the effectiveness of their slide show as a visual aid that actually enhances their presentation. Creating an effective slide show starts with mastering the basics and concentrating on the *message,* not the medium.

The Elemental Slide

Because of space limitations, slides often need to display talking points in outline format, which also serve as notes for the presenter. Slides also display graphics (such as charts, photos, and illustrations), videos, sound files, and hyperlinks to other slides, files, or web pages. The *weight* of each slide needs to be appropriate for the amount of time the presenter will spend talking about it: The audience will read all the text that fits on a slide in seconds, a fraction of the time it will likely remain up. Graphics provide *balance* for the text and convey far *more information* in as much space, occupying viewers' attention far longer.

The Look

A simple, clean, bright background design provides high *contrast* and readability for dark text. Many built-in PowerPoint *templates* (ready-made designs) are too dark or busy. Consistent background and layout of slides draw less attention away from content. A custom layout of larger text boxes makes better use of space than the small boxes used on templates. In addition, an image related to the content used as the graphic background of every slide can be added to the master slide for a strong custom-made look.[4]

First-time users might be attracted to the "AutoContent Wizard," which works like a web page *wizard*—with similarly uninspiring results. This utility assists in creating a slide show by offering a limited set of choices in a step-by-step procedure. The user chooses a basic layout type and design from among a few generic choices. The wizard creates slides with placeholder text and image boxes that you replace with your own. You will still need to change some elements to fit your exact content. The familiarity of the stock design to many audiences and the awkward fit of your content may expose your use of this novice device. The wizard is found in the New File dialog box or Office Project Gallery.

---

[4]A background image needs to be *semi-transparent* to allow it to recede into the background. Right-click (PC) or Control-click (Mac) on an image to **Show Picture Toolbar**. Click the Color button and choose **Washout** or **Watermark.** Or, use brightness and contrast buttons to customize the effect.

Built-in templates are more modest in what they offer: ready-made designs that you populate with your content, replacing the placeholder text on each slide with your own, but without assistance with the actual content. While many of these templates employ a layout that wastes space (thus the need to use key words and compressed phrases), they do offer sound design examples vis-à-vis color contrast of text and background and text size. Templates might be best used as examples of designs to peruse while gathering inspiration for a custom design more specifically suited to your subject and audience. They can also be harmlessly employed while learning the mechanics of the software and creating practice slide shows.

Thinking Outside the List

Many PowerPoint users feel compelled to contort their information into the hierarchical bullet list format of the built-in templates. Bullets shun complete sentences to conserve room, but it's the embedded hierarchal format resulting from the indented list that crowds to the right side of the slide, leaving a large empty space on the left (see Figure 7.8). Instead, display the data in a format most appropriate to its analysis—a table, schematic, flowchart, clustering bubbles, or other visual representation—using complete sentences if your meaning would be distorted or diluted with compressed headline phrases.

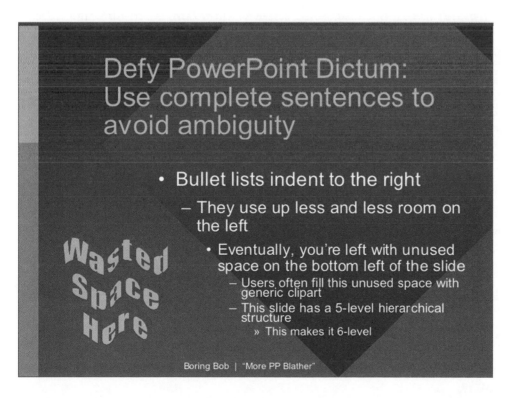

Figure 7.8 ■ Bullet lists use slide space inefficiently, compressing text to the lower right corner, leaving the void filled by unhelpful clip art.

The Gimmicks

Software developers may add features to programs for marketing purposes without any demonstrated *reason to use them*—PowerPoint being a case in point. To keep students thinking about their content instead of amusing themselves with gimmicks, tell them what to avoid.

- **Animating** text or pictures with a variety of speeds and visual effects adds little but distraction and delay and contributes to a frivolous feel. Functional animations, however, such as one that delays text or pictures in order to evoke an audience response first, may contribute to the effectiveness of a presentation.

> **PowerPoint Features to Avoid**
> - animations
> - clip art
> - sound effects
> - elaborate transitions

- Most built-in **clip art** in slideware is generic enough to add nothing illustrative to the slide and goofy enough to threaten the credibility of the presenter. Instead, use your own images that illustrate specifically what you're talking about.

- Adding **sound effects** to distracting animations builds on the frivolity effect to a gratuitously annoying intensity.

- Subtle **transitions** have a purpose. Some resemble ones familiar to film and video: fades, dissolves, iris open or close. And just as film and video editing observe a *grammar* of such techniques, so do professional-looking slide shows. A transition should provide an appropriate segue to the next slide and signal a change in the slide, not draw attention to the transition effect itself.

The Dangers

Props up poor presentations. Some inexperienced presenters, particularly those using a second language, mistakenly see slideware as a crutch they can lean on to prop up poor presentation or language skills. This notion assumes that what's on the screen will divert the audience from the presenter. On the contrary, coordinating a slide show with an oral presentation while attempting to keep the audience involved complicates the task.

Encourages teleprompter presentations. A nervous presenter might be tempted to read the slides verbatim as a teleprompter—an excruciatingly annoying practice to any audience—rather than use them as an outline of a more complete narrative.

Distorts preparation. Obsession with the appearance of a slide show can distort preparation if a presenter focuses disproportionately on creating the slide show itself (especially one laden with effects) at the cost of thinking about what he or she is going to say.

Components of a Slide Show

Slide: what you view one at a time like a single page in a word-processing document; a slide show comprises a sequence of slides.

Master slide: the slide that all others are based on, containing repeating elements—presentation title, presenter name, slide number, company logo—that automatically appears on every new slide.

Template: a ready-made design with text and graphic boxes already in place.

Wizard (or "AutoContent Wizard" in PowerPoint parlance): a utility to assist in creating a slide show by offering a limited set of choices in step-by-step procedures by having the user choose a basic layout type and design from among a few generic choices.

Background: a custom image used as the graphic background on a slide (usually the master slide). These images need to be semitransparent to recede into the background and keep foreground text readable.

Text box: holds text that can be formatted just as in a word processor and can be moved around the slide and reshaped, which affects how the text flows; several text and picture boxes can coexist on a slide.

Picture box: holds an image from an existing image file, the clipboard, or clip art.

Animation: the orchestrated movement of text or pictures on a slide with varying speeds and visual effects.

Sound effects: added to animations or transitions to accompany movement.

Transition: visual effect of one slide going to the next.

Hyperlink: linked text or graphic that jumps to another slide or opens the designated page in a web browser.

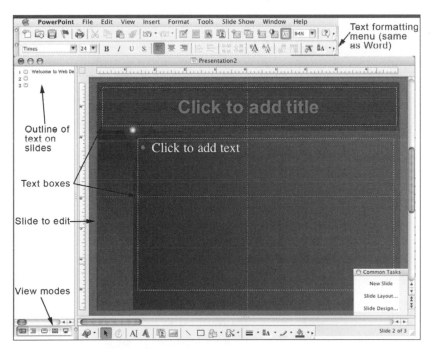

Figure 7.9 ■ Microsoft PowerPoint slide in single slide edit mode.

Discourages interaction. Slide show presentations often represent presenter-centered, one-way communication. When the lights are turned out, interaction with the audience is further put off or made awkward. Without interaction, then, the process becomes one of transferring information in one direction but without a suitably capable means of doing so: the information format is reductionist, the graphics simplified and low resolution.

Sells better than explains. The information design theorist Edward R. Tufte, in a stinging indictment of PowerPoint, suggests that imposing the bullet list format on users organizes information simplistically, defying analysis of complex relationships, and is suited to *selling* an idea but not *explaining* it.[5] The problem, he concludes, has to do with the relative "density" of information that can fit on a slide—a paucity—particularly on a generic PowerPoint template, compared to the printed page or even a web page.

Fragments information. Because each slide holds so little information, many slides must be used, fragmenting information and making comparisons or meaningful analyses of large amounts of data impractical. The greatest damage, therefore, results from the design of the software guiding or limiting what would otherwise be an analytical approach, rendering a presentation far less effective at transmitting information than one where a paper handout was distributed, which could display in one view much more information for comparison and analysis.

So why use PowerPoint at all? Because a particular tool has the potential, even the tendency, to be misused doesn't alone justify dismissing it; it confirms the importance of proper training. Slides simply aren't suitable for presenting all information, which seems to be a problem with the *choice* of the medium, not the medium itself.

🗒️ Activity 9 ■ Creating a Slide Show with Stock Content
Teacher skills: basic presentation authoring
Student level: intermediate to advanced
Content objective: mechanics of presentations
Software: slide show program

As we did with web and video projects, our first slide show project focuses on the *mechanics* of creating a slide show and modifying its appearance. Again, the idea is to separate the *content creation* aspect of a slide show from the *mechanics* of how it goes

---

[5] Tufte, E. R. (2003). *The cognitive style of PowerPoint.* Self-published monograph. www.edwardtufte.com

together. Once students master the mechanics, they can create slide shows with their own content without the challenges of one process interfering with the other.

Teacher Preparation

As the teacher you need not be a whiz with all of the fancy features of the program because we're trying to avoid those distractions. You should have a good understanding of the program and be able to create slides with text, graphics, some functional text animation, and simple transitions. You will need to construct a simple presentation on some topic of interest to your students, one that includes five or more slides combining text and graphics on a custom master slide. This slide show will serve as the example to demonstrate and, later, for students to reconstruct. The content—text and image files but not the demonstrated slide show document—should either be distributed to students or made available in a shared network location.

Source files should include

- images for the slides in any supported graphic file type
- image to be used as a background on the master slide
- text file in outline format of the text used on the slides, including
  - a title slide (e.g., title, presenter name, class, image representing subject)
  - main content slides
  - closing slide (e.g., information for further reading: books, articles, websites)

Steps for Students[6]

- Open a new, blank slide show document (**File > New**).
- If prompted, choose a slide **layout** (arrangement of text and graphics) appropriate for the content. The default layout is usually one heading and an indented bullet list in one column. Graphics can be inserted and placed anywhere on the slide they fit or cover the entire slide.
- Go to the master slide (**View > Master > Slide Master**):
  - Insert a graphic image appropriate for a background for all the slides (**Insert > Picture > From File**).
  - Resize or crop it to fill the slide.
  - Lighten the image by reducing its opacity with the watermark effect (**Format > Picture...Picture > Image Control > Color: Watermark**).
  - Close the master and open a new slide, the first slide (**Insert > Slide**).

---

[6]These steps refer specifically to PowerPoint for Mac OS X but apply with little or no modification to other versions of PowerPoint as well—for Macs and PCs—and, in concept if not exact procedures, to other presentation programs.

- Type or copy and paste the slide text (heading separate from list items) from the text outline document. Replace the placeholder text on each slide in the same way.

- Add additional slides (**Insert > New Slide**).

- Add the image that goes with each slide (**Insert > Picture > From File...***browse for image file)*. Resize, crop, and arrange images on slides as needed.

- Animate text on slides with bullet list items to make each appear one at a time with a mouse click and then dim as the next appears.

  - Click on a text box containing the list.

  - Create a custom animation (**Slide Show > Animation > Custom...**):
    Effects: Entry=Appear; After animation=*choose gray color*.
    Order and Timing: Start animation on mouse click.
    Options: Text enters all at once; bullets grouped by 1st level.

  - Repeat for all similar slides with bullet lists or set up animations on text box of slide master.

- Add transitions. Between the title slide and the first content slide (i.e., the first and second slides), add an "iris open" transition (signaling the opening of a topic). Similarly, before the closing slide, add either an "iris close" transition or a slow fade. Between all others, use a "push left, fast" transition to signal a new slide.

- Go to Slide Sorter view (see **View Modes** sidebar).

  - Click on the thumbnail of the first content slide (after title slide).

  - **Slide Show > Slide Transition...**

  - Set Effect=box out or iris open; Speed=medium.

  - Repeat for second to last slide, Effect=iris close or fade; speed=slow.

  - Select all other slides in the middle (to select multiple slides, hold the **Shift** key while clicking slide thumbnails), Effect=push left or wipe left; Speed=fast.

- Compare finished slide show to the teacher's demo slide show.

View Modes

PowerPoint has several ways of looking at a slide show. Choose a *view mode* by clicking on its icon on the bottom left corner of the window (see Figure 7.9 on page 157).

Single Slide (or *Normal,* the default view): View and edit a single slide.

Outline: Enter or edit text in this outline showing only the text from all slides on one page.

Slide Sorter: View small images *(thumbnails)* of all slides in one window and reorder, delete, or copy them, or apply transitions between them.

Slide Show (or Presentation): Shows the full-screen presentation (without menus) used to preview the final appearance and to give the presentation.

🔖 ACTIVITY 10 ■ Creating an Original Slide Show	
	Teacher skills: basic presentation authoring, master slide setup
	Student level: intermediate to advanced
	Content objective: presentation content creation, organization
	Software: presentation program

While people might learn how to create web pages just for the sake of having that skill, such as in a course or workshop, they might learn how to use slideware for a specific purpose at hand, whether an upcoming conference or lecture (for teachers) or a class presentation (for students). Choosing and developing a topic for a website, therefore, may appear to some to stand as an obstacle in the way of the fun stuff, authoring the pages, while slideware represents a simpler means of satisfying an immediate need of presenting information already prepared. Using slideware, moreover, is considerably less complicated than web authoring. Thus, students can begin creating their own slide shows as soon as they complete an outline, familiarize themselves with a few pointers about communicating with this medium, and learn the mechanics of a basic slide show, such as with the previous activity of recreating a slide show with stock content. This activity helps students develop a topic for a presentation.

Steps for Students

Topic selection

■ Choose a topic that is narrow in scope, perhaps a research topic or something already familiar to you.

Topic ideas

- research-related report
- historical event or holiday of the target culture
- comparison of a custom in your native culture and the target culture
- description of something of interest to you:
  - a tour, personal vacation, or field trip
  - a job you've had or an occupation you aspire to
  - a person (teacher, parent, friend; artist, political, or historical figure)

- a place (monument, park, building, neighborhood, city)
- a hobby (sports, music, pastime, reading interest)
- an object (car, motorcycle, family heirloom, painting)
- sales pitch for a business plan, product, service, or idea
- local business, what they do, for what market, and how well

Outline

- Include the points to discuss using key words, *if appropriate,* that you will connect and explain in your oral presentation. Otherwise, use complete sentences to express important ideas that would be diminished in a compressed form.
- Group the points. Only about six lines fit on an average slide. Use as much text as will fit.
- Use tables, charts, flowcharts, and other means of organization, not just the bullet lists.

Illustrations

- Collect as many useful, relevant illustrations as possible—photos, drawings, and graphs from the Internet, scanned pictures, and digital camera pictures. Save these together into a project folder.
- Decide which illustrations will accompany text on slides and which will fill the screen and stand alone.

Your site should include

- a title slide with your name, presentation title, and class information
- body slides, including ones with the text outline and illustrations
- closing slide with your contact information and resources for further information

Internet References

PowerPoint presentation software, Microsoft, *www.microsoft.com*

Keynote presentation software for Mac OS X, Apple, *www.apple.com*

Slide Show presentations, an integrated part of AppleWorks, Apple, *www.apple.com*

Presentations presentation software, Corel, *www.corel.com*

SMART Board™ interactive whiteboards, SMART Technologies, *www.smarttech.com*

Survey Projects

A survey project essentially organizes students around ideas to query others on. Students then analyze and present the results, which could become part of a class book, semester book, class website, other project or publication, or simply stand on its own.

Pedagogical Rationale

A survey project involves students in survey techniques, interaction with respondents, analysis, writing, and spreadsheet use. Students work in pairs or small groups on small surveys or as part of a larger class survey where teams take responsibility for different parts (e.g., a range of questions) or different stages (as described further in this section). While the project can take many forms and adapt to different levels, populations, and computer abilities, the stages remain the same.

Stages of a Survey Project

1. *Formulate* coherent questions about interesting topics relevant to the survey population and those who will see the results. For example, in a second language environment, where students might come from a wide range of countries, questions that get at the diversity of the student body (backgrounds, expectations, personal opinions) might appeal to students conducting the survey and those viewing the results. Demographic facts—the statistical makeup of the target population (countries students come from, their first language, gender, marital status, level of education)—are more appropriate for a direct analysis of student records, not information normally available to students.

2. *Conduct* the survey using face-to-face, paper, e-mail, or web form collection methods, keeping in mind the effect different methods may have on results. The paper and web form methods ensure anonymity, while the face-to-face and e-mail methods do not—a factor that may affect responses.

3. *Analyze* the results and write a summary analysis of the meaning of the numbers. While objective data is readily quantified (e.g., 22 percent of the students are from Korea or 18 percent want to pursue a degree in information technology), results from subjective survey questions (e.g., How do you feel about . . . ?) don't lend themselves to quantitative summary or graphical analysis but instead involve more complicated collection, analysis, and summary—perhaps more appropriate for advanced students.

4. *Present* the results in an understandable and accurate format, ideally including graphic charts (for objective-type questions).

Technical Requirements

Conducting the Survey

Stage 2 can vary widely in technical demands.

- *Face-to-face surveys:* A low-tech collection method could entail stopping people on campus, on the street, in a shopping mall, or other locations and asking the questions. Alternatively, paper surveys could be distributed, completed, and returned to a person or drop location later. The former method may call for brief surveys and questions that would not take a lot of time or embarrass the respondent.

- *E-mail:* More elaborate surveys and ones that potentially reach more people, e-mail surveys consist simply of a set of questions that the respondent answers in a reply to the message. Addresses of potential respondents (e.g., students, faculty, and staff from the program) would have to be available. (Use the *BCC* recipient line for such mass e-mailings—see Appendix C, A Thinking Person's E-mail.)

- *Web forms:* The most elaborate and possibly most effective survey method—in terms of offering anonymity in exchange for forthright answers—is a web page form that respondents fill out and submit. While creating a web page that includes *form objects* isn't difficult for those with some experience with HTML authoring, most forms rely on a type of application that runs on the web server called a *CGI* (common gateway interface) program. This CGI processes the coded input from the form as filled out by a visitor to the page and sends it to the form administrator (the person collecting the responses) via e-mail in a format that can be easily read or imported into a database. Most web hosts available to consumers provide basic CGI programs, such as this forms processor, in their service plans. Institutions that provide web hosting for faculty, staff, and students may make forms processing available as well.

Presenting Results

Stage 4 provides an opportunity to learn the basics of creating a simple spreadsheet and producing visualizations of the data, graphs, from the results. Popular spreadsheet programs, such as Microsoft Excel and AppleWorks, offer wizards that guide you step-by-step through the process of creating a graph from spreadsheet data and are perhaps the best first approach for those unfamiliar with spreadsheet programs. Each question can be represented by a graph, such as a pie or bar chart (see Figure 7.10). Some word processors, such as Word and AppleWorks, can even insert a spreadsheet or graph as an object, which can be modified directly in the word processor. Graphs can also be saved to an image format for inclusion in printed or web-based results.

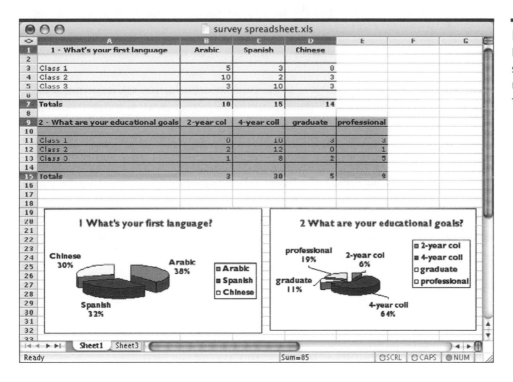

Figure 7.10 ▪
Microsoft Excel spreadsheet and graphed results from two objective survey questions.

✦ ACTIVITY 11 ▪ Conducting a Survey	
	Teacher skills: basic understanding of a spreadsheet program and graphs
	Student level: low-intermediate to low-advanced
	Content objective: survey techniques and process; spreadsheet use
	Software: word processor, spreadsheet program

Spreadsheets range from simple to complex. Results from a survey can be entered into a simple spreadsheet with questions and graphs included.

Spreadsheets—A Primer

A spreadsheet is a grid of individual *cells,* similar to cells in a table, for either numerical values or words (called *alphanumeric* data). Horizontal rows of cells run across the *X axis,* where vertical columns of cells run down the *Y axis.* Each cell is identified by an address expressed as coordinates, with columns using letters and rows numbers. So the first cell at the top left corner of a spreadsheet would have the address A1. The cell in the second column, third row would be B3. (See Figure 7.10 on page 165.) Data can be put anywhere on the spreadsheet, but for the sake of organization, data is grouped in rows and columns. Mathematical *formulas* are entered into cells where the sum or some other functions are to appear. For example, to display the total of a column of values in Microsoft Excel, a formula might look like this:

=SUM(B2:B10)

This formula will add up the values in a part of the second column, cells B2 to B10, and display it in the cell where the formula is located (usually the bottom of the same column). To get the average of the previous values, use the averaging formula:

=AVERAGE(B2:B10)

In most cases, you don't have to write this formula but select the cells to compute and choose a function. Popular spreadsheet programs, such as Microsoft Excel, AppleWorks, Corel Quattro® Pro, and Lotus® 1-2-3, work very similarly, although specific formula syntax may differ from one to the next.

Graphing Results

To make a graph, select the rows and columns containing the data you want graphed and use the program's chart-making command. In Excel, choose the **Chart Wizard** button on the toolbar or choose **Insert > Chart…**, then choose the type of chart graphic you want (bar, pie, line, area), add a *legend* (what values the colors in the chart represent), choose how to chart the data (by X- or Y-axis, as appropriate), and make other style choices. The preview of the chart as you progress through the wizard will make these choices easier. If you plan to print in black and white only, choose graphic patterns (bars, checks, dots) instead of colors.

> **TECHNOTE** ■ **Multiple Selections**
>
> To select an item in most applications, click on it. To select items next to it at the same time, hold the **Shift** key and select them as well. If the items abut on any side, they are *contiguous* and can be selected with **Shift**-click. But to select items that are not together, or *non-contiguous,* use the **Ctrl** key (PC) or **Apple** key (Mac) and click. Thus, to select the relevant data for Question 1 in Figure 7.10 on page 165, two non-contiguous rows, click and drag the mouse from A1 to D1, then, holding the **Ctrl** or **Apple** key, click from A7 to D7.

Teacher Preparation

- Put students in pairs or groups for survey projects.
- Prepare to help teams decide on an appropriate topic to survey and how to formulate unbiased questions.
- Choose and plan methods to conduct the survey (see Conducting the Survey on page 164).
- Demonstrate how to make a spreadsheet with the application the students have available. For practice, re-create the simple worksheet data in Figure 7.10 and create various graph types from it.

Steps for Students

Stage 1

- Decide on an interesting topic to survey, and write clear questions.
- Determine the survey population—whom to survey.

Stage 2

- Determine how you will conduct the survey: face-to-face interviews, questions on paper, e-mail, or a web form.
- Conduct the survey according to the plan described in this section.

Stage 3

- Create a spreadsheet for question responses similar to Figure 7.10.
- Enter the numbers for responses in the appropriate cells.
- What do the numbers mean? Can you draw conclusions about your survey population based on their responses?

Stage 4

- With the spreadsheet program, create graphs from the responses to illustrate them.
- Include these graphs with your written analysis by copying and pasting them into your text document.

Internet References

Excel, Microsoft, *www.microsoft.com*

AppleWorks Spreadsheet, Apple Computer, *www.apple.com*

Quattro Pro, Corel, *www.corel.com*

Lotus 1-2-3 in IBM Lotus SmartSuite®, *lotus.com*

8

Text-Based Activities

❖ Without buying expensive programs, what activities can my students do to focus on vocabulary?

❖ Where can I find sources of usage of specific vocabulary, grammar, and punctuation as examples for students?

❖ What's LexisNexis? If my school doesn't subscribe to it, what alternatives are there?

We have come to think of the computer as a powerful tool for language learning, partly for its ability to access and deliver multimedia material. Yet valuable learning opportunities remain using technology that predates this capability. In the days before the graphical user interface *(GUI)* for computer applications, when computers operated with a fraction of the processing power common today, text manipulation gave a glimmer of the possibilities posed by computers for language learning.

Computers perform simple, tedious tasks fast and accurately, such as spell-checking a paper, counting words, and finding words—tasks that tire the human brain but tax the computer hardly at all. In fact, purely text-based programs do things with text in a split second that would take days for a human to accomplish.

Concordance

A concordance is a list of occurrences of a specified word or phrase along with a piece of the passage where each occurs from a large body of texts, or *corpus*. Any electronic text document in any language could serve as a source of language to be searched, but a corpus, or *corpora* (plural), of sufficient size and comprising a variety of authentic texts, should afford a representative sample of usage.

The search itself works like the word **Find** command in a word processor (**Edit > Find**), except that a concordance displays in a list of their original sentence contexts all occurrences of the search term within the corpus (see Figure 8.1). A word processor highlights or displays the search term in the open document in serial fashion—one occurrence at a time. A concordance application can perform many other functions, such as using elaborate search criteria, sorting results, varying the length of the context shown with the search term, making word or frequency lists, comparing texts, and saving lists.

While concordances are widely used in linguistic study and the study of usage for reference, few language teachers have students use them in the classroom. The obscurity of this tool is no measure of its usefulness. Some activities that are as simple as a web search can provide examples of usage for vocabulary, grammar, and even punctuation.

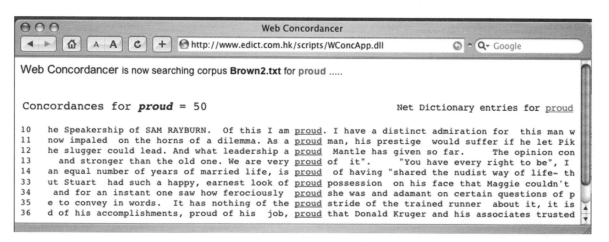

Figure 8.1 ■ A selection from a concordance of "proud" with the online Edict VLC Concordancer. The list can be sorted by what comes before or follows the search term. Click on the term in a citation to get the fuller context. *(www.edict.com.hk/concordance)*

Concordance Terms

corpus: a collection of texts, sometimes from a specific source or field (e.g., medical, literary, British-spoken) in the form of a single computer-readable file or database.

corpora: plural of corpus or generally denoting many texts from a variety of sources.

concatenate: link together into a chain, as individual text files are concatenated to form a corpus.

collocate: place side-by-side; a collocation of a word shows words appearing frequently near it.

KWIC (key word in context): a common option for displaying search results for text databases. For a concordance, the search term appears in the center of each line, in colored or bold text, with the surrounding sentence context to the right and left. The list can also be sorted by words to the left or the right of the search term.

ASCII (American Standard Code for Information Interchange): a common character set supported by all computers, representing 128 English letters, numbers, and symbols. Any text editor can open an ASCII text file, and most can save in this format (also called "text only"). Corpora concatenate texts in ASCII format only.

wild card: a character in a search, often a question mark (?) or asterisk (*), that represents an unknown (or any) character.

ACTIVITY 1 ■ Online Concordance	
	Teacher skills: web browsing, word processing
	Student level: low-intermediate to advanced
	Content objective: finding usage and vocabulary examples with online tools
	Software: web browser

Several websites offer free concordances with established corpora—an easy introduction to sample the utility of concordances without purchasing or installing software. Although an online concordance offers fewer searching and sorting parameters than a full concordance application installed on your computer, you don't need to worry about building, obtaining, or loading your own corpus for a local application. Corpora exist in many languages and operate similarly. In most searches, you enter your search string—a word, idiom, or phrase, with or without wild card characters—and hit the search button.

Two examples of online concordance engines include:

- Edict Virtual Language Centre (VLC), *www.edict.com.hk/concordance*
- Collins Cobuild Concordance Sampler, *www.collins.co.uk/Corpus/ CorpusSearch.aspx*

VLC has an easy-to-use concordance with options. The corpora, though small, are in English, French, Chinese, and Japanese. Choose the corpus to search. Some single-author collections provide a limited source for the search term. Expand the concordance to produce the entire sentence or paragraph context for a term and see its definition. *Parameter* settings for the search include sorting by the word occurring before or after the search term, which tends to group patterns in usage (Figure 8.2).

Figure 8.2 ■
Creating a concordance with parameters by specifying search term, corpus, length and number of resulting lines, sorting alphabetically by the word to the left or right of the search term, etc.

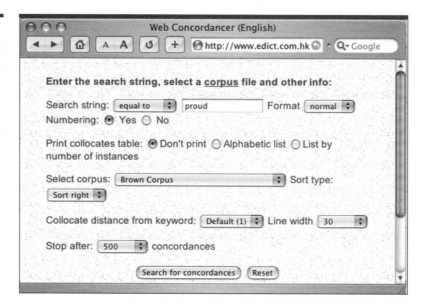

The Collins Corpus Concordance Sampler draws on a much larger corpus, 56 million words of contemporary written and spoken English. Words in the corpus are *tagged* for their part of speech, allowing a search using tags to differentiate uses:

- Search for "help/NOUN" to return   *I need some* help *with my homework*
- Search for "help/VERB" to return   *Can you* help *me with my homework*
- Search for "boring/JJ" (adjective tag) to return   *It was a* boring *movie*

These tags limit searches to specific parts of speech to return only uses of particular interest. The free Collins sampler, however, only returns 40 lines, has a short citation line of 70 characters, and does not link to the larger context citation or dictionary definition as VLC does.

The following concordance activities use examples for learning English specifically but apply in principle to using concordances in other language corpora to demonstrate vocabulary, grammar, punctuation, and usage.

Activities

Vocabulary on Demand

Students infer word meanings from their contexts, a challenging proposition, but one facilitated by multiple KWIC examples and the option of seeing the wider context of any term. Expand or adapt this activity to focus on any lexical or grammatical item.

> **Using Wild Cards in Searches**
>
> Wild cards stand in for any character and return a concordance of multiple forms of a word. For example, *big**, where the asterisk represents our wild card, could return concordance citations with *big*, *bigger*, *biggest*, *bigot*, and other words beginning with *big*. Wild cards are also useful in providing examples of words formed with the same prefix, such as *dis**, *un**, *in**, *mis**, etc. Focus on *dis-* in adjectives, for example, with *dis*ed*. Some online concordance engines and applications use parameter settings in the search instead of a wild card. For example, search for *dis* with the parameter setting *Starts with*.

Teacher Preparation

- Give students several new vocabulary words or phrases to look up.
- Pair words to be differentiated, such as *franchise* and *license* in business English, or similar phrasal verbs, such as *run across, drop in, look up* (as well as the more common past tense forms).
- (For all activities) Demonstrate use of the online concordance, how to set parameters for particular results, which corpus to use (where a choice is available), and how to read the results.

Steps for Students

- Enter each vocabulary item in the online concordance, choose a corpus (that the teacher recommends), and search.
- Based on the examples in the KWIC list, try to infer the meaning of each by establishing patterns of its usage.
- Double-click on the concordance word in any citation in the KWIC list to get a larger context (if feature available).
- Write each new item in an original sentence.
- Compare your sentences with your partner's sentences.
- Use an online dictionary to confirm your definitions and uses (see Figure 4.8 on page 41).

Count/Non-Count Nouns

This activity gives students practice in differentiating *count* from *non-count* nouns based on multiple examples, which articles are used for each, and how the use of *a* vs. *an* can aid pronunciation of the noun that follows.

Teacher Preparation

- Give students a list of nouns to concordance, mixing count with non-count nouns (e.g., *help, jewelry, advice, equipment, idea, problem, car*).
- Have them limit results to nouns by using a part of speech tag, if available (see previous section), such as with the Collins concordance (e.g., help/NOUN).

Steps for Students

- Perform a concordance for each vocabulary word.
  - Sort the results by the word to the left (in front of the search term).
  - Use the /NOUN tag to limit results to noun uses.
- What article is used before the word? What does that mean about the noun?
- Why is *an* used instead of *a*?
- Does the word also occur with a plural *–s* on the end? What does that mean?
- Verify your answers with a partner.

Collocations

Search for words that frequently occur with particles in a given meaning. A search for *interested,* for example, should result in a concordance showing this word's collocation with the particle *in*.

Teacher Preparation

- Create a cloze exercise with the particles that collocate with vocabulary items missing.
- Some particles should collocate for one definition while their absence indicates another, so for a more challenging exercise, some blanks in the cloze may not need to be filled in, depending on the context and meaning. For example,

  I believe _____ *Jim took it*. (no particle needed)

  I believe _____ *reincarnation*. (in collocates with believe)

Steps for Students

- Search for each term to create a concordance.
- Does a particle occur with the term? Is this use similar to the sentence in the activity?
- Verify your answers with a partner.

Reference for Correcting Papers

Identify mistakes in student writing and let them find the correct usage or form by searching for examples using a concordance of the term. This won't work for all mistakes but may be effective for problems of word choice, collocation, and articles. By using a concordance to see numerous authentic examples and struggling to infer the meaning, students assume responsibility for correcting their mistakes and may discover the logic behind the usage with more examples than textbooks provide.

Consider the common confusion in ESL/EFL over the past and present participle and their roles, respectively, describing an *experience* versus the *cause* of it:

I was boring *in class. I am* interesting *in Cuba.*

The speaker *was bored. It was an* interested *film.*

Without the benefit of part of speech tags used in the concordance, a search for *bored* will display the verb form in addition to the adjective:

The teacher bored *us*

as well as other meanings of the verb form altogether:

The bit bored *through the rock*

So students will need guidance interpreting a concordance and knowing which usages to look for.

Identifying Use of Punctuation

Use a concordance of punctuation marks to identify their various uses, especially less commonly used ones, such as (in ESL/EFL) the colon and semicolon. Using a good variety of corpora, students should see usage of the colon, for example, to introduce lists or statements, represent a ratio or time, and identify biblical verse. (Add a space after the colon in the search to eliminate ratios and biblical or time citations.) The citations also show proper typography: In English prose, there is no space before the colon but after.

Steps for Students

- Create a concordance for a colon (:).
- Where is it used?
- Is it used with numbers and words?
- What uses did your partner find?

Distinguishing Semantic Differences

Language students often have difficulty determining usage of words of similar meaning, such as (in ESL/EFL) *fix, repair,* or *mend*. In what context is each used?

Teacher Preparation

- Write a list of several groups of words with similar meanings for students to look up.
- Have students pair up for this activity.

Steps for Students

- Perform a concordance for each word in the group of similar word meanings. Start with *fix, repair,* and *mend.*
  - Sort the results for each word by the word to the right (after) the search term to group *what* people fix, repair, or mend.
  - Use a wild card character (* or ?) after the base form of the words (e.g., fix, repair, mend) or use the search parameter "Starts with" to return uses such as *fixes, fixed,* and *fixing* as well.
- From the concordances, find several things that are *fixed,* things that are *repaired,* and things that are *mended.* Make a list of each.
- With a partner, try to establish patterns of usage for each word.

Material Preparation

Provide examples for answers. When correcting student writing or exercises, questions about grammar or vocabulary usage may require further examples to illuminate. A concordance can quickly demonstrate a variety of contexts as examples of a rule.

Provide authentic examples. Concordance vocabulary or grammar items can generate authentic examples for material or quiz preparation. Lines of citations can be copied and pasted into a word processor, or more elaborate concordance applications can generate cloze, matching, and other activities from the citations.

> **Length of Citation**
>
> Most concordances, using KWIC citations by default, display *n* characters to the left of the search term and *n* characters to the right, a number that can be varied in some concordances, regardless of where the sentence begins. To get full-sentence examples instead of fragments—ones that can be copied and pasted into a word processor—switch to a view of the larger context, such as the entire sentence where the item occurs or use the greatest line width (see line width parameter in VLC, Figure 8.2). Create a cloze exercise as desired, such as by removing the search term or collocation item.

Internet References

ONLINE CONCORDANCE

Edict Virtual Language Centre. Corpora in English, French, Chinese, and Japanese. Also available are concordance programs (PC), and papers on using concordance, including a student's guide, *www.edict.com.hk/concordance*

Collins Cobuild Concordance and Collocation Sampler. Free, online concordance form. The Wordbanks *Online* English corpus claims to have 56 million words of contemporary written and spoken text to demonstrate English usage. (For full access to the Wordbanks Online corpus, including French and Spanish corpora and use of their concordance tools, subscribe to the fee service.) *www.collins.co.uk/Corpus/CorpusSearch.aspx*

Software

Concordance, R.J.C. WATT, (PC, free), *www.rjcw.freeserve.co.uk*

Concordance, Jean-Daniel Fekete (PC/Mac, free), *www.lri.fr/~fekete/concordance*

Concorder (Mac, free), *www.crm.umontreal.ca/~rand/CC_an.html*

Conc (Mac), SIL International Software, *www.sil.org/computing/catalog*

MonoConc Pro (PC), Athelstan, *www.athel.com*

Papers on Using Concordance for Language Study

Ball, Catherine N. *Tutorial: Concordances and corpora. www.georgetown.edu/ faculty/ballc/corpora/tutorial.html*

Godwin-Jones, Bob. Tools and trends in corpora use for teaching and learning. *Language Learning & Technology,* Vol. 5, No. 3, September 2001, *llt.msu.edu/ vol5num3/emerging*

Information and Communications Technology for Language Teachers. Using concordance programs in the modern foreign languages classroom, *ICT4LT Module 2.4, www.ict4lt.org/en/en_mod2-4.htm*

Dyck, Garry N. Concordancing for English Language Teachers paper, TESL Manitoba, February 15, 1999, *home.cc.umanitoba.ca/~gdyck/conc.html*

Stevens, Vance. Concordance and collocation resources, *www.geocities.com/Athens/ Olympus/4631/textanal.htm*

📖 Activity 2 ■ Other Internet Resources for Language Contexts	
	Teacher skills: web browsing, word processing
	Student level: intermediate to advanced
	Content objective: finding usage and vocabulary examples with search engines and specialized databases
	Software: web browser

As we realized in Chapter 5, the Internet is one massive language resource for reading and listening in many languages. So while online concordance, as in Activity 1, provides sophisticated searching and sorting of language in context, many other resources on the Internet also provide contexts for language usage. Students and teachers can find contexts for usage on specific websites or by using a web *search engine* (such as Google or Yahoo), a news search, a search of online literary works, and, for subscribers, a search of the powerful LexisNexis database. These better-known sources, while lacking the control over the format of search results that a concordance excels at, provide instead a wider context of the search term.

Pedagogical Rationale

This activity seeks to demonstrate the usefulness of a wide range of Internet resources for delivering examples of usage of specific language. Like activities in web searching techniques and evaluation of Internet sources in Chapter 5, Activity 2 will provide students with the ability to expand their knowledge of the target language by seeing terms of interest used in a variety of contexts. Use these resources just as the concordance engines were used in the previous activity to help students learn vocabulary and usage through analyzing multiple occurrences.

> **Online Dictionaries**
>
> Free online word references abound, including dictionaries with word origins, usage examples, audible pronunciation, related words, and hyperlinked definitions (where each word in the definition is linked to its definition), and specialized dictionaries (e.g., law, medicine, religion, computing, beer brewing). Some dictionaries also provide a thesaurus, word-of-the-day feature, and links to multilingual dictionaries. (See Internet References on page 180.)

General Internet Search

Searching for a vocabulary term with a web search engine will return *links to pages* that contain that term, not the terms themselves in citations (at least not ones of a useful length). To find the search term you would have to (1) follow a link that looked promising from the results page and then (2) conduct a find operation (**Edit > Find**) in the browser to locate the term on that web page.

In other words, the web search engine gives you links to pages that contain the term but no further help in identifying the term. While such a search would turn up the search term in a page, considering the lack of control over the context (what page it turns up on) and the limited occurrences (perhaps one per web page), the following methods might be more fruitful for the time spent.

News Search—Google

Some web search engines offer specialized searching within particular categories of information available on the Internet. In addition to a general web search, a news search engine searches only online news sources, such as newspapers, magazines, television stations, and Internet news outlets. Search these news sources for the occurrence of language of interest.

The popular search engine Google has a news search engine that takes your search term and produces results where that term appears from among thousands of news sources around the world. Google News returns a KWIC list of articles where the search term appears, in bold (see Figure 8.3). Each article headline appears with its synopsis and a

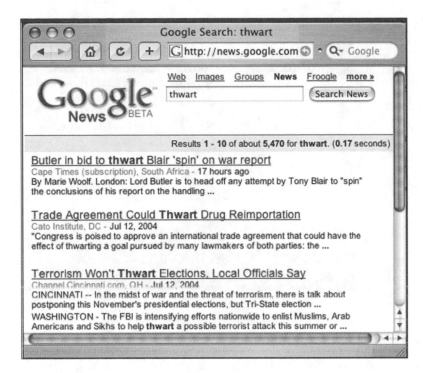

Figure 8.3 ■ A search for "thwart" on Google News lists news articles containing that term with synopses showing a short context for the term, in bold.

link to the full news article. This news search is available in many country versions in the local language.

News Search—LexisNexis

This massive database of news and other published business, legal, and medical reports is available by institutional subscription, usually to universities, media outlets, research institutes, and law firms. (Inquire at your school's library or information technology department to see if your school subscribes.) A LexisNexis search can produce various lists of search terms.

Use the Quick News Search or Guided News Search function to enter a word or phrase. The Guided News Search allows you to search particular news categories (e.g., world news, news transcripts) and sources for that category (e.g., major papers, NPR transcripts) as well as a specific publication name, date or date range, and multiple keywords. Sources include material in English, Dutch, French, German, Italian, Portuguese, and Spanish. The search results can be formatted in one of four formats, including a KWIC list displaying one article at a time with excerpted passages where the search term occurs in bold.

View the LexisNexis search results in the Expanded List format (see Figure 8.4), which displays one article at a time with excerpted passages where the search term occurs in bold.

Figure 8.4 ■ Results in "Expanded List News" format from a Quick Search in LexisNexis. The search term, "thwart," appears in bold in short excerpts from the full text of articles.

Literary Collections

Works published in the United States before 1923 or outside the United States before 1909 have expired copyright protection.[1] These works, in the public domain, are fair game for online availability in their entirety. Many sites offer free access to the full text of a particular author's selected or complete works or works by a collection of authors. Most of these sites can be searched for a term, producing some kind of KWIC list showing the search term in a brief context as well as the name of the work it comes from and a link to that passage.

Searching such a limited corpus for a term will likely result in far fewer, if any, results for a given term. Also, the contemporary usage for a particular term may have changed from its usage in a text in cases over a century old. Nonetheless, these online collections present yet another searchable source of language usage, not an exclusive source, to supplement textbook and real-life examples. See the following Internet References for a selected list of such online collections.

Internet References

NEWS SOURCES

Google News Search, *news.google.com*

LexisNexis (available by institutional subscription), *web.lexis-nexis.com/universe*

---

[1] To determine whether a work is copyright protected at all, see "Copyright Term and the Public Domain in the United States," Cornell Copyright Information Center, *www.copyright.cornell.edu/training/ Hirtle_Public_Domain.htm*.

ONLINE DICTIONARIES

Merriam-Webster online, *www.m-w.com*

Longman Web Dictionary for ESL/ESL students. Includes usage examples, related words, and pronunciation, *www.longmanwebdict.com*

Dictionary.com. Multilingual dictionaries, specialized dictionaries, translators, and more, *dictionary.reference.com*

SEARCHABLE BOOKS ONLINE

ClassicReader.com. Search or read the full text of hundreds of works in the public domain (copyright protection has expired) including works of fiction, nonfiction, children's books, poetry, short stories, drama, and classical, *www.classicreader.com*

BibleGateway.com, *bible.gospelcom.net*

William Blake poetry, *www.english.uga.edu/Blake_Concordance*

T. S. Eliot poetry, *www.missouri.edu/ tselist/tse.html*

🕮 **ACTIVITY 3** ▪ Typing Practice	
	Teacher skills: typing, general computer use
	Student level: beginning to advanced
	Content objective: learning to type and use other keyboard and mouse functions
	Software: typing practice

It's hard to imagine typing, or **keyboarding,** not being an essential skill today for just about everyone, not just those going on to further academic work. The time invested in becoming familiar with keyboard functions and proficient at touch typing will undoubtedly pay off in greater efficiency. Language students faced with learning a character set different from their native language (e.g., Arabic or Chinese speakers learning English) need more help than those used to the same characters from their first language.

Pedagogical Rationale

Typing practice has benefits beyond increasing a student's keyboard proficiency. Repeating practice words and sentences reinforces spelling rules and vocabulary, and following instructions exercises reading or listening comprehension. The game-like interface of many typing tutor programs also offers an attractive warm-up or *buffer* activity to students that have finished one activity and are waiting for others before moving on to the next (see **Buffer Activity** on page 77). Most applications offer a choice of keyboard layouts for different languages, practice for all levels of typing, and allow students to save their progress or record on lessons.

Teacher Preparation

While most typing programs are *tutorial* in nature—students can use them on their own with little assistance—students may still benefit from some instruction:

- Instruct students on proper finger placement on the keyboard.

- Demonstrate how to use numeric keypad functions (/ * - +) as well as other common characters (parentheses, brackets, slash, asterisk).

- Demonstrate left and right mouse button functions (or **Ctrl**-click for the one-button Mac mouse).

- Demonstrate use of typing tutor program, including saving of progress record (or "workbook").

Internet References

Typing Instructor, Individual Software, Inc. (PC), *www.individualsoftware.com*

Mavis Beacon Teaches Typing® (PC/Mac), The Learning Company, *www.mavisbeacon.com*

Type to Learn (PC/Mac), Sunburst Software, *www.sunburst.com*

Touch Typing (PC), *www.tutor-typing.com*

9

Content Activities

❖ What language programs should we use in class?

❖ Besides language learning programs, what others are useful for language students to use?

❖ I like to create my own material. What are my options for creating computer-based lessons?

While pedantic language or content programs belong primarily in an open-lab (self-access) setting instead of class, teachers can provide added value to these programs by assigning specific parts to work on and instructing students in their proper use. Such programs supplement classroom language activities, provide additional target language models and practice, assist the teacher as a language reference, and can also serve as a curricular buffer.

✦ ACTIVITY 1 ■ Grammar, Content, Skills, Integrated-Skills Programs, and Games
Teacher skills: basic computer use, use of multimedia programs
Student level: high-beginning to low-advanced
Content objective: grammar, skills, vocabulary
Software: various commercial programs

This book aspires to help language teachers retool for the computer classroom by presenting specific activity ideas and pedagogical approaches they can adapt for their own classes. Learning to use new teaching tools effectively and creatively, however, does not translate into handing the job over to pedantic software programs with "canned" (ready-to-use) content that teaches language—a mode of computer use classified as *tutorial* in that the computer offers instruction and interaction in place of a teacher. (See Chapter 2 for a discussion of the *tutor* versus *tool* mode of computer use.) Why, then, add a chapter on such tutorial programs to a book on CALL *class* activities?

Pedagogical Rationale

- *Supplemental role.* Content programs can provide supplemental instruction, models, alternative approaches, and practice to related class material and activities.

- *More target language.* Where target language stimuli outside the classroom is hard to come by, students might benefit from supplemental materials, especially when tied to class activities.

- *Resource to introduce.* Teachers often take time to introduce students to the library or other outside resources. Pedantic language programs represent such an extracurricular resource, and students need a thorough orientation to what they offer and how to use them, which may encourage them to take more control of their learning by taking advantage of available resources, especially ones not used in class regularly.

- *Teacher assistance.* Teacher training and experience vary widely in second and foreign language instruction. Good commercial language programs may offer the expertise in grammar instruction or vocabulary lacking in teachers better described as facilitators of self-study activities and native models of the target language.

- *Curricular buffer.* In some environments, particularly intensive language programs, high weekly contact hours for teachers may make some class work on canned programs appealing to reduce lesson planning to a manageable level and break up rigorous class activities.

The question is not whether pedantic programs are appropriate to use in teaching across the board, but rather how they should be used in connection with regular teacher-led lab class activities. Most of the time spent on these programs in class, after all, would be at the expense of human instruction time—what students are paying for. Having students spend regular class time on canned content is like having them go through exercises in their grammar workbook, reducing the teacher to a study hall monitor, not effective duty for a trained, experienced language teacher.

Language teachers recognize the paradox of the ultimate tutorial language program: If it were truly effective enough to replace flesh-and-blood teachers, they wouldn't want it anywhere near their students. Not to worry. These programs can't converse with students, evaluate their speaking skills and pronunciation, or correct their papers. They do excel, however, at tirelessly providing examples, repetition, practice exercises, immediate feedback from objective questions, glossaries, and transcripts, all under the control of the individual student. Ideally, a variety of these language instruction programs, as well as a target language dictionary, thesaurus, and encyclopedia, would be available in an open (self-access) lab, one staffed by a lab monitor to assist students on technical if not language issues.

Grammar Programs

Choosing Pedantic Language Programs

There are hundreds of language instruction programs. (See Internet References at the end of this section, for sources of objective language software evaluations.)

Factors in choosing pedantic programs
- **Content:** What are the target language, level(s), and skills covered?
- **Technical:** Can the lab computers run the software (consider platform, processing power, memory, network requirements)?
- **Responding to needs:** What are teachers' preferences?

- **Users:** What's the technical proficiency of students and teachers? Will they need additional training?
- **Mode of use:** Will the programs be used for classes, self-study, or both?
- **Cost:** What's the cost of the software for the number of computers it will run on? How does this purchase impact others?
- **Compatibility:** Will this software necessitate hardware upgrades or other purchases or changes to the existing setup?

Content Programs

Content programs can take many forms and include authentic material designed to inform the user about a topic (i.e., not language instruction) as well as content designed for second language learning.

EXAMPLES OF AUTHENTIC CONTENT PROGRAMS
(ONLINE OR CD/DVD-BASED)
- encyclopedia
- interactive atlas
- history, geography, culture of the target language country
- educational subjects, e.g., math, music, science, social studies
- cooking, wine education, home improvement, landscaping

EXAMPLES OF LANGUAGE INSTRUCTION
- second language interactive talking picture dictionary
- programs of exploration, adventure, or searching that teach language as a means to solve problems. For example,
  - ESL: Longman English Interactive
  - French: A la rencontre de Philippe
  - Spanish: Nuevos Destinos

Skills Programs

Skills programs can round out a good collection of language learning resources in a lab. In a second language learning environment, where L1s may vary widely in class, students' needs will vary, with some needing more practice with spelling and others needing more practice with pronunciation. The teacher's role becomes one of resource expert in diagnosing a student's particular needs and referring him or her to the appropriate program and unit.

EXAMPLES OF SKILLS PROGRAMS
- pronunciation
- spelling
- vocabulary, including idioms and slang (see Figure 9.1)
- typing
- test preparation, e.g., TOEFL®, TOEIC®, SAT®, ACT®, GMAT®, GRE®, foreign language proficiency tests
- language for specific purposes: business, medicine, law, science, technology, aviation

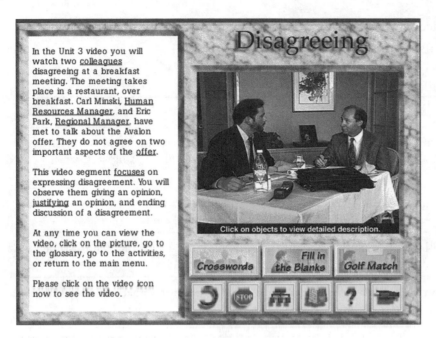

In the Unit 3 video you will watch two colleagues disagreeing at a breakfast meeting. The meeting takes place in a restaurant, over breakfast. Carl Minski, Human Resources Manager, and Eric Park, Regional Manager, have met to talk about the Avalon offer. They do not agree on two important aspects of the offer.

This video segment focuses on expressing disagreement. You will observe them giving an opinion, justifying an opinion, and ending discussion of a disagreement.

At any time you can view the video, click on the picture, go to the glossary, go to the activities, or return to the main menu.

Please click on the video icon now to see the video.

Disagreeing

Click on objects to view detailed description.

Crosswords · Fill in the Blanks · Golf Match

Figure 9.1

Business English Meetings teaches ESL students about the language and culture of North American business meetings, including vocabulary and idioms, through video scenarios. Transcripts, a glossary, and exercises accompany each video topic. (English Language Centre, University of Victoria. *www.uvcs.uvic.ca/cdroms*)

Comprehensive Language Learning Systems/Integrated Skills Programs

Some pedantic language learning software combines all skill areas in a holistic approach. Usually called "language learning systems" or "integrated-skill programs," they offer a rich mix of audio, video, and text content; instruction and practice; and feedback and context-sensitive help, such as a grammar handbook. Though best suited for self-study, these programs need to be demonstrated to students. Teachers should demonstrate useful features and show students how to navigate its content, access the program's multimedia, get feedback, and other aspects of functionality to ensure effective use.

Subscription Content

We have three primary options for accessing content with computers:

- *local* applications installed on the hard drive or run from a *CD/DVD*
- free access websites
- subscription-based websites

The last, subscription-based content, refers to websites that charge a fee to users to access, usually for a specified period of time. Users register for the service, pay the fee, receive a login name and password, and then begin to access the site and use the material.

A school might pay for access for students, or students might be responsible for paying individually, just as they purchase class textbooks on their own.

TABLE 9.1 ■ Subscription-Based Web Content

Advantages	Disadvantages
No software to install, configure, and maintain.	Cost of subscription may not be substantially cheaper, if at all, than purchasing software to install, keep, and reuse.
Content can be corrected, updated, and expanded at any time by publisher.	No tangible product as with a textbook or software purchase.
In the absence of a school lab, students could access content from any computer.	Subscriptions may not be refundable to students changing or dropping class.
Distance learning students could access material from their own computers, where they normally interact with the class.	Users resistant to pay for something they think they might get for free at other sites.
	Access expires at a certain point, imposing time pressure on its use.
	Access depends on continued operation of the company providing the service and a reliable Internet connection.

Games

Language games provide a diversion from involved projects and rigorous activities and act as a buffer between activities for students who finish before others. Games with a text focus can also introduce and reinforce language, especially categories of vocabulary, in the form of crossword puzzles, word search puzzles, hangman, wheel of fortune, as well as more elaborate games where the user must use clues to find or solve something. A MOO (discussed in Activity 7 in Chapter 5) is a type of online language game where a student navigates within a virtual environment and makes queries to reach a certain location or find an object or person.

Many games are structured around the completion of a single puzzle at a time, so they can be used for short periods of time. Except for complicated environments (like the MOO), most games also don't require much, if any, instruction to begin playing; all the directions a user needs are given on-screen.

Teacher Preparation/Activity

- Demonstrate use of the program: navigation, activities, correction, getting feed-back, context-sensitive help, and saving workbooks.

- Assignments:

  - Assign supplemental exercises as homework that *correspond to class work,* if possible.

  - Assign *specific* exercises to supplement teaching and other class materials or address L1-specific issues you diagnose—the value-added element the teacher provides when using any software.

  - Avoid simply assigning work on the program for a specified period of time ("busy work" that has no learning objective).

- If necessary and available in the program, students can print out section quiz results or a log of their activity to attest to the homework being done.

Internet References

TESOL CALL Interest Section software list, Deborah Healey and Norman Johnson, editors. Short summaries of ESL software, *oregonstate.edu/dept/eli/softlist*

ESL and CALL software reviews. Free-ESL.com, *www.free-esl.com*

Computer Assisted Language Instruction Consortium (CALICO) software reviews. Thorough evaluations based on a standard form, *calico.org/CALICO_Review*

CALL@Chorus software reviews, *www-writing.berkeley.edu/chorus/call*

Language Learning & Technology (LLT) software reviews, *llt.msu.edu/archives/software.html*

Virtual CALL Library, *www.sussex.ac.uk/languages/1-6-6.html*

CALL@Hull. Centre for Modern Languages, Language Institute at the University of Hull (UK), *www.fredriley.org.uk/call*

Technology & Learning Magazine online. Search for software reviews and articles by subject, computer platform, and student age, *www.techlearning.com*

SuperKids® educational software review. Reviews and ratings of educational software, tools for online and offline use, news about important educational issues, views of visionaries and policymakers, *www.superkids.com*

INTEGRATED-SKILLS PROGRAMS—ESL

Ellis Language Systems. (PC and Mac) A variety of products, including packages designed for children and English for academic purposes and business, *ellis.com*

Longman English Interactive. (PC only) A multilevel, video-based, integrated-skills program that includes more than 100 hours of instruction per level. Pearson Longman, *longman.com*

English Discoveries. (PC only), *www.englishdiscoveries.com*

Business English Meetings. English Language Centre, University of Victoria, *www.uves.uvic.ca/edroms*

OTHER CONTENT RESOURCES

Computer Enhanced Language Instruction Archive (CELIA). Archive of mostly older ESL and foreign language freeware, demos, and games maintained at the Institute for Education, La Trobe University, Melbourne, Australia, *www.latrobe.edu.au/education/celia/celia.html*

Nuevos Destinos. (Mac and PC) WGBH television/McGraw-Hill, *main.wgbh.org/wgbh/learn/ndestinos*

	ACTIVITY 2 ■ Custom-Authored Lessons
	Teacher skills: comfort with general computing, some experience with authoring (such as web pages), willingness to learn new applications on own
	Student level: all
	Content objective: grammar, vocabulary, listening
	Software: various authoring programs

For some teachers, one appealing aspect of teaching with computers lies in the potential to create custom lessons. Just as teachers have long used word processors to write their own materials, they can use multimedia or web authoring tools to create focused, relevant materials for their students. Although the range of technical involvement stretches from relatively simple projects accessible to any motivated teacher familiar with basic computing, word processing, and web browsing, other projects can challenge the most technically inclined. So while it's not for everyone, it's also not limited to technophiles.

Authoring projects can range in complexity from a slide show presentation or voice recording to a class website or lessons involving audio, video, and interactivity created with a multimedia authoring program (see Figure 9.2—Hot Potatoes). Skills teachers gain in learning to create this material, moreover, can be passed on to students in project activities.

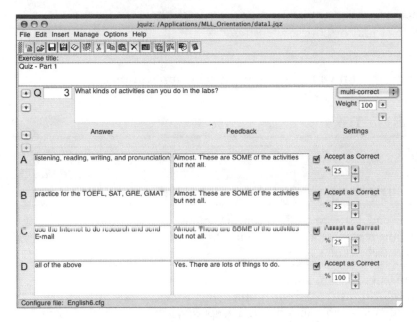

Figure 9.2

Hot Potatoes, an easy-to-use JavaScript-based authoring tool for self-correcting web quizzes. (Half-baked software, Inc., *web.uvic.car/hrd/hotpot*) This multiple-choice exercise can score partially correct answers and provide feedback. (From the Java HotPotatoes Alpha G version for Mac OS X.)

There isn't space here to detail *how* to create custom multimedia materials, but this section should give you an idea of the possibilities. Lab personnel or experienced CALL teachers should be able to help you create some of the lesson types in Table 9.2. For more involved endeavors, such as creating a website or using multimedia authoring programs, you might want to take a workshop or course, traditional or online, perhaps one at an adult education center or at the academic computing support center if you teach at a large college. Self-learners can work through any one of the hundreds of books on computing topics available in large bookstores and computer stores or use free or fee-based application training materials available online.

Table 9.2 shows a range of custom lessons that teachers can create. The *types* represent a sample of possibilities, while the *technical difficulty* refers to the teacher's expected technical proficiency. Specific software titles used to author lessons are listed by lesson type in Table 9.3.

Teacher Preparation

- Decide on the type of lesson to develop: presentation only, interactive content, or test.
- Decide on the type of media to use: text, images, audio, or video.
- Find the appropriate program(s) to author the lesson.

- Get training in the use of the program:
  - colleague or lab personnel experienced in the program
  - workshop or course
  - web training
  - primers: Some educators share application primers with their students and others via their professional or course websites.
  - books
- Use a lesson idea as a project on which to learn the new application.

TABLE 9.2 ■ Selected Custom Lesson Types

Custom lesson type (software used)	Class activity	Technical difficulty (1–5)
Voice recording (sound editor, audio format compressor/encoder)	Students listen to audio recordings made by the teacher, e.g., for pronunciation or comprehension.	2
Audio dubbing (sound editor, audio format compressor/encoder)	Students listen to audio clip digitized from tape or transferred from another source (e.g., textbook audio, radio broadcast, speech, lecture).	2
Video clip (video editor, media converter)	Students view small part of larger program digitized from video tape.	3
Custom video (video editor, video camera, media converter)	Student video project, where they use still images, video, titles, voiceover narration, and a soundtrack to create a original short video production.	3
Class website (HTML editor or courseware account)	Students use teacher's class website for assignments, announcements, syllabus, files (sound, text, graphic), communication (bulletin board, chat), and related links.	4
Quizzes (quiz-maker application or online tool)	Students take quizzes to test their understanding or completion of class, homework, or buffer activity.	3
Puzzles (puzzlemaker)	Students work on word-based puzzles as a focused vocabulary or buffer activity.	1
Slide show (presentation or "slideware")	Teacher uses slide show as instructional aid or to demonstrate for students slide show projects.	2
Interactive multimedia project (multimedia authoring program)	Students use self-contained lessons for focused language practice.	5

TABLE 9.3 ■ Selected Authoring Software

Name	Company	Description	Platform
Sound (Waveform) Editors			
Audio Recorder	*versiontracker.com*	(Free) Record directly to AIFF or MP3.	Mac
Audacity	SoundForge *audacity.sourceforge.net*	(Free) Simple waveform editor, saves to MP3.	PC/Mac/ Linux
Amadeus	HairSoft *hairsoft.com*	Sound editor/analyzer w/MP3 support.	Mac
Simple Voice Recorders			
DL-Recorder	Dartmouth College *schiller.dartmouth.edu/ dl-recorder*	(Free) Record and play MP3 and wav audio in simple interface emulating an analog lab recorder.	PC/Mac
Windows Sound Recorder	Microsoft Corporation *www.microsoft.com*	(Free) Recorder bundled with Windows OS. Saves as WAV, MP3, MP3, WMA.	PC
GoldWave	GoldWave Inc. *goldwave.com*	Fully featured digital audio editor with simple interface; records, saves to, and opens many formats, including MP3.	PC
LangLab	E-LangLab *www.elanglab.com*	Simulates analog lab tape deck.	PC/Mac
Audio Compressor/Encoders			
RealPlayer Plus	Real Networks *www.real.com*	Plays many audio formats; records voice.	PC
QuickTime Pro	Apple Computer *www.apple.com*	Edits, encodes many video formats, including QuickTime streaming and MPEG.	PC/Mac
iTunes	Apple Computer *www.apple.com*	(Free) Converts to MP3 in batches, plays many formats, and creates playlists.	PC/Mac
Video Editors			
iMovie	Apple Computer *www.apple.com*	Intuitive, drag and drop editing with built-in MPEG4 encoding. Bundled with Mac OS.	Mac
Windows Movie Maker	Microsoft *www.microsoft.com*	Bundled with Windows OS.	PC
Final Cut Pro®	Apple Computer *www.apple.com*	Professional video editing.	Mac

TABLE 9.3 ■ Selected Authoring Software *(continued)*

Name	Company	Description	Platform
Final Cut® Express	Apple Computer *www.apple.com*	A cross between the ease of use of iMovie and the power of Final Cut Pro.	Mac
Adobe Premiere	Adobe Systems *www.adobe.com*	Fully featured video editing software.	PC

Video Compressors/Encoders

Cleaner	Discreet® *www.discreet.com*	Video encoding into all major video formats, including streaming web video.	PC/Mac

Media Converters (Hardware)

Dazzle Digital Video Creator	Pinnacle Systems *www.dazzle.com*	USB2 analog-to-DV real-time converter.	PC/Mac

HTML Editor

Composer	Mozilla (Netscape) *www.mozilla.org*	(Free) Open-source development of one of the original WYSIWYG editors.	PC/Mac
Dreamweaver	Macromedia *www.macromedia.com*	Leading professional WYSIWYG HTML editor.	PC/Mac
GoLive	Adobe Systems *www.adobe.com*	Fully featured professional editor.	PC/Mac
FrontPage	Microsoft Corporation *www.microsoft.com*	Also part of the Microsoft Office suite.	PC/Mac

Courseware Packages[*]

CourseInfo	Blackboard, Inc. *www.blackboard.com*	Courseware packages help faculty manage courses on the Internet entirely through a browser (no software to install). Communications tools include announcements, calendar, bulletin board, chat, e-mail, and whiteboard. Assessment tools support multiple question formats and automatic grading. Other features include a gradebook and use metrics.	PC/Mac
WebCT	WebCT *www.webct.com*		PC/Mac
ANGEL	Angel Learning *angellearning.com*		PC/Mac
Internet Classroom Assistant	Nicenet *www.nicenet.org*	(Free) Nonprofit-based courseware site to manage communications for a course.	PC/Mac

[*] By institutional subscription or limited free version by individual. Compare features of dozens of courseware suites, including free services, at EduTools, *www.edutools.info/course/compare/index.jsp.*

TABLE 9.3 ■ Selected Authoring Software *(continued)*

Name	Company	Description	Platform
Stand-Alone Quiz Maker			
Hot Potatoes™	Half-baked Software *web.uvic.ca/hrd/hotpot*	(Free for education) One of the easiest to use quiz-making programs for the web. Creates quiz and web page. Just upload the resulting page to your website and refer to it.	PC/Mac
Online Quiz Maker			
Quiz Center	Discovery Channel School *school.discovery.com/ quizcenter/quizcenter.html*	(Free) Online quiz maker. Make a quiz and set up a group to access it.	PC/Mac
Languages Online	E.L. Easton *eleaston.com/quizzes.html*	(Free) Online multilingual quizzes and quiz makers.	PC/Mac
Makers	Interactive Exercise Maker Mellon Tri-College Language Grant *lang.swarthmore.edu/makers*	Make quizzes online. You can then move the completed quizzes to any other server.	PC/Mac
Puzzle Maker			
Crossword Compiler	Crossword Compile *www.crossword-compiler. com*	Create crossword puzzles to print out or upload to your website to do online.	PC
Slide Show Presentation			
PowerPoint	Microsoft Corporation *www.microsoft.com*	Also part of the Microsoft Office suite.	PC/Mac
Keynote	Apple Computer *www.apple.com*	High-quality 3-D presentations for OS X.	Mac
Slide Show	Apple Computer *www.apple.com*	Part of the AppleWorks suite.	Mac
Presentations	Corel *www.corel.com*	Part of the Corel Office suite that includes WordPerfect.	PC
Multimedia Authoring Environments (for Content Delivery and Test Creation)			
HyperStudio	Roger Wagner Publishing *www.hyperstudio.com*	HyperCard-like authoring environment popular with school teachers.	PC/Mac

Table 9.3 ■ Selected Authoring Software *(continued)*

Name	Company	Description	Platform
ToolBook Instructor	SumTotal Systems *www.sumtotalsystems.com*	Fully featured interactive multimedia content creation tool for local applications, CD, or the Internet.	PC
Authorware	Macromedia *www.macromedia.com*	Visual authoring tool for creating rich-media e-learning applications for lab servers, CD/DVD, or the Internet that comply with learning management system (LMS) standards.	PC
Director	Macromedia *www.macromedia.com*	The Cadillac of multimedia authoring environments. Professional level, high-learning curve.	PC/Mac
The Authoring Suite	WIDA *www.wida.co.uk*	Classic language lesson authoring environment, includes text reconstruction program, test maker, and many question types.	PC
Questionmark Perception	*questionmark.com*	Create and deliver secure quizzes, tests, surveys, and assessments over the Internet.	PC
Test Pilot	Clear Learning *www.clearlearning.com*	Create tests or assessments, or deliver content from any server platform.	PC/Mac
MetaCard	Runtime Revolution *www.metacard.com*	Multimedia authoring tool and GUI development environment for building graphical applications, computer-based training (CBT), and other applications.	PC/Mac
Author Plus online	Clarity Language Consultants *www.clarity.com.hk*	Easy authoring environment using text, audio, video, and graphics to make lesson and quizzes with feedback.	PC
MaxAuthor	Computer Aided Language Instruction Group University of Arizona *cali.arizona.edu/docs/wmaxa*	(Free) Windows and Internet-based multimedia language authoring system. Without programming, creates language instruction courseware for dozens of languages, utilizing audio, video, footnotes, graphics, test questions, and flash cards.	PC

PART 3

Technical
Considerations

10 Platform and Computer Compatibility

> ❖ My department uses Macs, but I have a PC at home. How can I work on my files in both places?
>
> ❖ Won't I need a PC to use Microsoft Office and the Internet and to support foreign languages?
>
> ❖ Isn't there more software for PCs than Macs?

I t's difficult to discuss the use of computers in education for long without the topic of *platform* coming up. Platform is the operating system the computer runs on, such as Microsoft Windows, Apple Macintosh, Linux, and various versions of UNIX®. Platform in education is an issue, sometimes a contentious one. For many people, even regular computer users, the platform argument, popularized as the "Mac vs. PC debate," is esoteric; for others, narrow experience may limit their ability to fairly judge the merits of one choice over the other. Although deciding on the platform of a computer for home use generally involves personal predilections and doesn't impact others, making that decision on behalf of others in the workplace can take on near religious overtones.

For some, an uncompromising allegiance to one over the other can lead to the kind of narrow-minded thinking that is anathema to rational decision-making.

Yet platform, as a *problem,* is often a red herring masking the more common source of problems encountered in personal computing: a user's lack of knowledge, experience, or patience. This chapter aims to shed light on this dimly lit subject for teachers as well as administrators by debunking some popular myths and suggesting a rational framework for decision-making. We also discover how easily educators and students can work harmoniously together with different computers.

Platform—A Primer

- *Computer platform:* The base system on which a computer operates, or operating system *(OS).* Applications, such as a word processor, run within this environment. The most common operating systems for personal computers are Microsoft Windows and Apple Macintosh. Linux is another but has not yet penetrated the market for non-technical users. *Servers* (computers that function as file, web, and database servers, etc.) also run versions of software from Microsoft and Apple as well as various versions of UNIX. (See **Linux** sidebar.)

- *PC:* Personal computer. *Around* the mid-1970s, computers designed for personal use, called "microcomputers," were collectively labeled "personal computers," or PCs, including ones by IBM, Apple, Compaq, Tandy, Atari, Commodore, Osborne, and Texas Instruments. Microcomputers were small and self-contained, as

Linux

Linux is an operating system (OS) based on UNIX, an industrial OS running most of the world's largest, most powerful, and critical servers. Linus Torvalds, as a computer science undergraduate in Finland, developed Linux as an alternative OS for personal computers because of his familiarity with UNIX and his dissatisfaction with Microsoft's DOS, which he felt was buggy and unstable. He distributed it to other programmers around the world to tweak and improve, part of the **open source** software movement (a community of programmers jointly developing software, which is freely distributed). Linux is especially attractive for its power, stability, large base of application developers, open source roots, and low licensing costs (free, in many cases). More and more software companies are developing applications for Linux, but its ease of use and application support for consumers have not caught up with Windows or Macintosh.

opposed to large mainframe computers or the terminals ("workstations") that connected to them. The eventual reduction of the personal computer market to those running Microsoft or Apple operating systems, for the most part, saw the term "PC" come to represent the former and Macintosh, or "Mac," the latter. This usage has not become entirely standardized, though PC *usually* refers to computers running the Windows OS, which also goes by Windows-, Intel-, or Pentium-based PCs, or, more colloquially, "Wintel" machines.[1] We will use "PC" here to refer to computers that run a Windows OS and "Mac" for Apple computers running a Macintosh OS. The Mac OS only runs on Apple computers (or *hardware*), for the most part, where the Windows OS runs on PCs made by many companies. Microsoft does not make a computer.

| TECHNOTE | ■ **Processors** |

PCs and Macs run on different microprocessors, also called central processing units *(CPU)* or simply "processor" or "chip." These chips employ different computing architectures. The Mac's "PowerPC" chip uses an efficient "reduced instruction set computer" (RISC) technology where PC chips use "complex instruction set computer" (CISC) technology. RISC draws on fewer instructions to execute compared to CISC, thus a RISC chip of much lower *clock speed* (instructions per second, measured in megahertz [MHz] or gigahertz [GHz]) than a CISC chip might accomplish the same net processing in the same time. Chips of lower clock speed may mean cooler operating temperatures and lower power consumption, hence their suitability for portable computers.

Factors in Deciding on a Computer Platform

There are many factors to consider in an intelligent choice of computer platform for an individual, and especially for a lab, department, or company. Unfortunately, many *irrelevant* factors commonly emerge driving or justifying platform decisions by individuals or administrators, even including information technology (IT) personnel. We can begin by separating the wheat from the chaff. (See Table 10.1.)

---

[1] Intel, the company that makes the microprocessor chip, or *CPU*, used in Windows-based PCs, is not the only company that produces microprocessors for these computers (AMD, Transmeta, and VIA are others). The Pentium class is not the only chip produced by Intel (Celeron is a less expensive class of chip).

TABLE 10.1 ■ Irrelevant and Relevant Factors in Deciding on Computer Platform

Irrelevant factors	Relevant factors
compatibility	software availability
workplace model	multilingual support
upgradability	ease of use
cult of personality	cost
financial prognosticating	setup and support
prevailing myths	history
one-size-fits-all recommendations	servers
	networking

Irrelevant Factors in Platform Decision-Making

1. *Compatibility.* Despite the fact that millions of documents, e-mails, instant messages, and media files are sent between Macs and PCs every day, with little or no problem, myths about incompatibility persist.

   - *Application compatibility.* Most programs that are available in both platforms (and most popular programs *are*) use the same *file type.* For example, a Microsoft Word, Excel, or PowerPoint document created on a Mac is the *same file format* as one created on these programs in Windows, and vice-versa. The characteristics of a file are inherent in the type (denoted by its **file extension,** e.g., doc, xls, pps, gif, jpeg, html), not by its platform of origin. Problems of compatibility arise between *versions* of the same application more than which OS it runs on.[2] Most applications cannot open documents created with a more recent (i.e., newer) version of the application (known as *forward compatibility*), though they can usually open documents created with a previous (older) version *(backward compatibility).* So Word 6.0 will not open Word XP documents (without special converters installed), but the reverse is possible.

---

[2] In fact, a very common incompatibility issue arises *within* Microsoft products running on Windows: a Microsoft Works Word document cannot be opened by Word in Microsoft Office.

The inability of a Mac to read documents created on a PC, or vice-versa, appears when the document was created with a program that runs on one platform but not the other *and* is a *proprietary* file format—not a common occurrence. A *proprietary* file format, such as Quark (file extension .qkd) or Adobe PhotoShop® (.psd), can generally only be opened by the program that created it, regardless of platform. An example that came up in the past in education, where Macs and PCs share space much more commonly than in large businesses, was a Mac not being able to open a Microsoft Office document when that Mac only had Apple's Office-like suite AppleWorks installed, which comes free on Macs. Of course, this wasn't a *platform* problem at all but one of not having the application installed. Another PC without Office installed on it wouldn't be able to open the document either. A workaround for ensuring compatibility among word-processing documents has long been saving in the **rich text format (RTF)**, a cross-platform, cross-application text document format that can be opened by most word processors. (See **TECHNOTE: File Format** in Chapter 4 on page 36 for more on RTF.)

- *Fonts*. PCs and Macs share many fonts but even these may be rendered slightly differently on each platform, resulting in *slight* differences in spacing and page layout over long documents.

- *Media*. Macs and PCs format their media (disks) differently. For most of its existence, however, the Mac has been able to read Mac- *and* PC-formatted media (floppy disks, CDs, *flash drives,* etc.), so transferring files regularly between Macs and PCs is accomplished simply by using PC-formatted (DOS) media for both or a "hybrid" format for CDs or DVDs. Conversely, PCs cannot read Mac-formatted media without the use of a third-party utility.

- *Hardware-software integration*. Not all compatibility issues are between Macs and PCs but relate to the fit between the hardware and software on the same platform. Windows runs on computers made by many companies (Dell, Hewlett-Packard, Compaq, Sony, etc.). Microsoft makes the OS and some application software but *not* the hardware (except a game box). In this tangle of manufacturers, incompatibilities arise. The components within PCs, such as the sound card, video card, Ethernet card, **CD** and **DVD** drives, are usually not made by the same company that made the computer. So while the PC world offers a great variety of competing computers, models, and components, even the option of building your own—often resulting in more options and lower prices—this hodgepodge of hardware and software cannot always be tightly integrated. One of the great advantages of the Mac has been the tight integration of hardware and software (the OS and some applications), since they are developed in tandem by the same company, Apple, resulting in ease of setup and reliable performance. Macintosh software developers can limit their design for and testing on a limited set of hardware and system standards.

- *Internet standards*. The Internet makes a good argument for the irrelevance of platform. In most cases, it makes no difference which OS one uses provided that the media players, or **plug-ins** (helper applications for web browsers that play or display special audio, video, graphic, or text content), are available for Macs and PCs. The vast majority of audio and video content on the Internet is delivered in only a few media formats: RealPlayer, QuickTime, Windows Media, Flash, and Shockwave. All of these formats have players or web browser plug-ins for Macintosh and Windows (most for Linux, too). Some less common A/V media formats, however, are only available for Windows, though these tend to be for private or corporate intranet content. More compatibility issues arise from the choice of **web browser** (Internet Explorer, Mozilla, Safari, etc.) than computer. The original concept of web content, going back to the networked information project led by Tim Berners-Lee at CERN,[3] was driven by a need to overcome platform incompatibilities to communicate by open standards, such as HTML and **TCP/IP**. Thus, websites or resources limited to a particular platform run counter to the spirit of the web and information sharing in general.

2. *Workplace model*. Some argue that students should use in school the computer they will more than likely use in the workplace. What does this argument assume they'll be doing? Most major applications, such as office productivity suites and authoring tools, are available for Macs and PCs. This argument might apply to a computer science major or a technician training to work on a specific system or hardware but not someone using applications that look and behave almost identically on Macs as on PCs. Moreover, consider the larger mission of education: Is it a place to limit choices for students, insulate them from different approaches, and conform to someone else's model—all without challenge? They're in school to learn and approach new experiences and ideas with an open mind. The same argument applied to language learning would maintain that teaching a child more than one native language will confuse him or her.

3. *Upgradability*. How *upgradable* a computer is generally refers to the hardware, both replacing components superceded by more powerful ones, such as the processor and hard drive, or *expanding* capabilities with additional components, such as more temporary memory (random access memory, or **RAM**), an extra internal hard drive, a video card for high-performance graphics rendering, wireless networking card **(Wi-Fi NIC),** etc. External **peripherals** can also expand the capabilities of a computer: a printer, scanner, removable drive (e.g., **USB** flash drive), media converter (for video digitizing), etc.

    In practice, more people expand their computer than upgrade it. They take advantage of built-in **expansion slots** and connections, such as USB, **FireWire, PCI,** ATA, PCMCIA (for laptops), etc., to add components and peripherals as

---

[3] European Organization for Nuclear Research, Geneva, Switzerland.

discussed.[4] All of these connection ports for plugging devices into are common on Macs and PC. Upgrading or replacing internal components, especially the cpu (*logic board* or *mother board*), can be especially difficult and expensive in some cases and not always a wise proposition as computers become cheaper and more powerful. The total performance of a computer depends not on one single component but on a whole system of complementary components.[5] Simply upgrading one component without regard for how it interacts with others may lead to minimal performance improvement, perhaps at great cost and with considerable technical difficulty. Still, in some cases, you might be able to upgrade the computer's processor for less than the cost of a new computer—an event much more likely on a PC than a Mac. If you build computers for a hobby, you'll likely understand how each ingredient affects the whole stew, but most users don't. They need a computer to be productive, not tinker with it as an amusing end in itself.

Upgrading the components, with the exception of adding RAM, is far less likely, rendering the upgradability factor of little actual consequence. Considering that we invest in computers periodically, perhaps every three to five years, the greater the investment we make in each computer, the *harder it may be to justify or afford its replacement*. Still, because their market offers many competing makers, PCs generally, but not always, offer systems with more upgrade options than Macs. This limitation is especially relevant for the one-piece, compact Macintosh models, such as the iMac® and eMac™, as opposed to tower designs.

As with any purchase, what's important is what you'll actually *need* and *use*. Buying overcapacity in computers accounts for a great deal of unnecessary expenditure.[6] For example, when computer makers first started phasing out floppy drives as outdated and inadequate for removable storage (led by Apple in 1998 with the iMac), many people continued to insist on the drives, either installed internally or as add-on external devices, reasoning that someone sometime might have a floppy disk they need to read. In that an expenditure on one piece of equipment comes at the expense of something else (a zero-sum model), this overcapacity represents waste. The question is not, "Will I ever use this option?" but "Is what I spend on this equal to what I'm giving up, given the probability of its need?"

---

[4] FireWire (aslo known as IEEE 1394) is an external connection port. PCI and ATA are internal connections (most hard drives and CD/DVD drives connect to the ATA bus). PCMCIA is an external connection on laptops (such as for WiFi NICs).

[5] Such as a fast processor, a fast system *bus* (the connection for data on the motherboard), fast RAM type (not simply amount of RAM), sufficient level-2 or level-3 cache (known as L2 or L3 cache—fast, temporary memory to facilitate processing), a fast hard drive (measured in rotations per minute, RPMs, and low *seek times* for data) and hard drive bus, etc. So, improving overall performance can be complicated.

[6] Excess processing power also accounts for waste in new computer purchases. Getting the highest processing speed (measured in Ghz) available at a given time results in a much lower overall computer value for most users as the slim difference in speeds is indiscernible in most operations and will be moot in a matter of months with the next speed boost of new chips.

4. *Cult of personality.* Some associate Bill Gates or Steve Jobs, the cult-like personalities representing Microsoft and Apple, respectively, with the superiority of PCs over Macs, or vice-versa. The same approach would lead one to prefer one make of car over another based on its celebrity spokesperson. Which CEO we respect more as a businessperson or idolize more as an icon of cool or genius has no bearing on the fit of their products for our needs.

5. *Financial prognosticating.* Over the years, proponents of one platform have predicted the downfall of the other with the accuracy of a palm reader. If experienced financial analysts on Wall Street—with immense experience, education, and resources—cannot reliably foretell the future of companies, why do some school administrators and IT departments imagine they can? The financier J. P. Morgan saw financial dilettantes offering advice as an ominous sign: He pulled his investments out of the stock market shortly before the crash of 1929 after getting a hot stock tip from the man shining his shoes.

    Moreover, would the financial viability of a computer company even impact the usability of its product if it was *already* operating productively? Not really. Computers have a short life. They depreciate to zero value on the books in about three years, and their hardware capabilities render them less and less compatible with newer, more demanding software. If a computer company folded the day after your purchase, would the machine suddenly stop working? Of course not. It's not like your gym closing the day after you buy a lifetime platinum membership with cash. With a computer, there's a built-in productivity window that cannot be closed by industry developments.

    Finally, in a market driven by image over substance, does the financial success of a company and its marketing effectiveness necessarily correlate with the quality of its product? If it did, perhaps Cokes and Big Macs would make people fit and attractive (like the people in their ads), Gap T-shirts would outlast Fruit of the Loom, and Budweiser would offer taste.

6. *Prevailing myths.* Misconceptions about PCs and Macs abound. The motivations range from a lack of knowledge—few people are very familiar with *both* platforms—to insecurity and a need to justify choices already made. Why else do such myths prevail? Since 90 percent of personal computers on earth run Windows,[7] there's momentum behind such an overwhelming majority presence, an attitude that may see safety in numbers and have faith by proxy in decisions made by the majority as necessarily being the right decisions for them, too. The dominance Microsoft enjoys quantitatively in the market, then, feeds its spin. Thus, many people buy a computer not after an informed choice among OS options, but because they believe it to be the only game in town—a notion not intended to dismiss the *rational* reasons for buying a PC. How Microsoft came to dominate

---

[7]The Windows global market share does not reflect the share of the *language lab market,* particularly since the latter was dominated by Macs originally as was the early education market generally.

the market speaks of its business acumen and tenacity (and Apple's frequent lack thereof), not the *technical prowess* of the product. Bill Gates understood early on how to commodify computers, often by making the innovations of others commercially successful for Microsoft.

7. *One-size-fits-all recommendations.* No two language lab environments or teacher requirements are identical. The needs of faculty, staff, and students, as well as the institutional support and financing, present enough variables to render unique each program's or individual's decision challenges. Blanket recommendations are often proposed by those basing decisions on what they already know instead of doing homework on what they don't. Be wary of simple answers to complex issues and the agenda of those making recommendations.

Relevant Factors in Platform Decision-Making

A rational framework for decision-making begins with access to complete information about all available choices. What differentiates Macs and PCs and might make one a wiser choice in a particular situation than another? Consider the following factors in the context of your actual use of computers.

1. *Software availability.* An argument is often put forth that there are more applications available for Windows than Macintosh. Whether true or not, is this relevant to you? Only the programs you *actually use* need to be available in your OS. Most of the major programs for office productivity, web development, design, multimedia creation, and language learning content are available for Macintosh and Windows at about the same time. While subtle differences in interface and file management exist, the applications are otherwise nearly identical. Many of the PC programs (counting Windows and DOS) that help make up a greater number of software titles are variations on the same functionality or otherwise have little or no applicability to CALL labs. For example, are the dozens of file transfer protocol *(FTP)* programs for Windows really an advantage over one really good, intuitive one that does the trick on the Mac, such as Fetch? Many Mac titles, furthermore, going back to the mid-1980s, were written specifically for educational purposes, and they still run on the latest version of the Mac OS and offer a diverse assortment of learning content.

   Moreover, since the new generation of the Mac OS,[8] OS X, is built on UNIX, the most powerful industrial operating system in the world, the reverse argument could now be made. Macs can run not only the thousands of Mac OS applications that have been around since 1984 and newer OS X applications but also UNIX

---

[8] Mac OS refers to versions of the Macintosh operating system released between 1984 and 2001, the final being Mac OS 9. Mac OS X (Roman numeral 10) reinvented the platform based on a version of UNIX (BSD), which can run all old Mac OS applications (in *Classic* mode) as well as applications written or modified to run on OS X. OS X provides dramatic improvements in power, stability, and extendibility of the Mac.

programs, opening up specialized applications that have been used over the last 30 years.[9] The point remains that Macs run most anything you'd need in a CALL lab, even discounting the Virtual PC option. (Virtual PC is a program that runs on Macs and allows the Windows OS to run within the Mac OS in *emulation* mode, where Windows applications can run.) With this problematic arrangement, you're paying nearly as much as a low-end PC would cost, thus getting one computer for nearly the price of two.

Still, some programs important to some users run only on PCs, such as certain database and communications programs, language software, and multimedia games. Again, what's important is whether this affects you and your language lab. Though some important applications have not been available for the Mac in the past, Mac OS X has brought many new developers to the Mac and more applications and compatibility to the platform. You would need to contact the administrator of relevant databases at your institution to find out what operating systems are supported by databases you may need to access. If you or your students don't need to access these databases, then this concern is irrelevant. Ironically, while PC users have long trumpeted their quantitative edge in software titles, studies have shown that Mac users actually use *more* programs because they experience fewer problems with them and face less intimidation in learning them.[10]

Windows users enjoy far more games than Mac users, but we're talking here about tools for language learning and teaching, not for an arcade at the mall. So while your 14-year-old may make compelling use of the "more games" argument for a PC at home, in the context of education the specter of irrelevancy rises again.

2. *Multilingual support.* Someone in a second language teaching environment (e.g., ESL in the United States) may have the luxury of not worrying about foreign language support on computers, but for those involved in foreign language instruction (e.g., Chinese in the United States), it might be a deciding factor in whether one uses PCs or Macs. If we want students to be immersed in the target language, then we need the OS and all or most applications used, particularly the word processor and web browser, to support the target language. The Windows and Mac operating systems come in many *localized* versions; that is, the versions sold in Japan have a Japanese interface (menus and dialog boxes in the target language), and so on for many other countries.[11] They both also support character sets (see **TECHNOTE: Character Sets** on page 211) used to represent Roman and

---

[9] These UNIX programs won't run "out of the box" under Mac OS X; they would have to be recompiled specifically to run under OS X (using a free Apple utility).

[10] International Data Corporation. (1997). *Understanding the total cost and value of integrating technology in schools*. White paper.

[11] Actually, Mac OS X and Windows XP (Professional Edition) build multilingual support into a single version, allowing the user to switch to many different languages without buying separate country versions.

non-Roman languages, displaying other languages in applications and allowing input of the characters.

Issues in Multilingual Support

Operating system support. The OS must be able to correctly read the character set required to display the letters or characters of the language. There are many different encoding sets, and some operating systems don't support all of them or interpret certain values in them differently.

Application support. Even if the OS supports a given character set, a particular application might not, or it might not support a right-to-left direction, such as for Arabic or Hebrew. You need both to support the language you're teaching. For example, a Microsoft Word document created in Windows XP and utilizing Unicode as the character set (see **TECHNOTE: Character Sets** on page 211) would only appear the same on a Mac running Microsoft Word if it also supported Unicode.[12]

Proofing tools. Teachers and students expect proofing tools (spell-checker, dictionary, thesaurus, hyphenation, grammar-checker) for the target language in their word processor. Even if the OS and word processor support character sets with the foreign characters, the application might not include proofing tools. Sometimes these are available as custom-installed components from the original application CDs or available for purchase from a third party.

Portability. When you send a document with foreign characters to someone else (such as by e-mail attachment), the recipient needs to be using a computer with an OS and application that support the same character set used to encode the document in the first place. If he or she doesn't, the recipient will see gibberish. The portable document format *(PDF)* addresses this problem by embedding fonts in a document, so that it travels with everything it needs.

Input language. When you type in another language, you might want to use the keyboard layout for that language instead of the "qwerty" (or standard) keyboard layout used for inputting Roman character sets in U.S. English. With Windows and Macintosh, you can switch between keyboard layouts for many languages from a desktop menu (after configuring the OS for keyboards to display).

Interface language. The U.S. versions of the Windows and Macintosh operating systems have the ability to display menus and dialog boxes in dozens of languages.[13] Using the target language in the interface helps create an immersion environment in the labs. (See Figure 10.1.) The applications that you and your

---

[12]As of this writing, Microsoft Office for Mac OS X is Unicode compliant; however, it won't support right-to-left text.

[13] For Windows XP Home Edition, you must purchase the Windows Multilingual User Interface Pack separately. Mac OS X comes with a built-in multilingual interface support.

Figure 10.1 ■ The OS interface in Mac OS X and Google language preferences changed to French. Note the menu items in the Safari web browser are in French as is the Google News in the French site.

students actually use should fully support the language you teach. Some teachers of non-Roman languages have, in the past, opted for PCs because of their more thorough *application* support of the language—a disparity gradually disappearing as more and more applications for Macs and PCs support Unicode.

3. *Ease of use.* At one time, when the choice in personal computing was between MS-DOS and Macintosh, Mac users enjoyed a superior, more capable OS and a clearly intuitive GUI unknown in the PC world. With the development of *GUI* Windows versions 3.1 and beyond, however, the ease-of-use playing field began to level. Apple and Microsoft continued to develop their own GUIs, borrowing concepts and features from each other.[14] Apple focuses a great deal of attention on intuitive graphical interfaces geared to how humans interact with functional elements (and wrote a well-regarded book on it titled *Macintosh*

---

[14] Apple, in fact, sued Microsoft for infringing on their trademark interface concepts, a battle they eventually lost. One of the key arguments centered on original creation and ownership of certain concepts, some of which Apple appropriated from an interface prototype developed earlier by Xerox's Palo Alto Research Center (PARC), making Apple's complaint seem disingenuous to many critics.

| TECHNOTE | ▪ **Character Sets** |

A character (letter, number, punctuation mark, or symbol) on a computer is represented in code by a number, because computers only understand numbers. There are many different systems used to encode characters, and some of the values in these **codepages** or **character sets** conflict with each other by assigning the same index number to define different characters. The OS and applications use these character sets. The most basic and common of these sets is *ASCII* (American Standard Code for Information Interchange), which has 128 characters with values 0–127 that represent English letters, numbers, punctuation, and special characters. (Don't confuse these character sets with *fonts*. A font is a piece of software describing a particular typeface *design* for characters in a character set. A set can be rendered in thousands of fonts.)

Example of ASCII code values

character	code value
a	97
A	65
1	49

Extended ASCII, a set that adds 128 more characters to handle accented letters in some European languages, also consists of 128 numbers with values 128–255.

Example of Extended ASCII code values

character	code value
ç	135
Ç	128
ß	225

Other sets are required to support non-Roman languages (with PC-specific and Mac-specific sets). The revolutionary improvement in this regard is Unicode, an encoding system powerful enough to assign a unique number to all of the characters of the world's languages, which formerly required many smaller, separate, often conflicting character sets. Current Windows (XP) and Mac (OS X) operating systems support Unicode, though many applications do *not* yet.[15]

---

[15] The Unicode Consortium provides information about Unicode as well as an up-to-date list of systems and applications that support it (*www.unicode.org/standard/WhatIsUnicode.html*).

Human Interface Guidelines), attention that carries over to their case designs. But which is easier to use? It depends on what you do with your computer and whom you ask. Most people find what they're already used to is easier—not as a result of a comparison, just a natural aversion to change. There's a great deal of subjectivity involved until we look at usability studies that, for example, count how many clicks of the mouse or key strokes it takes to accomplish common tasks, differences that add up. Some studies have shown Macs to accomplish tasks with fewer clicks or key strokes than the same task in Windows.[16] Others indicate more convincingly that users of Macs make fewer calls to help desks, have their problems solved more quickly than Windows users, and that new computer users are less confused when using Macs than when using PCs.

CALL is seeing greater involvement of faculty and staff in multimedia development for curricular projects. The programs used in multimedia development present some of the greatest demands on the processing ability of the hardware, on integration with the OS, and on a user's ability to understand an application's interface well enough to focus on the content of the project without being distracted or discouraged by technical challenges. In other words, we use applications on the computer to accomplish something *else,* the creation of some project or work. The measure of an OS's ability to help you do that is how much it stays out of your way. So ease of use in multimedia programs often determines not simply how readily a project is accomplished but whether it gets done at all. The Mac OS has long enjoyed an advantage in many areas of multimedia development, and for many reasons, but tight integration of its hardware and software and an obsession with the user's visual experience with the interface rank foremost. Nonetheless, few multimedia development tools are Mac-only anymore, reflecting the wider market for PC software.

4. *Cost.* Because of greater competition in the PC world, PCs, as well as their components, often carry a lower price tag than the same for Macs—a factor that has contributed to the Mac's lower market share in the past. PCs would be even cheaper were it not for the virtual monopoly Microsoft enjoys in the OS market, allowing it to set higher licensing fees for Windows preinstalled on PCs than it could in a more competitive market, a situation that has spurred interest in OS alternatives, such as Linux, which brings the cost of a PC down considerably from one with Windows installed.

At times in its history, a Mac was up to two or more times more expensive than a comparable PC. Macs didn't start to compete on price with PCs until Apple's brief flirtation in the mid-1990s with granting cloning licenses for other companies to build computers that ran the Mac OS (such as Motorola, Power Computing,

---

[16]*Macworld* and other magazines for the Macintosh community have conducted and published such practical studies.

and Umax). While this venture proved a failure for Apple financially, it was soon followed by their single most successful product, the iMac—in fact, the single most successful computer model in history. The iMac brought a powerful, compact, visually stunning computer to market at a price that could meet or beat a PC with comparable options. For these reasons, it also represented a dream machine for labs that buy computers by the dozen.

While initial hardware costs are easy to compare, they don't represent the true cost of operating the equipment over its lifetime, a calculation known as the "total cost of ownership" (TCO). TCO takes into account "all costs associated with using and maintaining networked computers,"[17] such as hardware, software, training, technical support, repair, and maintenance—factors actually amounting to more than the purchase price of the equipment. A lab's investment in computers, then, isn't finished after the boxes of computers arrive. The value of a computer is realized only in its use for productive purposes. A computer taken out of service for hardware failure or software glitches offers no value until it is repaired. The true cost of such downtime includes the repair and loss of productivity.

Studies by industry analysts, such as IDG and the Gartner Group, have shown that Macs require lower technical expertise and qualifications to set up and run, require significantly less maintenance, are brought back online faster after repair, remain in service longer, and enjoy a higher resale value. Thus, while Macs may have a higher initial cost (and not in all cases), their TCO is significantly lower.[18] When multiplied by dozens of machines in a lab, these savings become substantial.

5. *Setup and support.*[19] A critical factor in the choice of technology involves understanding the challenges of setting up and supporting various systems. Designing, installing, configuring, and supporting a networked computer lab is not for the technically faint of heart. Whatever is installed must be supported, which means that if you do not have access to dedicated technical support staff, then you cannot install a system requiring their support. And every computer, even the one at home, needs support. A language lab at a well-funded school may have the

---

[17](July 2001). *Taking TCO to the classroom: A school administrator's guide to planning for the total cost of new technology.* Consortium for School Networking white paper.

[18]Gartner studies include a 2002 report for Apple on TCO of Macs and PCs at Melbourne University, Australia. IDC studies include a 1997 white paper that found that TCO in education differs substantially for education than for business, where education TCO is about half of what business pays per unit. The ease of use of Macs in education was found to increase the effectiveness of technical support, lead to greater user satisfaction, and result in greater numbers of applications used than in a PC environment.

[19]Shawn Provençal, the systems administrator in the Geddes Language Center at Boston University, provided valuable feedback in this chapter, particularly his views on the control available in maintaining PCs over Macs on a network, of less-than-stellar technical support offered by Apple, and of using Windows 200x servers instead of Mac servers in a mixed-client environment, especially when integrated into a larger, Windows-dominated institutional environment. Mac OS X server, however, has greatly enhanced multiplatform, multi-protocol support.

technical resources to draw on to solve complicated problems, and they may be able to afford *in-house* support—someone who works on-site for the department or program. Without in-house support, systems need to be more reliable, less complicated, and require less support. Teachers in some environments may not have centralized technical resources available. An objective, informed determination of the level of support required should precede any investment in a system. After all, should teachers spend their time dabbling in troubleshooting or teaching their subject?

Matching a system with available support, then, may be the single most significant determinant of platform, which is why many educational settings, especially grade and secondary schools, chose Macs in the past.[20] Many industry reports have found that Macs are easier to set up and maintain over a network, have greater network compatibility for a cross-platform environment built-in, suffer from less down time per unit, and require less technical sophistication to fix.[21] For the same reasons, some small businesses equip their offices with Macs. More often than not, they cannot afford a large or full-time technical support staff, must set up and maintain their own systems, have far less ability to carry on business with computers down, and give little computer training to employees.[22]

6. *History.* If a program has used one platform exclusively, then a change should only be undertaken with careful consideration of all the factors by knowledgeable people. Changing platform (swapping the Macs for PCs, or vice-versa) involves technical staff being up for the challenge of new equipment and systems, retraining users, replacing or converting materials, licensing new software, and making provisions to accommodate differences that remain. In most programs of more than a few teachers, some will likely be PC users and some Mac users, either in the office or at home. Few are likely to change what they use at home to suit choices made for them at work. Accommodating faculty, staff, and students who use computers at home different from what's supported at school presents few real problems and is, moreover, an obligation in the responsible management of computer support in education. Education presents a special case for a mixed-platform environment.

---

[20] A *Consumer Reports* survey ("Desktop computers: Readers report," June, 2003) found that Apple computers had the lowest rate of required repairs to original hardware components, significantly lower than Dell, Hewlett-Packard, IBM, Compaq, Gateway, and Micron—all PC manufacturers. Apple also outperformed all reported PC manufacturers in customer satisfaction with its technical support.

[21] Again, considering the integration of computers into an existing network structure, especially the institution's network beyond the lab's LAN, brings factors into consideration that go beyond this book, are changed by upgrades in operating systems, and require a case-specific analysis. Some lab managers may well argue at this time that sending "disk images" out to workstations, for example, is easier and more reliable with PCs because of the availability of a greater variety of competing network management utilities for Windows than for the Mac. On the other hand, Macs generally experience fewer problems requiring such drastic reformatting.

[22] Aron, L. J. (2002, December 17). Should you switch to a Mac? *Fortune Small Business,* p. 385.

Teachers are freelancers who pick their tools. Dictating computer choice to them is as odious as it is unnecessary and rejecting their choice of tools and techniques may not only prove unproductive and costly but also runs counter to respect for academic freedom.

We can extend the issue of one's history with computers to their prevalence in a field. Apart from the argument of how easily PCs and Macs can coexist, they each have tended to prevail in certain fields. Macs have long enjoyed a strong presence in creative fields, such as design, music, filmmaking, publishing, multimedia production, as well as in education, especially grade and secondary, but also in post-secondary schools of education, communication, fine arts, and language teaching. Less well known is the prevalence of Macs among U.S. lawyers and in certain hard sciences.[23] The success of the UNIX-based Mac OS X attracts converts from other sciences as they realize they can use the UNIX programs they've relied on for decades but now on a Mac sporting the most elegant and intuitive interface ever for that most stable and powerful of computing platforms.

PCs running Windows dominate corporate environments, and corporate IT decision-makers have little choice in the matter. They also attract computer enthusiasts interested in building their own systems and have a presence in all of the fields previously populated mainly by Macs.

7. *Servers.* Before Mac OS X, this category wasn't necessary for a serious discussion on platform because Apple's servers, though easy to set up and run, suffered from slow, unstable performance and a near-pariah status in the industry (though far more secure against viruses or hacking than Windows). Unlike personal computers, none of a server's features, including ease of use, matter as much as power and stability. Apple servers offered neither by comparison and were shunned, except for low-demand, uncomplicated environments where ease of setup was deemed more important than power or stability. But for these small and low-demand networks, Macs offered very easy file sharing among other Macs without the need of a dedicated server, network hardware, or much technical experience.

Many language labs or other network environments that used PC and Mac clients (see **TECHNOTE: Client-Server** on page 216) have used Windows servers, with a smaller number using Linux or UNIX. Apple's OS X server changed this situation. OS X server software, running on familiar Macs, offers the ease-of-use Macintosh experience and thoughtful interface design on top of the most powerful, stable, and mature operating system, UNIX. OS X server is also compatible with the widest variety of networking protocols and client operating systems but does not suffer from the notorious security bugs of Windows servers. OS X servers represent not just a better choice now for Mac-based labs but counter to some extent the argument for using Windows clients based on the desirability of using

---

[23] Apple Myths, *www.apple.com/myths*

| TECHNOTE | ■ **Client-Server** |

On a network, some computers act as **servers** to serve requests for files or permissions from other computers, known as **clients**. The client-server arrangement can be *local,* such as in a lab or department where the group of servers and clients form a **local area network** (LAN), or it can span multiple networks or even the Internet.

Common computer lab servers

authentication server: manages user logins, passwords, and access to applications and files

document server: stores folders for users to save their work

file server: a central storage location for files, with much greater storage capacity than a client computer

database server: hosts databases and controls access to them

web (also HTTP) server: hosts HTML and related files on the Internet accessible with a web browser application

e-mail server: maintains e-mail accounts and stores mail for users

backup server: provides a network storage location for backing up files from client computers or other servers

software archive: a repository for all software purchased by a lab so that installations of applications can be made over a network instead of with CDs or DVDs one client at a time

Windows servers. Whether OS X servers offer the full complement of required services to Windows clients would need to be evaluated on a case-by-case basis by a knowledgeable network administrator.

8. *Networking.* A network connects computers and users and enables the exchange and transfer of files. The challenge of networking comes with setting up and maintaining servers and clients to communicate. Servers can be set up for many purposes (see **TECHNOTE: Client-Server**). The more of these capabilities that exist in-house, the more highly trained the technical staff need to be to manage them and the greater their numbers and salaries. Systems that are set up and maintained with greater ease by less technically oriented staff may prove to be cheaper to maintain overall and contribute more toward productivity. While Windows and UNIX offered more powerful server options for many years, Linux and Mac OS X now match that power, with equal stability and, in the case of Mac OS X, lower technical skill requirements of administrators.

The Internet has facilitated certain communications and interoperability that formerly fell on the shoulders of LAN management software. For example, most files can be easily moved between Macs and PCs as e-mail attachments, on PC-formatted USB flash drives or CDs or DVDs. This easy movement of files between computers, however, opens them up to the devastating effects of computer viruses. Macs face a substantially lower vulnerability to viruses than do PCs for a variety of reasons, not least because there are far more programmers, including hackers, for Windows. While antivirus programs can counter this threat, they can only do so with a vigilant maintenance routine where programs are installed and properly configured and run on all computers on the network to scan all disks and downloaded files, and updated regularly or automatically with current virus profiles (called *definitions*).

Why Alternatives to Windows?

Just as choice among hardware vendors in the PC world brought their prices down below Apple hardware prices, so too would real choice (especially for traditional PC environments like large corporations) in the OS market among competitors drive innovation, compatibility, stability, and security up and prices down. In other words, the best thing for the Windows world is competition that people feel free to choose, be it Linux, Apple, or something else.

Apple has always impressed users with its innovation and design, setting technological and design trends in the industry far out of proportion to its market share. Macs brought many innovations to the market, including the first personal computers with color, sound, a mouse, a graphical user interface, a universal user interface across all applications, text-to-speech and speech recognition, plug-and-play hardware expansion, built-in networking, a 3½" floppy drive, a built-in CD-ROM drive, multiple monitor support, FireWire peripheral ports, easy and affordable wireless networking, color and design in cases, illuminated keyboards on laptops, etc. Apple also brought the first personal digital assistant (PDA) to market, the Newton®—long before the market was ready for it—and the iPod made MP3 personal music players wildly popular. The Mac OS was Y2K compliant from the start.

Who Should Decide?

The decision on platform must be informed by facts, not whim, and made by the people who will use and support the computers, rather than micromanaged by administrators above. There are consequences with any choice, and decision-makers need to enter into the process enlightened and open minded. After all, can you say that you exercise choice when you are not fully aware of alternatives?

A Note on Perspective

My computing experience began with typing history papers in FORTRAN (a programming language for science) on a Telex terminal, then moved into personal computing with MS-DOS and Apple II, then Macintosh and Windows. For the multimedia, print, and web development work I do, my Mac rules. But I've also always had a PC at home (and not just to run Microsoft Flight Simulator). I'm as curious about the capabilities of and differences between Macs and PCs as I am about differences among languages and cultures. A more diverse environment—of computers and cultures—makes for a richer experience.

This book was written in Microsoft Word on a Mac (first OS 9 then OS X) by day and Microsoft Word on a PC (Windows XP) by night. Screen shots were taken of application windows and edited in Adobe Photoshop on whatever computer I was writing at the moment, Mac or PC. All files were transferred via a 128MB USB flash drive plugged into the extra USB port on my Mac's keyboard or the USB port on the front of my PC's case. Working with both computers, there were no formatting issues, no software to install, no file incompatibilities, no problems.

Keyboard Shortcuts

For many users, the mouse has taken over all input functions except for entering letters or numbers. It's often faster, however, to execute the same commands with a "keyboard shortcut," pressing a combination of keys instead of searching through menus with the mouse. PCs and Macs share most of the same keyboard shortcuts for common application commands. Press the Control (**Ctrl**) key on the PC or the **Apple** key on the Mac along with the letter keys for shortcuts (see Table 10.2). Furthermore, many of the command options accessed on the PC with a right button click of the mouse are available on a single-button Mac mouse with **Ctrl**-click or clicking and holding the mouse button down a few seconds. Though Macs don't ship with a two-button mouse with a scroll wheel, you can plug a USB model into a Mac and get full function out of both buttons and the scroll wheel (for vertically scrolling of documents or pop-up menus), leaving few functional differences between using a Mac and PC.

Table 10.2 ■ Common Keyboard Shortcuts Using **Ctrl** (PC) or **Apple** (Mac) Key

O	open document	P	print	V	paste
N	new document	A	select all	Y	repeat last action
S	save	X	cut	Z	undo last action
F	find	C	copy		

PART 4

Appendices

A Glossary of Terms

Italicized words in definitions are also glossed items.

address: see URL.

AIFF (audio interchange file format): common uncompressed audio format.

analog: an information storage system consisting of a continuous signal and using magnetic tapes, such as for audio (e.g., cassette) or video (e.g., VHS).

anti-aliasing: a process of smoothing the appearance of text onscreen by blurring character edges into the background, filling the *pixel* steps between contrasting colors with intermediate shades.

ASCII (American Standard Code for Information Interchange): also called *text only* or *plain text,* a common character set supported by all computers and text editors, representing 128 English letters, numbers, and symbols.

aspect ratio: the proportions of an image expressed as a ratio of width to height. The aspect ratio of most computer monitors is 4:3 (e.g., 1024×768).

asynchronous: communication with a delay between sending a message and responding to it, such as e-mail mailing lists (*listservs*).

attachment: a separate computer file, such as an image or word processing document, attached to an e-mail message.

authenticate: to demonstrate that you're authorized to access information or services through a *login*.

BCC (blind carbon copy): similar to *CC* except that all addresses on this line are hidden from recipients.

binary: a system where only two units are used to represent on and off (or charged vs. uncharged in electrical terms) represented by 0 and 1 in digital information.

bit (*bi*nary digi*t*, usually represented by a lowercase *b*): the base unit in computing, a value of 0 or 1 (representing on or off). Bits combine for more meaningful code: Most characters are represented by 8 consecutive bits. Basic digital measurements: 8 bits = 1B (byte); 1024 bytes = 1 kB (kilobyte); 1024 kB = 1 MB (megabyte); 1024 MB = 1 GB (gigabyte); 1024 GB = 1 TB (terabyte). Transfer rates are expressed in *bits* (10Mb/s *Ethernet*), disk capacity in *bytes* (80GB hard drive).

bookmark: to save the web address, or *URL*, of a particular web page using the *web browser*'s "Bookmarks" or "Favorites" options.

boot: to start a computer up.

browse: to locate a local file by searching through folders or following links on web pages to locate information (also, *surf*).

buffering: the pre-loading of a percentage of streaming media into memory so that when the clip begins playing, it can play continuously through short network interruptions.

byte: see *bit*.

CC (carbon copy): an additional, not primary, recipient of an e-mail message.

CD-ROM (compact disk-read-only memory): optical media that holds about 700MB of audio, video, or data files. CD-R (record) is a CD that can be written to, or *burned*,

but only once; CD-RW (re-writeable) can be recorded over and over.

CGI (common gateway interface): a program that runs on a web server and allows users to interact, such as processing input from web forms and sending the data to an administrator.

chat: synchronous, spontaneous communication between two or more people using a text, audio, or audio/video forum.

client: in a client-server network arrangement, a computer served by or connected to a *server*; software run on a client vs. a server, such as an *FTP* client.

clock speed: the processing power of a *CPU* measured in instructions per second, *MHz* (megahertz) or *GHz* (gigahertz).

codec (*compression/dec*ompression): the scheme used to compress files to make them smaller for storage and playing over a network *(MP3, MPEG)*.

context-sensitive: the availability of relevant help file information, commands, and toolbars based on a user's specific location or operation in a program.

courseware: a web server–based software package for education that enables teachers to post course materials, calendars, quizzes, etc., and set up communication forums among students.

CPU (central processing unit): also *processor* or *chip*, the microprocessor that provides the processing power for a computer (Pentium, PowerPC).

CRT (cathode-ray tube): a tube-based display technology used in conventional computer monitors and TVs. A moving electron beam illuminates active portions of the screen, drawing lines from top to bottom.

CSS (cascading style sheet): custom style definitions that can be applied across an entire website to automatically set the appearance for text on every page.

default: an automatic setting software assumes until you change it, such as the default font in a word processor.

Desktop (PC) or *Finder* (Mac): the view onscreen before any applications are launched. Files saved to the Desktop are actually saved to the computer's hard drive and organized under the user documents folders.

dialog box: a box that appears when certain commands are invoked, such as **File > Save As...**, asking for further user input, such as the name and location of a file to be saved.

digital: an information storage system consisting solely of discrete units, 0s and 1s (*binary* information) in its base form and residing on magnetic media (hard drives) or optical media (CD or DVD disks).

digitize: to convert from analog form to a computer-readable format, such as scanning a picture from a book and converting it to an image file (JPEG, GIF, TIFF).

domain: a unique name that identifies a website. For example, in the address *www.apple.com, apple* is the domain and *.com* is the top-level domain (TLD) or domain category.

download: to get a copy of a computer file from another computer, such as a server, usually via a web page or FTP client.

dpi (dots per inch): number of *pixels* in a horizontal inch.

DV (digital video): the format of video shot with a digital video camera or edited on a computer.

DVD (digital versatile, or video, disk): optical media of higher capacity than CD, about 4.7GB. Some versions are recordable (DVD-R, DVD+R) and some can be recorded multiple times (DVD-RW, DVD+RW).

encode: to compress an audio or video file to make smaller using a particular *codec.*

Ethernet: a fast local area network (LAN) connection from one computer to others or to the Internet. Data transfer rates, measured in megabits/second (Mb/s) range from 10Mb/s to 100Mb/s (Fast Ethernet) to 1,000Mb/s (Gigabit Ethernet).

expansion slot: an open internal connection *(bus)* for expanding the capabilities of a computer, such as memory *(RAM).* The *PCI* slot, found on many desktop computers, can be used to add a network card, more powerful graphics card, or external connection port, such as FireWire or USB.

file extension: the three- or four-character suffix applied to computer file names after the period (e.g., *.doc* identifies a Microsoft Word document).

Finder: See *desktop.*

FireWire: also known as IEEE 1394, a high-speed external port for connecting external drives, DV cameras, and other equipment.

flame: to post a scathing message to a *listserv,* particularly with inflammatory accusations about another list member.

flash drive: key-size portable storage device that connects to a computer's USB port.

font: often used interchangeably with *typeface,* which describes the design of characters in a set, such as Arial; *font* is actually the final appearance of characters in a given typeface at a specific size when attributes like bold and italic are added.

freeware: copyrighted software made available on the Internet free of charge by its developer.

FTP (file transfer protocol): a two-way file transfer—uploading to and downloading from a server—requiring a login. Some HTML editors have FTP capabilities built-in.

GB (gigabyte): see *bit.*

GHz (gigahertz): 1,000MHz. (See *MHz.*)

GIF (graphics interchange format): a web image format that supports limited colors, one a transparent color, used for drawings and line art.

GUI (graphical user interface): an easy-to-use icon-based computer interface navigated with a mouse (Windows) instead of a text-only command line interface using keyboard input only (DOS).

hard return: pressing the **enter/return** key at the end of a line of text, such as at the end of a paragraph, instead of letting the text wrap automatically to the next line.

hardware: physical equipment, such as a computer (or *cpu*), keyboard, monitor, disk drive, printer, etc.

HTML (hypertext markup language): the plain text code of a web page defining how it displays in a *web browser.*

HTTP (hypertext transfer protocol): A *protocol* is a standard of communication. HTTP defines how files are transmitted from an HTTP (web) server to a computer running a *web browser.* HTTPS refers to a secure web server using encrypted transmission of data.

hyperlink (also, **link**): a non-linear connection from one object to another in an electronic document, *software,* or on the Internet. Internal links use *relative paths* (folder/filename); external links use *absolute paths* (complete *URL*).

IM (instant messaging): a *synchronous* private chat of two or more people using an IM application, such as AOL Instant Messenger (AIM), Yahoo! Instant Messenger, MSN Messenger, or iChat (Mac).

ISP (Internet service provider): provides users with access to the Internet; usually a telephone or cable company, school or employer.

JPEG (Joint Photographic Experts Group): efficient web image format that supports true color, has variable compression levels, and is used mostly for photos.

kb (kilobyte): see *bit.*

keyboarding: use of the computer keyboard (letters, numbers, other characters and function keys) as well as the mouse.

keypal: a penpal via e-mail.

keyword: a central term used to represent a topic in a search, such as with a *search engine.*

KWIC (key word in context): a common option for displaying search results for text databases where the *keywords* appear in excerpts from the text.

LCD (liquid crystal display): a display technology used in laptops and flat screen monitors. Each picture element, or *pixel,* is continuously illuminated with only the color value of each *pixel* changing.

listserv: an automatic mailing list service for a particular interest group. Messages are read and posted to members through regular e-mail. A message to the listserv gets broadcast to the entire member community.

local: referring to the computer you're using (such as the hard drive) or office or department network (local area network, or LAN).

location: see *URL.*

log on: to provide a user (login) name and password in order to gain access to a computer network, information, or functionality.

MB (megabyte): see *bit.*

menu: a horizontal bar at the very top of most applications with categories of commands (**File, Edit, View, Help**) that appear when one category is clicked.

modem: a device enabling an Internet connection with a regular *(analog)* phone line, which converts outgoing digital computer data to analog waves to travel over a connection and convert incoming wave information to digital.

mouseover: to pass the mouse pointer over an object, such as a *hyperlink* or toolbar button, to reveal a description or action that would occur by clicking.

MP3: audio layer 3 from *MPEG* video, a high-quality compressed audio format for music and voice. To reduce file size, this *codec* eliminates redundant and irrelevant parts of a sound signal that the human ear can't perceive.

MPEG (Moving Picture Experts Group): a high-quality *codec* for digital video that compresses video efficiently by only storing changes from one frame to another rather than all the information in each frame.

multimedia: some combination of media types—text, audio, video, graphics—in a presentation or program.

NIC (network interface card): an Ethernet or WiFi card installed in a computer to allow it to access a LAN or the Internet.

open source: software whose source code is publicly available for free so programmers can collaborate on improving and sharing it with users at no charge.

OS (operating system): the base system on which a computer operates. Applications, such as a word processor, run within this environment. (See *platform*.)

parameters: settings or limitations, such as in a search.

path: the location of a file on your computer or a server expressed with folder and file names. (See *hyperlink*.)

PC: Personal Computer, as opposed to a mainframe computer, but sometimes specifically referring to personal computers that run the Microsoft Windows *OS* as opposed to the Apple Macintosh *OS*.

PCI (peripheral component interconnect): an internal *expansion slot* connection *(bus)*.

PDF (portable document format): similar to a word processing document in that it can contain text and graphics, except that the PDF format embeds all information needed (such as fonts and images) so that it appears exactly the same on any computer (as displayed with Adobe Acrobat Reader and other applications).

peripheral: equipment, such as a scanner, printer, or drive, that is not built into the main case of a computer but connects to it via a port, such as *USB* or *FireWire*.

pixel (*pic*ture *ele*ment): a single illuminated dot on a monitor.

platform: the operating system *(OS)* a computer runs on, such as Microsoft Windows, Apple Macintosh, Linux.

plug-in: a helper application that works within another application, such as a browser plug-in (QuickTime Player, Flash Player, Acrobat Reader) that enables a web browser to present various types of media.

PNG (portable network graphic): a web image format that combines features of *GIF* (transparency) and *JPEG* (support for true color).

pop-up menu: a list of choices that appear in a small box when the mouse is passed over or clicked on certain objects. For example, right-clicking on an image on a web page brings up a pop-up menu of options to save or copy the image or location.

port: an external connection point on a computer to attach peripherals, such as *USB* or *FireWire,* or make other connections, such as to a network or phone line.

portal: a website that offers a wide array of resources, such as news, information, and a search engine, sometimes for a particular audience.

RAM (random access memory): fast, short-term memory used by a computer to process commands, run applications, and work on documents. Something held in RAM, such as a document not yet saved to a local drive, is lost when the computer shuts down.

random access: the ability to instantly locate information without following a linear or sequential *path* to it.

reboot: to restart a computer already running.

refresh rate: in a *CRT*, the frequency of the display being redrawn as measured in hertz (Hz). A common refresh rate for computer monitors is 75Hz, or 75 screen redraws per second.

right-click: using the right-side button on a two- or three-button mouse (or **Ctrl**-click on Macs) to access properties and context-sensitive commands.

robot: a computer software program that performs a task automatically, such as a robot to subscribe new members to a *listserv*.

RTF (rich text format): a text document format readable by most word processors, one that retains formatting, such as character, line spacing, and alignment.

sample: to take snapshots of a continuous analog signal in order to convert it into discrete digital values. The rate is measured in samples per second, or hertz (Hz).

sans serif: see *serif*.

scale: to change the size of an image while maintaining its proportions, or *aspect ratio*.

search engine: usually a web-based utility (Google, Yahoo) to locate web pages or other resources using *keywords* to return a list of matches.

search string: *keyword* phrase used in a search.

serif: non-ornamental typefaces are broadly divided into *serif* and *sans* (without) *serif* types. The strokes of a *serif* typeface have ornamental feet at the ends; *san serif* type-faces have plain members without orna-ment. Times New Roman is *serif* and Arial is *sans serif*.

server: a computer that serves files or services (web server, file server, e-mail server) to connected computers, or *clients*.

shareware: inexpensive software download-able from the Internet directly from the developers. The try-before-you-buy distrib-ution relies on the honor system.

site: a website comprises many related and linked web pages (HTML documents) and other files.

software: data stored electronically, such as an operating system or program.

spam: unsolicited junk e-mail, usually trying to sell something, often illegitimate.

streaming media: a method of playing audio or video efficiently over the Internet with-out downloading, or copying, the file to the user's computer (commonly employed by online media outlets).

suite: a package of related programs from the same company that work together to some degree (Microsoft Office).

synchronous: communication happening at the same time (real time) by senders and receivers, such as on the telephone or in an instant messenger *(IM)* chat.

tag: in HTML source code, a command describing how a part of the page should be displayed. The <TITLE> tag holds the page title, displayed on the top frame of the web browser.

TCP/IP (transfer control protocol/Internet protocol): the communications protocol for transmitting data over the Internet and most networks.

template (also *stationary*): a document, usually locked or read-only, that serves as the basis for other documents by opening as an untitled copy of the original.

thread: e-mail messages or bulletin board postings and replies grouped by topic.

TIFF (tagged image file format): a high-quality, uncompressed bitmap image format for printing.

toolbar: usually a row of buttons, with graphical icons identifying their functions, located at the top of an application window below the *menu,* representing common commands, such as Save and Print. A floating toolbar can be moved around the screen to rearrange the workspace.

upload: to send a copy of a computer file to another or remote computer, such as a server, usually via an *FTP* client or web page.

URL (uniform resource locator): the exact address or location of a web page, usually beginning with "http://."

USB (universal serial bus): a high-speed external *port* for connecting a keyboard and mouse as well as storage devices (such as a *flash* drive), digital cameras, and other equipment.

utility: a type of software, usually small, that serves a specific function in maintaining the computer, such as a disk utility that repairs hard drive errors.

volume: digital storage media, such as a hard drive. A disk drive can be partitioned into multiple volumes.

VPN (virtual private network): software that establishes an encrypted (secure) connection, often to a *WiFi* (wireless) network, and *authenticates* users (makes sure they belong to the organization and are authorized to be on the network).

WAV (*wav*eform audio format): common audio format for Windows *PCs*.

waveform editor: an audio editor that displays the sound signal graphically to make it easier to locate points to edit.

web browser: an application, such as Internet Explorer or Safari, used to view pages (HTML documents) on the World Wide Web and supported graphics (JPEG, GIF, PNG) and access other supported media.

web host: the company or service that maintains website files on its web server and makes them available on the Internet.

WiFi (wireless fidelity): a network connection using radio waves to transmit data instead of a wire.

window: a rectangular container onscreen that a *GUI* program runs in and typically includes its toolbar buttons. Windows and Macintosh can run several different programs at the same time, each in its own window.

wizard: a utility found in some programs to assist the user in completing a task through offering a limited set of choices in step-by-step procedures.

WYSIWYG (what you see is what you get): in an *HTML* editor, the graphical creation of web pages without resort to writing code. Pages look in the editor as they will appear in the *web browser*.

B File Saving and Sharing Options

Table B.1 shows common file-saving locations, including "removable media" (disks or drives that can easily move from one computer to another, e.g., *CD, USB flash drive*) and indicates common means of sharing documents, such as a text or audio file that a teacher creates and wants students to be able to access in class. The three-letter *file extensions* (e.g., .doc for a Microsoft Word document) represent examples of common file types within each category.

TABLE B.1 ■ File Saving and Sharing Options

Where saved/ how shared	Media capacity (1000bytes=1kB, 1000kB=1MB, 1000MB=1GB)	Practical for file types (with example file extensions) — small files (typ.)				large files (typ.)				Comments
		text (doc, xls, html)	slide show (ppt, pps)/ or PDF (pdf)	web graphics (jpg, gif, png)	print graphics (tiff, eps, pict, bmp)	audio (aiff, wav)	audio compressed (mp3, ra, wma)	video (dv)	video compressed (mpg, mov, wmv, rm)	
										File types matched to media that can hold them and are also the most practical for sharing information with a class. For example, though a text, slide show, or PDF file would fit on a CD, that media is impractical for regularly distributing such files to a class.
local hard drive	5–100GB+ avg.					X	X	X	X	Hard drive or "local" drive of student computer in lab; uncompressed audio or video files are too large to play over most networks.
network folder	1–50MB avg.	X	X	X	X		X		X	In a networked lab with a local file server, students access all but the largest files from individual or class folders.
courseware website	1–20MB avg.	X	X	X			X		X	Most efficient for small file distribution to students and among class, especially outside of class (distance learning).
e-mail attachment	0–5MB avg.	X	X	X			X		X	Fast and convenient for small files; some e-mail accounts have small space quotas.
removable media										
CD-R DVD-R	700MB 4.7GB					X	X	X DVD	X	These disks can only be written to once in a "session" (not a file at a time incrementally like other media). They require special disk "burning" software and can not be erased or rewritten.
CD-RW DVD-RW DVD-RAM	700MB 4.7GB 9.4GB					X	X	X DVD	X	While burning these disks is awkward, as above, they can be erased completely and reused for subsequent session burnings (about 100 times). Not all DVD disk types are compatible with each other.
USB flash drive	32MB–1GB	X	X	X	X	X	X		X	These key-size devices plug into any computer's USB port and appear as any other drive; compatible way to transport most files.
Zip disk	100–750MB	X	X	X	X	X	X		X	The Zip and other high-capacity magnetic disks need a compatible drive in each computer where used and are expensive, bulky, and supported less and less.
floppy disk	1.4MB	X	X	X						Too small and slow to be of wide use; phased out on many computers.

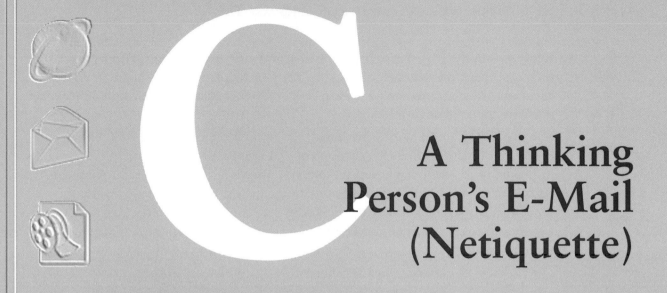

C

A Thinking Person's E-Mail (Netiquette)

These rules help keep communication via e-mail painless and efficient through common sense and courtesy. As with most rules, exceptions arise that justify breaking them.

1. **Use salutations and closings.** Include the name of the person you're writing to and your name to close. Except in informal correspondence, such as frequently e-mailing close friends, a simple salutation and closing personalize the message and suggest that a human wrote it.

2. **Reread and spell-check.** E-mail takes a certain informal tone, but that doesn't mean it should be hard to read, full of mistakes, or otherwise show evidence of carelessness. Unless writing to a close friend or regular correspondent, reread and spell-check your message before sending it.

3. **Watch your tone.** E-mail, by its nature, can seem terse. Your words stand on their own; they are not softened by a wink or a nod, and you can't adjust your message midway based on feedback you get from the recipient.

4. **When in doubt, be formal.** Though e-mail seems informal, not all of your communication with it actually is. Responding to a potential employer, for example, warrants formality. Using *emoticons* (symbols in place of words, such as [:-)], which appears as a smiling face if viewed sideways) or e-mail shorthand (e.g., BTW for "by the way") isn't a part of formal writing.

5. **Reply promptly.** If you expect people to send you e-mail and respond to yours, then read your messages regularly (i.e., daily or thereabouts). When you go on vacation, use an automated vacation reply. Whether justified or not, people expect swift responses from e-mail.

6. **Use the BCC line.** In addressing a message to multiple recipients, *BCC* (blind carbon copy) functions like *CC* (carbon copy), except that each recipient sees only his or her name in the TO (addressee) line, not anyone else's, whereas all recipients' addresses on the CC line are visible to *all* recipients. In fact, when you use the BCC line, the recipient doesn't even know that you sent this particular message to anyone other than him or her. Use BCC instead of CC for multiple recipients for three reasons:

   • It keeps the message header shorter.
   • Some recipients might not want others to see their e-mail address.
   • A recipient who intends to respond only to you could inadvertently respond to all other recipients on the CC line (by using Reply All) and reveal personal information or bother others with an irrelevant message.

   Nonetheless, the CC line lets all recipients know who has been notified of a certain message. Keep it short (half dozen or so recipients).

7. **Double-check your recipients.** You can't get a message back once it's sent, so be sure you've said what you want to say to the person you want to say it to. Many e-mail programs have an auto-complete feature when typing names from the address book in the recipient line. Check to make sure that the address matches the right person.

8. **Use a descriptive subject line.** Summarize your topic as succinctly as possible for the subject line, especially for posts to listservs. Be sure to change the subject line in responses after they get bounced back and forth a few times and have moved beyond the original topic.

9. **Don't use HTML mail.** Or at least don't set it as your default message format for all messages. *HTML* e-mail is essentially a web page. It's bigger than plain text messages, downloads more slowly, and has to be viewed with an HTML-capable e-mail application, such as Outlook Express®, OS X Mail, Mozilla Messenger, AOL, and web mail services (e.g., Yahoo Mail). People who access their mail with a text-only application, such as telnet, won't be able to read your HTML mail at all and will have to use another application (an *FTP* client) to get the file as an attachment. Spam often comes as HTML mail.

10. **Don't further quote quoted text.** When you forward or reply to a message, many e-mail programs put the original message text in quotes, placing a > character at the beginning of each line. They serve a useful function of indicating the original text, but each subsequent forward or reply will embed them (place a new set of quotes at the beginning of a line). After being passed around a few times, this text becomes painful to read—for those who trouble to read it. Instead, simply copy and paste the original single-quoted text into your message, and use only what you're specifically responding to, not necessarily the entire message.

11. **Use e-mail text rather than attachments.** When possible, paste text into an e-mail message rather than sending it as a separate *attachment*. Attached files may get corrupted in transit (by e-mail *servers*) or present other problems to the recipient, some of whom may deny all attachments as a virus protection measure or not have the application to open it. It's also faster and easier to download and access text in e-mail than in an attachment and, therefore, more likely that the recipient will read it. There are, however, many reasons to keep the text in the original format, such as a Word document if it is highly formatted, includes footnotes, or if you're using the Comment or Track Changes features, for example.

12. **Send images as is.** Many people send pictures inserted into Word or PowerPoint documents, requiring the recipient to have these applications. Your recipients will have fewer problems accessing your pictures if you simply attach the original *JPEG*, *PNG*, or *GIF* format images to your message, that is, without putting them inside another document.

13. **Keep paragraphs short.** Reading on-screen is harder on the eyes than reading print. The columns tend to be wider, further complicating the task of returning from the end of a line to the beginning of the next. Short paragraphs, such as in newspaper articles, are easier to follow visually. Keep the message as a whole short as well. The medium thrives on speed and brevity.

14. **There's more spam than sirloin.** Chances are, if you don't know the sender of an e-mail message, it's unsolicited junk mail, or *spam*. Don't waste time or put your computer at risk opening unknown message attachments. Use a spam filter on your e-mail application.

15. **You're responsible for your own well-being.** E-mail has been around since the last century, as have news reports about the destructive capability of viruses, which makes it perhaps fair to say that if you open every attachment sent to you, whether you know the sender or not, and you don't vigilantly maintain up-to-date virus protection on your computer, then you might find sympathy from others lacking when you're victimized by a destructive virus and suffer a loss of files or other computer damage.

16. **Don't forward virus warnings.** Forwarding virus warnings or outrageous stories (urban legends) you receive marks you as a cyber neophyte. The Internet is awash in unsubstantiated rumors. If you hear of a virus or e-mail hoax, confirm the facts first:

    Symantec Anti-Virus Center, *www.symantec.com/avcenter/hoax.html*

    The Department of Energy's Computer Incident Advisory Capability (CIAC) Hoax Pages, *hoaxbusters.ciac.org*

    Internet ScamBusters, *scambusters.org*

    Urban Legends Reference, *snopes.com*

17. **When in doubt, be skeptical.** Chances are that if you get mail announcing something you've never heard, be it a miracle cure for illness, a vacation prize, an investment opportunity, a class action suit, or some "shocking truth," it's a scam. Unfortunately, e-mail is the best thing for scam artists since Charles Ponzi. Furthermore, any phrase related to "a friend at the company checked it out and it's true!" appearing in the message should confirm it as a scam. A note to those skeptical of such skepticism: The second largest industry in Nigeria, after oil, is Internet scams, usually taking the form of a government official trying to get "legitimate funds" out of the country. If you're not looking for it, don't buy it and don't subject your friends and coworkers to a possible scam by forwarding it. More than putting them at risk for falling for the same scam, you risk looking gullible.

18. **Don't rehash jokes.** It's unlikely that the joke you get by e-mail that you want to forward to your friends and coworkers hasn't already been seen several times by 90 percent of them.

19. **Flaming never pays.** To "*flame*" someone is to send them a scathing e-mail, usually in response and often in a mailing list (listserv). You'll almost always regret it, and that missive will live on electronically at innumerable locations indefinitely, longer than you'll likely hold those feelings, especially postings to *listservs*. Use the "Save as Draft" function in your e-mail program. Write what you want, get it off your chest, and then sit on it for a day or so before mailing, if at all. Also, be careful about trashing someone in an e-mail to a third party. E-mail gets around far more than letters ever did, sometimes inadvertently.

D
Web Browser Basics[1]

Browser Window (see Figure D.1)

Location line (also, address or URL): Where the web page address appears or a new one can be typed (hit the **return/enter** key to load the new page). You don't need to type the *http://* part of the address. (See Figure D.2 for a breakdown of the parts of a *URL.*)

Status bar: A message line in the bottom frame of the browser *window,* it shows the progress of page items loading and can state whether the web *server* has been found or if a request has stalled. When you *mouseover* a link on the page, the address of that link appears here, showing you where you'll go whether it's an internal link (within the same site) or an external one.

Scroll bars: The vertical scroll bar on the right and horizontal scroll bar on the bottom of the browser window shifts the view to unseen portions of the current page. They do not appear if the entire page can be viewed in the given window size.

Linked text: Hypertext links used to be underlined and blue by convention, but more and more may be a different color and not underlined. Increasing use of cascading style sheets (*CSS*—a custom definition of styles on a site) creates more appealing functional options, such as changing text color when you mouseover or click on it.

---

[1] Some items depend on browser and version used.

Figure D.1 ▪ The Mozilla web browser window in Windows XP, with buttons and layout typical of most browsers. Browsers allow some features, such as *menus* and buttons, to be added or removed through the View menu or application preferences.

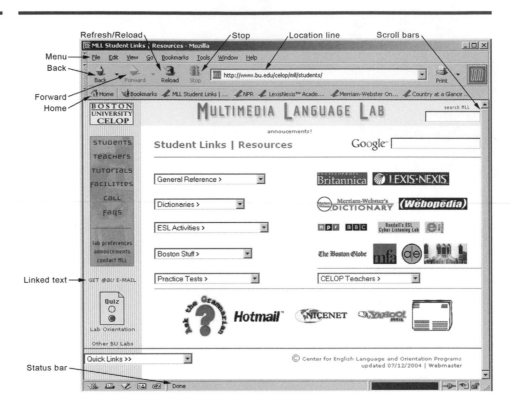

Figure D.2 ▪ Breakdown of a web address, or URL. Only part of the URL is case sensitive: all letters following the *domain* category, *edu* here.

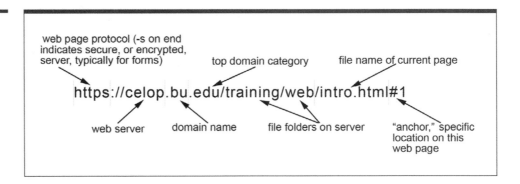

Common Toolbar Buttons

Back: Goes back to the previous web page viewed. A small arrow at the bottom corner of this button lists previously visited pages, with the most recent at the top.

Forward: Similar to the **Back** button, but it goes to the next page visited in a sequence of pages already visited and therefore is only available after you have used the **Back** button and want to move forward again.

Refresh/Reload: Forces the current page to load again from the web server, useful for stalled pages, to force database or form results to reappear, or to view recently updated pages. In some browsers, you must press the **Shift** key while clicking **Refresh** to force the browser to download the page anew from the web server instead of the browser's local cache (temporary storage of recently viewed items).

Home: The *default* page that displays when the browser launches, as set up by the user in the browser preferences. Often a custom home page (such as a lab page), **search engine,** or news site relevant to the computer's use.

Stop: Stops the current page from loading from the server, also stops animated *GIFs* from moving and some automatic background sounds from playing.

Find (under **Edit** menu if not on toolbar): Searches for word(s) in a **search string** on the current web page like a word search in a word processor. It's *not* an Internet search.

Common Menu Commands

File > New Window: You can have several browser windows open at once in separate windows or *tabs* of one window, sometimes helpful if you don't want to lose what's on the current page, such as a chat window, a form that has been partially filled out, or the results of a database search or form post.

Open > File or *Page:* Open a file located anywhere on your computer that your web browser can read (.html, .txt, .gif, .jpg, .png).

Save (as file or web page): Save a web page in its entirety, graphics and text ("source"), or save only the text ("text only") for archiving or viewing later *offline* (when not connected to the Internet).

Go: Reveals your browsing trail for most of the current session, similar to the session history list available with the **Back** button. Jump to any previously visited site by selecting it in this window, useful for going back to a site visited many pages ago without having to load all of the intervening pages.

Favorites or *Bookmarks:* Pages whose address you have your browser remember for a later visit. These lists can also be sent to others and imported into their menus.

Clear and Simple Web Authoring

These "rules" are meant as a starting point for creating durable web content for people new to web authoring. Some may apply to complex pages and designs, and some not. Like grammar rules, there may be good cause to break them at some point, to exercise poetic license, but only intentionally, by design, and for a reason, understanding the consequences and trade-offs. Procedures for *how* to carry out some of these suggestions can be found in the web authoring projects in Chapter 7.

Text

1. Use sans *serif* typefaces on-screen (e.g., Arial, Helvetica, Verdana), whose plain characters do not feature the ornamentation of serif fonts (e.g., Georgia, Times New Roman, Palatino), which offer greater readability in print but are blurred in the lower resolution of monitors. Use serif fonts for large-sized headings (size 4+), if desired.

2. Text in ALL CAPS is difficult to read, as is Text With Initial Capitals, where readers' eyes bump up and down while scanning across the line. Reserve these features for titles, headings, and links with few words.

3. Underlined text, never considered much of a looker in design circles, indicates linked text to many users, even if it's not, because browsers display linked text by default as underlined and blue.

4. Text pasted from a word processor into an *HTML* editor may include formatting or characters not supported by a ***web browser***. Check your pages thoroughly with a web browser using your HTML editor's **Preview in Browser** command.

5. Don't over-link text. Provide *relevant* links without giving visitors too many reasons to leave your page or distract them from reading. Have external links (ones outside of your site) open in a new browser window.

Images

6. Some people may connect to the Internet with modems or slow computers. The more images you use and the larger they are, the slower the page will load. Keep images small in file size by decreasing dimensions, reducing the number of images per page, or increasing image compression (using a lower-quality setting for *JPEGs* or fewer colors for *GIFs*).

7. Provide short, descriptive "alternative text" in the image properties box (see Figure E.1). This text appears before the image loads or if it doesn't load, also enabling screen reader programs of the visually impaired to read the page. Do not provide alternative text for transparent GIFs (spacer images used for layout).

8. Set the image border to 0 to avoid an unappealing blue box around the image (see Figure E.1).

Figure E.1 ■ The Image Properties box in Macromedia Dreamweaver. The alternative text (ALT) and border width (Border) are specified for the image.

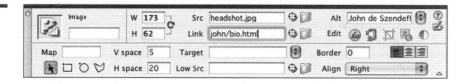

Layout

9. Sketch the layout of your page(s) by hand first. It's much easier to put a rough design or layout on paper with a pencil instead of with an HTML editor. When you have visualized a design first, the HTML editor becomes a tool to help realize that plan, rather than a cumbersome means of exploring design ideas.

10. Sketch a *site map* showing the organization of the pages within the site and how they're linked.

11. Sites constructed with frames may cause special problems. All browsers don't support them the same way, people have difficulty printing them (by printing the wrong frame unintentionally), and the specific page *URL* is hidden. A consistent navigation bar on every page of a ***template***-driven site accomplishes what most frames do.

12. Keep important information and navigation links "above the fold." Like the top part of a newspaper, the top of the web page will be seen when the lower parts are hidden, made available only by scrolling down.

13. For easier reading of large amounts of text, use narrow columns of about 50 characters (10 words). The longer the line of text, the more difficult it is for the eye to return to the left margin and locate the next line. Use the left side of the page for navigation links or graphics, and allow for buffer margins on all sides of text blocks (1/2" or more).

14. Consider putting large amounts of text on fewer pages or even one page rather than breaking it up into many pages. One page can be searched for a word or phrase and printed more easily.

15. Set page or table dimensions to accommodate a minimum monitor size and resolution (at this writing, typically 800 x 600 *pixels*). Pages wider than someone's screen resolution will require horizontal scrolling (going right with the scroll bar to read the whole page) in addition to vertical scrolling to go down. Vertical scrolling is expected, horizontal is not.

Design

16. Use high-contrast color schemes for text. Black type on a white background offers the greatest readability. Otherwise, use a dark text on a light background (e.g., maroon text on ocher background), and avoid jarring colors. Get opinions from others on your choices.

17. Consider how the readability of your text may change when it's an active link (medium blue) or a visited link (purple). Linked text changes to these default colors regardless of what color you've chosen for them. (Only the use of *CSS* on your pages reliably changes this default formatting to whatever you choose. A CSS page for your site defines the appearance of different kinds of text on all pages—headings, body text, links, etc.)

18. Focus on a layout that presents your information clearly without making *unnecessary* demands on the viewer to sort out a cluttered design, too much information in one view, or one with technical barriers (e.g., requiring a fast network connection, large monitor, specific operating system or browser, or browser plug-ins installed).

Functionality

19. Give each page a descriptive title in plain, concise language. The *page title* is not the same as the *file name*. The latter is only how the computer and HTML links refer to the page. Most *search engines* look for the text in the title (the <TITLE> tag in the <HEAD> of the HTML code) before anything else.

20. Always check your pages on other browsers, computer platforms, smaller monitors, and from a modem connection. The same web page may look different under different conditions.

Files

21. Keep files used for a website well organized and in as few subfolders as possible. They must be organized *locally* (on your hard drive) exactly as they will be *remotely* (on the web server). When you insert a graphic into a web page, you are establishing a *path* to where it's located. If the graphic is also in your website, then it's a *local path* relative to the referring page (the web pages it's inserted into). If the path refers to a location that changes when the files are uploaded, then the graphic will not appear on the page.

22. For easier site management, keep file names as short and descriptive as possible, and avoid uppercase letters. While URLs are not case-sensitive in the *domain* name (*www.bu.edu*), they are in the file path portion (*/celop/MLL/Students.html*).

23. File names cannot contain spaces or certain *illegal characters* (e.g., /\@!#%). Stick to letters, numbers, the dash (—), and underscore (_).

24. Each folder should have an "index" file, with the file name "index.html" or "default.html," depending on the web server software. Having such a file in each folder prevents a visitor from getting a directory listing of the files in that folder, routes them to the main page of that folder faster, and makes for shorter URLs, as most web server software will look for a file of that name by *default* if only a folder is specified. For example, the URL *http://celop.bu.edu/* will *resolve*, or redirect, to *http://celop.bu.edu/index.html* automatically, if such a file is present. Thus, you do not need to type that file name in references.

Internet References

An excellent, concise, well-known guide for web authors on the fundamentals of web design (especially for non-designers) is *Web Style Guide: Basic Design Principles for Creating Web Sites* by P. J. Lynch and S. Horton, 2nd ed, 2002 (New Haven: Yale). The contents of the book are also entirely online, *www.webstyleguide.com*

"Web Design for Instruction: Research-Based Guidelines," College of Education, University of Saskatchewan, *www.usask.ca/education/coursework/skaalid*

"Guidelines for Designing a Good Web Site for ESL Students" by Charles Kelly, Aichi Institute of Technology (Toyota, Japan), *iteslj.org/Articles/Kelly-Guidelines.html*

Site-Building Advice, Education World, *www.education-world.com*

Fair Use Guidelines for Educational Multimedia[1]

Language teachers have taken advantage of copyrighted material in all media—newspapers, magazines, books, songs, speeches, movies, TV programs—to provide native models of target language use as long as they've had the means to present or distribute it. And the Internet has added to these choices instant access to a tantalizing cornucopia of multimedia material to help educators illustrate and exemplify what they teach in interesting and relevant ways. At the same time, the Internet, combined with widely available technology that facilitates copying and manipulating multimedia material, has increased the potential to violate, inadvertently or otherwise, the copyright protections of the owners of this content. Simply having the *ability* to obtain the work of others, even works not explicitly copyrighted (such as some websites and unpublished work) or strictly for educational purposes, does not, by itself, confer a legal *right* to use it.

What Is "Fair Use" of Copyrighted Material?

What copyrighted content can educators use in authoring their own multimedia lessons or creating their own class websites? Federal copyright law, and specifically the fair use provision (17 U.S.C. §107), spells out legal reproduction and use of multimedia material for educational purposes. Other statutory provisions,

---

[1]David Bachman, in the reference department of the Pappas Law Library at Boston University, assisted me in finding resources for the Fair Use provision.

such as the Technology, Education, and Copyright Harmonization (TEACH) Act (2002), contain updated references concerning the Internet, particularly for distance education. These government documents can be obtained at many sites online. Many college libraries, furthermore, publish on their websites these legal texts as well as practical interpretations and examples to guide students and educators in their use of copyrighted materials in compliance with the law (see **Internet References** at the end of this appendix). Teachers are responsible for compliance and therefore need to take the initiative in determining what they can and cannot use without explicit permission. In some cases, teachers may need to seek the advice of the educational institution's copyright coordinator. A general reference librarian, law librarian, or your institution's office of academic computing may be a good place to start, or, for non-affiliated language programs, a reference librarian at a public library.

For the purposes of CALL, we're concerned not with simply viewing or listening to copyrighted material, be it a movie, song, web page, picture, etc., or even copying material for teaching in general, but rather with the copying, distribution, or integration *without explicit permission* of all or parts of the creative or intellectual work of others into curricular multimedia projects, including such projects by students. (The TEACH Act protects *displaying* or *playing* any copyrighted material in the classroom, in "face-to-face" teaching, without permission but imposes other liabilities on the institution for compliance.)[2] Examples could include using graphics found on the web (such as with a **Google > Images** search), a song, or scenes from a movie or TV program on a course website, a PowerPoint presentation, or a custom multimedia project. The Fair Use Guidelines for Educational Multimedia define the extent to which the rights of free speech and the public interest (i.e., education) precede copyright protections of the creator—how much copying teachers can legally get away with. Note that despite attempts to quantify amount of material and duration of use, fair use is still a subjective measure.[3]

Determining Fair Use Coverage

Four factors are used in determining what constitutes fair use of copyrighted work:[4]

(1) the purpose and character of use, including whether such use is of a commercial nature or is for nonprofit educational purposes,

(2) the nature of the copyrighted work,

(3) the amount and substantiality of the portion used in relation to the copyrighted work as a whole, and

---

[2] See the American Library Association for copyright discussions and summaries, *www.ala.org*.

[3] Background material gathered from Dartmouth College's Office of Academic Computing Web Teaching site, *www.dartmouth.edu/~webteach*.

[4] From the "Fair Use Guidelines for Educational Multimedia," "Preamble," section 1.1, as reproduced at *www.musiclibraryassoc.org/Copyright/guidemed.htm*.

(4) the effect of the use upon the potential market for or value of the copyrighted work.

To be in compliance with fair use, your project must

(1) adhere to certain limits as to the portion of the work you borrow (see Table F.1),

(2) have access restricted to your students only, and

(3) expire after two years (i.e., be taken offline or otherwise made inaccessible).

TABLE F.1 ■ Fair Use Guidelines for Educational Multimedia in a Nutshell— Limitations of Use[5]

Type of media	Amount permitted*	Stipulations
Motion (film, video) for all media	10% or 3 minutes	Attribute source in project (as in credits)
Music, lyrics, music video	10% or 30 seconds	Cannot change "basic melody or fundamental character of work"
Illustrations and photographs	5 images by one artist; 10% or 15 images from collective work	Unlike other fair use allowances, photos or illustrations can be used in their entirety
Text	10% or 1,000 words	An entire poem of fewer than 250 words but no more than 3 poems by single poet or 5 poems by different poets in anthology
Database	10% or 2,500 cell or field entries	

*The lesser of the two.

Using Graphics from the Web

In general, you cannot use graphics you find on someone else's website unless

(1) the owner explicitly states that they can be used (usually under the condition that they not be sold, such as in a clip art collection),

(2) you request and obtain permission for your intended use, or

(3) your use falls under fair use allowances.

Some cautious educators avoid #3 and insist that their students either use images from clip art collections or that they request permission to use the images from the owner.

---

[5] From the "Fair Use Guidelines for Educational Multimedia," "Preamble," Section 4, as reproduced at www.musiclibraryassoc.org/Copyright/guidemed.htm.

Students will have much less luck at the latter, however, when dealing with large corporate entities, such as media conglomerates (Sony, Disney, etc.), then they will dealing with non-commercial sites. There are thousands of clip art galleries online and others who freely share their work (again, under varying conditions of use). Searching for "clip art gallery" will turn up many results to sort through, but note that it's not unheard of for people to include in their online clip art collections works they do not own or did not obtain permission to share, and you may have no way of determining this.

Copyright law provides special provisions for the use of copyrighted work in nonprofit education, by students in the completion of coursework, and by educators as a teaching tool. Some educators who teach web page authoring, though, interpret fair use to mean that anything is fair game as long as it's for the noble purpose of education, and a quick perusal of faculty and student web pages will turn up many images and other material borrowed from other sites—evidence of this liberal interpretation.

As long as you're teaching students how to create web pages, why not also teach them about what they can legally use without violating the copyrights of others? According to fair use guidelines, up to five copyrighted photographs or illustrations from a single artist (or up to 10 percent or 15 images of a collection) can be incorporated into a teacher's or student's multimedia project (such as a web page) and used for up to two years without explicit permission. The source should be attributed and copyright information, if given in the original, should be displayed—though merely attributing the source alone does not confer fair use of copyrighted material. In addition to adhering to limits on the amount of material used, access to the project must also be restricted to the intended educational audience, the class, by way of a password-protected website.

Converting Analog Material to Digital

Scanning print pictures or digitizing audio from cassette tapes or video from videocassette tapes are examples of converting analog material to digital forms. The TEACH Act provides an exception for educators to this otherwise prohibited action under the following conditions:[6]

- The amount that may be converted is limited to the amount of appropriate works that may be performed or displayed, pursuant to the revised Section 110(2); and
- A digital version of the work is not "available to the institution," or a digital version is available, but it is secured behind technological protection measures that prevent its availability for performing or displaying in the distance-education program consistent with Section 110(2).

In other words, teachers can only digitize the portion or amount of material they actually need for the instructional purpose, within the limits of Section 110 of the Copyright Act of 1976, and access to it must be restricted to students in the class.

---

[6] Conditions quoted from "New Copyright Law for Distance Education: The Meaning and Importance of the TEACH Act," American Library Association, www.ala.org.

Avoiding Copyright Issues Altogether

The subjectivity inherent in the interpretation of what exactly constitutes fair use in a given circumstance, even to a qualified legal expert, leaves one certain method for avoiding the risk of violation altogether: Use only material that you create from scratch, not based on or derived from anyone else's work. For example, teachers often assign students a web project featuring the city they live in. Instead of looking for pictures of the city online or scanning ones in publications, students can take a camera and get their own pictures, ensuring not only ownership of the images but most likely ones that more accurately illustrate the point of the web page.

The fiction writer John Gardner once remarked that his memory for lines and phrases from other writer's works was so keen that he could inadvertently and unknowingly plagiarize others at length in his own writing.[7] Such possibilities, along with the copyright issues of concern to educators, make one wonder what in this information-saturated world can truly be said not to be derivative.

Internet References

Sources of Legal Text

Cornell Legal Information Institute. For copyright law, search for U.S. Code > Title 17, *www.law.cornell.edu*

United States Code, U.S. House of Representatives, *uscode.house.gov/*

Regulations of the Copyright Office, U.S. Library of Congress, Title 37 CFR, Parts 200–299, *www.access.gpo.gov/*

Colleges and Other Sites Providing Guidelines for Educators and Students

Copyright and Web Teaching, *www.dartmouth.edu/~webteach/articles/copyright.html*

University of Texas System, *www.utsystem.edu/ogc/intellectualproperty/copypol2.htm*

Explanation of TEACH Act, *www.utsystem.edu/ogc/intellectualproperty/teachact.htm*

American Library Association, *www.ala.org*

"Copyright 101 for Educators" by Wesley A. Fryer, *Technology & Learning* online, June 1, 2003, *www.techlearning.com*

To determine whether a work is copyright protected at all, see "When Works Pass into the Public Domain in the United States: Copyright Term for Archivists and Librarians," Cornell Copyright Information Center, *www.copyright.cornell.edu/training/Hirtle_Public_Domain.htm*

---

[7] From a *Paris Review* interview as compiled in Plimpton, G. (1989). *The writer's chapbook: A compendium of fact, opinion, wit, and advice from the 20th century's preeminent writers.* New York: Viking.

G Sample Letter to Secure Publisher Permission to Digitize or Distribute Material

A sample letter is shown on page 246.

[school letterhead]
[date]

[publisher]

Attn: Permissions Request

Dear Publisher:

We at [school] have adopted your textbook(s) listed below for the indicated
courses. These books have accompanying audio or video material
that is typically used either with tape recorders or video players in language labs.
We are asking your permission to transfer the audio or video on these [tapes] to a
digital format for similar use on computers in our [computer lab] as this is now our
primary means of audio/video delivery in our program.

Textbook Title	ISBN	Course Number

Access to these digitized audio/video files, either over the Internet or on our LAN,
would be restricted by a log-in and password system to only the students and
instructors in our program who are using the related text. There will be no copies,
digital or otherwise, made for student use outside the labs. Access would remain
the same as with traditional audiocassettes or videocassettes; *only the means of
delivery* (broadcast) would be changed. Student access to these files would end the
last day of each semester that they are enrolled in the course using this text.

We appreciate your cooperation and look forward to hearing from you. If you have
any questions, we will be happy to provide you with further information.

Sincerely,

[name]
Instructional Materials and Research Coordinator

H Selected CALL Resources

CALL Organizations and Conferences

International Association for Language Learning Technology (IALLT), *iall.net*

The Computer Assisted Language Instruction Consortium (CALICO), *calico.org*

European Association for Computer Assisted Language Learning (EUROCALL), *www.eurocall-languages.org*

Teachers of English to Speakers of Other Languages (TESOL), CALL Interest Section, *www.tesol.org/*

International Association of English Language Teachers of English as a Foreign Language (IATEFL), Computer Special Interest Group, *www.iateflcompsig.org.uk*

CALL Publications

Association for Educational Communications and Technology (AECT), *aect.org*

CALL-EJ Online. Bi-annual referred journal, *www.clec.ritsumei.ac.jp/english/callejonline*

Campus Technology (formerly Syllabus). Educational technology for administrators in higher education, *www.campus-technology.com*

Computer Assisted Language Instruction Consortium (CALICO) Journal, *calico.org/calicopubs.html*

Computer Assisted Language Learning: An International Journal, *www.tandf.co.uk/journals*

Educational Technology Review Online, *www.aace.org/pubs/etr*

ELT Journal. Quarterly journal for ESL/EFL professionals and related fields, *www3.oup.co.uk/eltj*

ESL Magazine, *www.eslmag.com*

International Association for Language Learning Technology (LLTI), *iall.net*

Internet TESL Journal. Articles, papers, lesson plans, classroom handouts, teaching ideas, and links for ESL/EFL teachers, *iteslj.org*

Internet4Classrooms. Resources for teachers using the Internet, *internet4classrooms.com*

IT Links. The online journal published by the Information Technology in English Language Teaching Special Interest Group of ELTeCS-East Asia, *www.it-links.org*

Japan Association for Language Teaching, CALL Interest Section, *jaltcall.org*

Journal of Interactive Media in Education, *www-jime.open.ac.uk*

Language Learning & Technology Journal, *llt.msu.edu*

ReCALL. Cambridge University Press journal of the European Association for Computer Assisted Language Learning (EUROCALL), *www.eurocall-languages.org/recall*

Teachers of English to Speakers of Other Languages, CALL interest section (TESOL-CALL IS), *darkwing.uoregon.edu/~call*

Technology & Learning. Sections for teachers, technology coordinators, and administrators. Educational technology news, software and product reviews, *www.techlearning.com*

Listservs

FL TEACH. Foreign language teaching forum, *www.cortland.edu/flteach*
>   To subscribe, send a message to
>   LISTSERV@listserv.buffalo.edu
>   In the message put only the following:
>   SUBSCRIBE FLTEACH firstname lastname

LLTI. Language Learning Technology International Information Forum, *polyglot.lss.wisc.edu/IALL/LLTI.html*
>   To subscribe, send a message to
>   listserv@dartmouth.edu
>   In the message put only the following:
>   SUB LLTI yourfirstname yourlastname

TESOL CALL IS, *www.uoregon.edu/%7Ecall/list.html*
> To subscribe, you must first be a TESOL CALL IS member. Subscribe to the listserv at above site.

CALL Labs and Practitioners Resources

CALL@Chorus by Jim Duber. College Writing Programs, University of California, Berkeley. CALL demos, technical tips, software and text reviews, *www-writing. berkeley.edu/chorus/call*

ESL Café Web Guide. Dave Sperling's CALL resources links, *eslcafe.com/search/CALL*

Ohio University ESL (OPIE). Resources for technology in language teaching by John McVicker, *www.ohiou.edu/esl/teacher/technology*

Oregon State University, English Language Institute (ELI). CALL papers and resources by Deborah Healey, *oregonstate.edu/~healeyd*

Randall's ESL Cyber Listening Lab. A huge collection of online ESL listening content and authoring tips. Randall S. Davis, *esl-lab.com*

Web Resource for CALL Lab Managers and Teachers and Learners of Languages Online by Vance Stevens, *www.geocities.com/vance_stevens/esl_home.htm*

Technical Magazines Online

Digital Education Network. Free online Microsoft software tutorials and courses, *www.actden.com*

eWeek Magazine. High-technology news, *eweek.com*

InfoWorld. IT news, *infoworld.com*

Macworld. News, reviews, resources, information, and how-to articles about Macintosh computers, *macworld.com*

SupportNET, technology support resources and links for educators, *supportnet.merit. edu/resources/supportsites.html*

Wired. Computing news and reviews, *wired.com*

ZD Net. Business related IT news, *zdnet.com*

References

Matisse's Glossary of Internet Terms, *www.matisse.net/files/glossary.html*

TechTutorials. Free computer, programming, networking and application tutorials, *www.techtutorials.info*

Webopedia. Dictionary of computing terms, *pcwebopaedia.com*

Whatis?com. A tremendous knowledge base for information technology, including an encyclopedia of technical terms, tutorials on technical topics, technical news, and links to other technology-related resources, *whatis.com*

Books

Beatty, K. (2003). *Teaching and researching computer-assisted language learning.* Upper Saddle River, NJ: Pearson ESL.

Boswood, T. (Ed.). (1997). *New ways of using computers in language teaching.* Alexandria, VA: TESOL.

Bush M., Terry, R. (Eds.). (1996). *Technology-enhanced language learning.* Chicago: National Textbook Company.

Bush, M., Terry, R. (Eds.). (1997). *Technology-enhanced language learning.* Chicago: National Textbook Company.

Chapelle, C. (2001). *Computer applications in second language acquisition: Foundations for teaching, testing, and research.* Cambridge, U.K.: Cambridge University Press.

Egbert, J. and Hanson-Smith, E. (Eds.). (1999). *CALL Environments: Research, practice, and critical issues.* Alexandria, VA: TESOL.

Hanson-Smith, E. (Ed.). (2000). *Technology-enhanced learning environments.* Alexandria, VA: TESOL.

Hanson-Smith, E. (1997). *Technology in the classroom.* Alexandria, VA: TESOL.

Levy M. (1997). *Computer-assisted language learning.* Oxford, U.K.: Oxford University Press.

Lynch, P. J., Horton, S. (2002). *Web style guide: Basic design principles for creating web sites,* (2nd ed.). New Haven, CT: Yale University Press.

Sperling, D. (1998). *Dave Sperling's Internet guide.* Upper Saddle River, NJ: Prentice Hall.

Warschauer, M. (1995). *E-mail for English teaching: Bringing the Internet and computer learning networks into the language classroom.* Alexandria, VA: TESOL.

Warschauer, M., Kern, R. (2000). *Network-based language teaching: Concepts and practice.* Cambridge, U.K.: Cambridge University Press.

Warschauer, M., Shetzer, H., Meloni, C. (2000). *Internet for English Teaching.* Alexandria, VA: TESOL.

Index